HARVARD STUDIES IN ADMINISTRATIVE LAW

VOLUME V

LONDON : HUMPHREY MILFORD
OXFORD UNIVERSITY PRESS

Judicial Control of the Federal Trade Commission and the Interstate Commerce Commission 1920–1930

A Comparative Study in the Relations of Courts to Administrative Commissions

By CARL McFARLAND

CAMBRIDGE
HARVARD UNIVERSITY PRESS
1933

PRINTED AT THE HARVARD UNIVERSITY PRESS
CAMBRIDGE, MASS., U.S.A.

CONTENTS

CHAPTER I

CHAPTER II

CHAPTER III

CHAPTER IV

CHAPTER V

JUDICIAL CONTROL OF THE FEDERAL TRADE COMMISSION AND THE INTERSTATE COMMERCE COMMISSION, 1920–1930

CHAPTER I

INTRODUCTION

Two theories of the relations of courts to administrative agencies are apparent in the writings of Anglo-American lawyers. One treats the justice dispensed by courts and the social control exercised by administrative tribunals as parts of a single system of law in which the courts wield ultimate authority. The other recognizes a dual system of public administration of justice and seeks a division of function between courts and administrative agencies so that some administrative determinations are final while others are subject to judicial supervision. The first of these theories is the older in American jurisprudence, growing out of the simple governmental organization of the first three-quarters of the nineteenth century when the conspicuous agencies of public administration were the courts. During the last half century administrative justice has been pressing for recognition, and in consequence there has been a development and readjustment of theory to admit the dual system which has been the concomitant of the change from individualistic political philosophy toward social legislation and public control.

Today theories of judicial relation to administrative tribunals emphasize some form of division of function to preserve to the courts their traditional duties as supervisors of the governmental machine and yet allow the purely administrative tribunals to build their own autonomous system. The relations of the newer administrative agencies to the courts [1] take the form of problems in judicial control or review,[2] administrative finality, rule and dis-

[1] Dickinson, *Administrative Justice and the Supremacy of Law* (1927), was written as an introduction to the subject of the relation of courts to administrative tribunals. Freund, *Administrative Powers over Persons and Property* (1928), treats the subject of administrative powers particularly from the standpoint of legislation. Other writings are listed below, p. 12 n. 25 and p. 24 n. 59.

[2] The phrases "judicial review" and "judicial control" are used interchangeably herein, although there is some tendency toward separate definition. With respect to deportation of aliens, enforcement of military discipline, granting of land patents, the use of the mails, and the like it has been said that "the function of the courts is not one of review but essentially of control — the function of keeping them within their statutory authority." Mr. Justice

cretion, and other conceptions of appropriate spheres of authority as between courts and administrative tribunals.

The preeminent examples of administrative tribunals in the federal government are the two independently constituted commissions charged with the regulation of trade and transportation — the Federal Trade Commission and the Interstate Commerce Commission. A comparative study of the relations of the courts to these commissions affords a stereoscopic view of the evolution of administrative justice in related fields. Legislative policy — which held attention during the closing decades of the nineteenth century and the opening decades of the twentieth — was of first importance, but the realization of that policy through administration, if not a tougher problem, is of no less consequence.

The Federal Trade Commission and the Interstate Commerce Commission arose from the same political and social movements, the trade commission was modeled after the commerce commission, and their duties and functions are similar in many respects — yet in their present stage of development they differ greatly. An examination of the relations of these commissions to the federal courts with particular reference to the decade 1920–1930 will disclose the nature of the judicial control and the measure of authority allowed the administrative tribunals. First, however, the shifting theory and inarticulate practice in judicial-administrative relations will appear in connection with a survey of the doctrines, principles, and policies under which the commissions have been treated.

Brandeis, dissenting, in Crowell *v.* Benson, 52 S. Ct. 285, 307 (1932). Compare also: "The use of the term 'judicial review' is sometimes misleading. It seems to be loosely applied, not only to the inquiry whether power to act is lawfully vested or exercised, but also to the process of nullifying the administrative action or of substituting a judicial determination in its stead." Powell, *Separation of Powers: Administrative Exercise of Legislative and Judicial Power*, 28 Pol. Sci. Q. 34, 47 (1918). There is an outline of the various formal methods of judicial review in Isaacs, *Judicial Review of Administrative Findings*, 30 Yale L. J. 781 (1921), and a more extensive treatment of the methods of control of administration is given in Freund, *Administrative Powers over Persons and Property* (1928), p. 227 et seq.

CHAPTER II

POLICY AND DOCTRINE

NOTWITHSTANDING the dangers and impracticable uses of doctrine for more than purposes of rationalization, discussions of administrative development ordinarily proceed in terms of the traditional principles and conceptions of public law. Accordingly, the doctrines which have been asserted in the political and judicial treatment of the Federal Trade Commission and the Interstate Commerce Commission must be touched upon before examination of the actual operation of the two commissions. There are obvious imperfections in the treatment of doctrine apart from the course of decisions, but a very brief preliminary enumeration and comment should clear the way for a study of judicial control in action — otherwise the problems would remain veiled in customary, but by no means solving, phrases.

I. SEPARATION AND DELEGATION OF POWERS

The time-honored division of the labors of government was the first obstacle to the existence of the Interstate Commerce Commission,[1] and other principles for the legal treatment of modern

[1] The doctrine of separation of powers was originally asserted to prevent a concentration of complete authority in any single branch of government. In the last century it came to be regarded as a rule of abstract and analytical operation. Compare: "There are, essentially inherent, in every system of government, three principal powers. . . ." Parker, *The Three Powers of Government* (1869), p. 3 (Lectures at Harvard Law School). And compare: "I have been surprised to see how many partisans the notion of a separation of powers rigid and perpetual — the judges the interpreters, the legislature the creator — is able even in our day to muster at the bar." Cardozo, *The Growth of the Law* (1924), p. 132.

In addition to the orthodox division into legislative, judicial, and executive functions, a two-fold division has been asserted. Goodnow, *Politics and Administration* (1900), pp. 9–10; MacIver, *The Modern State* (1926), p. 368. The courts themselves recognize a two-fold division into matters of judicial competence and matters of non-judicial competence. Luther *v.* Borden, 7 How. 1 (1848); Pacific States Telephone Co. *v.* Oregon, 223 U. S. 119 (1912). For an early study see: Bondy, *Separation of Governmental Powers*, Columbia University Studies (1896), v, 139.

The Supreme Court of the United States, however, has never treated the

administrative agencies are often related to the doctrine of separation of powers.[2] Now, however, the commerce commission is commonly taken as the outstanding example of the eclipse of the doctrine.[3] When the Act to Regulate Commerce, under which the commerce commission was established, was first attacked for infringement of judicial power, it was held that action or conclusion "upon matters of complaint brought before the commission for investigation, and which the act designates as the 'recommendation,' 'report,' 'order,' or 'requirement,' of the board is neither final nor conclusive; nor is the commission invested with any authority to enforce its decision or award. . . . The commission is invested with only administrative powers of supervision, which fall far short of making the board a court, or its action judicial, in the proper sense of the term."[4] Since this pronouncement, however, the orders of the commission have been made effective without judicial action and the commission has become an authoritative tribunal for the regulation of rates, practices, services, finance, and other matters affecting transportation. It adjusts differences even to the extent of making preliminary awards of damages which are *prima facie* evidence in jury trials. Excess earnings of carriers are "recaptured" and receipts from joint carriage are apportioned. With this experience behind them, the courts have sustained the

doctrine as a technical, legal rule. See: Frankfurter and Landis, *A Study in Separation of Powers*, 37 Harv. L. Rev. 1010 (1924). Compare: "All those administrative duties the performance of which involves an inquiry into the existence of facts and the application to them of rules of law" are "in an enlarged sense" judicial acts. "But it is not sufficient to bring such matters under the judicial power, that they involve the exercise of judgment upon law and facts." Den *v.* Hoboken Land and Improvement Co., 18 How. 272 (1856). For an analysis of the functioning of administrative agencies and comparison with the conception of a separation of powers see: Dickinson, *Administrative Justice and the Supremacy of Law* (1927), pp. 15–31. When the legal problem has been raised, the Supreme Court has rejected abstract application and decision has been given on consideration of the "necessities of the case." Buttfield *v.* Stranahan, 192 U. S. 470, 496 (1904).

[2] *Infra*, p. 12 n. 25.

[3] Compare: "As a functioning tribunal it oversteps at almost every turn the so-called separation of governmental powers. While apparently, as an administrative body, the Commission is but executing Congressional mandates, in its determination of controversies it is exercising judicial authority, and in its prescription of future adjustments it is itself enunciating legislative policy." Sharfman, *The Interstate Commerce Commission* (1931), I, 288.

[4] Kentucky U. I. Bridge Co. *v.* Louisville & N. R. Co., 37 Fed. 567, 612–613 (1889).

Federal Trade Commission Act with the simple assertion that "the Commission exercises only the administrative functions delegated to it by the act, not judicial powers." [5]

As a corollary to the doctrine of separation of powers, the doctrine of non-delegability of powers is often put forward to resist legislative grant of authority to administrative agencies. Here, as with separation of powers, the Supreme Court has been guided by the necessities of government.[6] As Chief Justice Marshall wrote in 1819, "the sound construction of the Constitution must allow to the national legislature that discretion, with respect to the means by which the powers it confers are to be carried into execution, which will enable that body to perform the high duties assigned to it. . . ." [7]

When the Act to Regulate Commerce was attacked for violation of the doctrine, the great Chief Justice was quoted and the act sustained.[8] And after the legislation of 1910 had conferred full authority upon the commission, the argument that the delegation was beyond the powers of Congress was held "without merit." [9] Commenting on this decision, Chief Justice Taft remarked that "the inevitable progress and exigencies of government and utter inability of Congress to give time and attention indispensable to the exercise of these powers in detail forced the modification of the rule [that no legislative power be delegated]. Similar necessity caused Congress to create other bodies with analogous relations to the existing legislative, executive, and judicial machinery of the Federal Government. . . ." [10] So far as the doctrine prevails in decisions involving orders of the Interstate Commerce Commission, the power of Congress is limited only to the necessity of prescribing a "standard" [11] — a specification of the subject matter

[5] Federal Trade Commission *v.* Eastman Kodak Co., 274 U. S. 619, 623 (1927).

[6] There is considerable literature on the "decadence" of the doctrine. For a recent discussion see: Duff and Whiteside, *Delegata Potestas non Potest Delegari: A Maxim of American Constitutional Law*, 14 Corn. L. Q. 168 (1929).

[7] McCulloch *v.* Maryland, 4 Wheat. 316, 421 (1819).

[8] Interstate Commerce Commission *v.* Brimson, 154 U. S. 447 (1894).

[9] Intermountain Rate Cases, 234 U. S. 476, 486 (1914).

[10] Proceedings on the Death of Chief Justice White, 257 U. S. v, xxv–xxvi (1922).

[11] ". . . Congress cannot delegate any part of its legislative power except under the limitation of a prescribed standard. . . ." United States *v.* Chicago etc. R. Co., 282 U. S. 311, 324 (1931).

and an authorization to make adjustments toward the attainment of some prescribed purpose is sufficient.

When in 1919 the first order of the Federal Trade Commission reached the courts, the statute was readily sustained. "Grants of similar authority to administrative officers and bodies have not been found repugnant to the Constitution. . . . With the increasing complexity of human activities many situations arise where governmental control can be secured only by the 'Board' or 'Commission' form of legislation." [12] The Supreme Court opinions do not discuss the constitutionality of the trade commission statutes. Validity has been assumed. When a circuit court of appeals held that the act had "so often been considered and held to be constitutional by the courts that it is not necessary now to consider these objections to its constitutionality," the Supreme Court refused to review the decision.[13]

But while the authority of the Interstate Commerce Commission is a delegated authority with which the courts ordinarily do not interfere, the authority of the Federal Trade Commission has been restricted to the exercise of only preliminary, investigative power. When the first order of the commission came before the Supreme Court, that tribunal explicitly determined that the exercise of the delegated authority was the ultimate province of the courts. "The words 'unfair method of competition' are not defined by statute. . . . It is for the courts, not the commission, ultimately to determine as a matter of law what they include." [14] And shortly after: "What shall constitute unfair methods of competition denounced by the act is left without specific definition. Congress deemed it better to leave the subject without precise definition, and to have each case determined upon its own facts, owing to the

[12] Sears, Roebuck & Co. *v.* Federal Trade Commission, 258 Fed. 307, 311–312 (1919). And see to the same effect: Arkansas Wholesale Grocers' Ass'n *v.* Federal Trade Commission, 18 F.(2d) 866, 870 (1927).

[13] Federal Trade Commission *v.* Balme, 23 F.(2d) 615, 621 (1928), *certiorari denied* 277 U. S. 598. "It may be true that the constitutionality of the act, instead of being directly decided, has rather been necessarily assumed . . . by the Supreme Court. Nevertheless we think the question cannot now be regarded an open one." Federal Trade Commission *v.* Arkansas Wholesale Grocers' Ass'n, 18 F.(2d) 866, 870 (1927), *certiorari denied* 275 U. S. 533. See also: Hankin, *Constitutionality of the Federal Trade Commission Act*, 19 Ill. L. Rev. 17 (1924); Tollefson, *Judicial Review of the Decisions of the Federal Trade Commission*, 4 Wis. L. Rev. 257, 266–271 (1927).

[14] Federal Trade Commission *v.* Gratz, 253 U. S. 421, 427 (1920).

multifarious means by which it is sought to effectuate such schemes. The commission, in the first instance, subject to the judicial review provided, has the determination of practices which come within the scope of the act." [15] Not only do the courts say what shall be "unfair methods of competition" or what restrains competition and tends toward monopoly, but they modify the orders of the commission.[16]

Administrative agencies are ordinarily created to exercise powers previously in the hands of legislatures, and on principle Congress cannot impose legislative functions on the courts. If the Federal Trade Commission Act, as was intended and as is generally assumed, delegates legislative power, then the courts have reached the curious result of taking that authority as a proper field of judicial competence to the exclusion of the administrative commission.[17] Notwithstanding the use of the words "judicial review,"

[15] Federal Trade Commission *v.* Beech-Nut Packing Co., 257 U. S. 441, 453 (1922).

[16] The act provides that, upon application to a court for enforcement of an order of the commission, the court "shall have power to make and enter upon the pleadings, testimony, and proceedings set forth . . . a decree affirming, modifying, or setting aside the order of the commission." *Infra*, p. 43.

The situation is not easily reconciled. Compare an effort to rationalize: "The power to modify the order of the Commission is given by statute, and includes the power to conform an order in point of law to the pleadings and findings. . . . Even where the court may remand, with instructions to modify in accordance with its opinion, the decree continues to be that of the court. . . . But . . . the jurisdiction of the court is original. . . . Where the fault of the Commission's order is in point of law, the court may correct it, but in doing so it recognizes that the Commission is purely a fact-finding body." Federal Trade Commission *v.* Balme, 23 F.(2d) 615, 618–619 (1928).

[17] The report of the Senate committee speaks in terms of delegation and compares the statute with the Act to Regulate Commerce. "The committee gave careful consideration to the question as to whether it would attempt to define the many and variable unfair practices which prevail in commerce, and to forbid their continuance or whether it would, by a general declaration condemning unfair practices leave it to the commission to determine what practices were unfair. It concluded that the latter course would be the better. . . . It is believed that the term 'unfair competition' has a legal significance which can be enforced by the commission and the courts, and that it is no more difficult to determine what is unfair competition than it is to determine what is a reasonable rate or what is an unjust discrimination." Report of the Senate Committee on Interstate Commerce, June 13, 1914, 63d Cong., 2 Sess., No. 597, p. 13. President Wilson recommended the commission "as an instrumentality for doing justice to business where the processes of the courts or the natural forces of correction outside the courts are inadequate to adjust the remedy to

the delegation and the authority have been construed as a devolution of power to the courts and not to the trade commission.[18] The administrative body exercises no more authority from a functional point of view than a public prosecutor. Undoubtedly, it is the broad scope of the delegated authority, comprising as it does the whole commercial field, that has moved the courts to take upon themselves the duty of restricting the statutes by way of "interpretation." It has been judicially pronounced that a broad construction "would bring within the disposition of the commission a vast number of subjects and controversies which in their

the wrong in a way that will meet all the equities and circumstances of the case. . . . There ought to be an administrative commission capable of directing and shaping such corrective processes, not only in aid of the courts but also by independent suggestion, if necessary." Special Address to Congress, January 20, 1914, *Messages and Papers of the Presidents*, XVII, 7916; Cong. Rec., Vol. 51, 1963. See also: Report of the Senate Committee, 63d Cong., 2 Sess., No. 597, pp. 8–9, 12.

However, the orders of the commission have no force until a decree is issued by a federal court. On application by the commission to the courts for enforcement of orders, the courts will determine whether "as a matter of law" the practice amounts to an unfair method of competition or tends toward monopoly. From an analytical or practical point of view this does not constitute a delegation of authority to the administrative commission.

Compare: "The courts may not, under the pretext of exercising judicial power, consistently with the decisions of the Supreme Court of the United States, set aside such orders when lawfully made, for nothing is more elementary than that power to make such orders may be conferred on such boards even when judicial power is expressly vested in the courts, as it is under the federal constitution. The right of the legislature to delegate such order-making power seems now to be as inherent to government as the right to trial by jury or the writ of habeas corpus." Cuthbert Pound, *Constitutional Aspects of Administrative Law* in *Growth of American Administrative Law* (1923), p. 130 (printed also in 9 A. B. A. J. 409).

[18] Compare this description of the paradox: "A common belief, shared in 1914 by almost everybody, was that the courts, in their handling of anti-trust problems, were not sufficiently expert and that to get away from the bondage of legal tradition, part of this labor should be undertaken by the Federal Trade Commission, which would approach these problems from the economic and business standpoints. This was the belief in which the Commission began its work and shaped its course during its critical first ten years. To the extent that the Commission has followed legal tradition, public opinion and the courts have always supported it. To the extent, however, that the Commission has departed from legal tradition, it has not been supported either by the Courts or by public opinion." Montague, *Anti-Trust Laws and the Federal Trade Commission: 1914–1926*, 27 Col. L. Rev. 650, 13 A. B. A. J. 328 (1927). And see: Dickinson, *Administrative Justice and the Supremacy of Law* (1927), p. 318.

nature belong to the legislative and judicial departments of the government." [19]

Although the doctrines of separation and non-delegability of powers have not prevented the existence of administrative tribunals, the terminology persists.[20] A superficial use of the words appears in customary expressions such as "quasi-judicial" or "quasi-legislative." The labelling of subject matter of functions as "legislative" may indicate some larger measure of discretion in the administrative agency,[21] but "the cataloging of the duties of an independent commission by tags representing the three traditional subdivisions of the Government is little more than an interesting mental exercise." [22] The break with the doctrine of delegation of powers has only been "softened by a *quasi*." [23] While, as has been said in another connection, "twistings of the watchwords and solving phrases of the past to meanings satisfying to the wants of today are among the staple modes of growth

[19] New Jersey Asbestos Co. *v.* Federal Trade Commission, 264 Fed. 509, 511 (1920).

[20] For example: "Each of the orders . . . was an exercise either of quasi-judicial function of determining controversies or of the delegated legislative function of rate making and rule making." United States *v.* Los Angeles etc. R. Co., 273 U. S. 299, 309 (1927). See also: Interstate Commerce Commission *v.* Humboldt Steamship Co., 224 U. S. 474, 484 (1912); Baer Bros. *v.* Denver etc. R. Co., 233 U. S. 479, 486 (1914); Interstate Commerce Commission *v.* Goodrich Transit Co., 224 U. S. 194, 214 (1912); Terminal R. R. Ass'n *v.* United States, 266 U. S. 17, 30 (1924); Assigned Car Cases, 274 U. S. 564, 583 (1927). And for a discussion of the functions of the Interstate Commerce Commission in terms of judicial, quasi-judicial, and legislative duties see: Needham, *Judicial Determinations by Administrative Commissions*, 10 Pol. Sci. Rev. 235 (1916).

But at times an "administrative" category appears: "The Federal Trade Commission exercises administrative, not judicial, powers." Chamber of Commerce of Minneapolis *v.* Federal Trade Commission, 280 Fed. 45, 48 (1922) "The commission is not a court; it exercises administrative, not judicial power." Eastman Kodak Co. *v.* Federal Trade Commission, 7 F.(2d) 994, 996 (1925), *affirmed* 274 U. S. 619.

[21] See *infra*, pp. 24–25.

[22] Commissioner Eastman, *The Place of the Independent Commission*, 12 Const. Rev. 95, 97 (1928). See also: Rosenberry, *Administrative Law and the Constitution*, 23 Am. Pol. Sci. Rev. 32, 36–38 (1929).

[23] "It is said that the powers of Congress cannot be delegated, yet Congress has established the Interstate Commerce Commission, which does legislative, judicial and executive acts, only softened by a *quasi*. . . ." Mr. Justice Holmes, dissenting, in Springer *v.* Government of the Philippine Islands, 277 U. S. 189, 210–211 (1928).

in law,"[24] continued use of the words is safe only when ideas of analytical or logical separation or non-delegability of powers are completely out of mind.

II. Other Doctrines and Considerations

But if the doctrines of separation and delegation of powers have fallen into disuse as working principles, there are other conceptions and doctrines under which administrative action is subjected to the test of judicial materials and technique.[25] Involved in several of these doctrines are natural law concepts. The personification

[24] Pound, *The New Feudalism*, 16 A. B. A. J. 553, 555 (1930). "... Our theory of application of law was made for rules of property, so that when, in the present century, we had to turn more and more to administration, for a time it was far from easy to adjust our legal ideas to the demands of a new type of tribunal." *Ibid.* 555–556.

[25] The constitutional doctrines as to the separation of powers, delegability of powers, due process, and as to the position of the courts as the ultimate interpreters of a written constitution are said to be "but the outworks of an elaborate structure devised to buttress from different sides the central doctrine of the supremacy of law. ..." Dickinson, *Administrative Justice and the Supremacy of Law* (1927), p. 75. "The trader is entitled to his day in court. ..." Sears, Roebuck & Co. *v.* Federal Trade Commission, 258 Fed. 307, 311 (1919). "The Federal Trade Commission exercises administrative, not judicial, powers. The act provides no penalties, nor has the commission power to make more than a finding of facts, which requires confirmation by this court before any burden is cast upon the parties. ... Full provision for review is made, confined, of course, to the limited right of courts to review administrative or legislative acts. Chamber of Commerce of Minneapolis *v.* Federal Trade Commission, 280 Fed. 45, 48 (1922).

Most of the aspects of the problem, now treated in current literature, were developed by Professor T. R. Powell two decades or more ago.

For examples of the approach to the study of administrative powers through the doctrine of separation of powers see: Powell, *Separation of Powers: Administrative Exercise of Legislative and Judicial Power*, 27 Pol. Sci. Q. 215 (1912), 28 Id. 34, 34–35 (1913); Berle, *Expansion of American Administrative Law*, 39 Harv. L. Rev. 430 (1917); Pillsbury, *Administrative Tribunals*, 36 Harv. L. Rev. 405 (1923); Rosenberry, *Administrative Law and the Constitution*, 23 Am. Pol. Sci. Rev. 32 (1929); Frankfurter and Davison, *Cases on Administrative Law* (1932). For an approach to the study of American administrative law through other doctrines see: C. Pound, *Constitutional Aspects of Administrative Law* in *Growth of American Administrative Law* (1923), and for studies in administrative finality see *infra*, p. 24 n. 59.

But the doctrine of separation of powers, considered either historically or logically, has not warranted judicial review in all governments. Compare: Ghose, *Comparative Administrative Law* (1919), Lect. V; and for an interesting

of "law" — in the inimitable words of Mr. Justice Holmes, a "brooding omnipresence" — does not in terms concern us here because, in treating the orders of the Federal Trade Commission and the Interstate Commerce Commission, the judicial expressions may be studied under more specific headings and the phrases have more tangible — if less soothing — meanings.

Judicial Supremacy. In the literature on the subject, however, in place of natural law conceptions, but not without some lingering philosophies, there is the definite policy embodied in such doctrines as "the rule of law,"[26] "supremacy of law,"[27] or "justice according to law,"[28] that judicially administered justice is superior to administrative justice and that therefore "no man can lawfully be made to suffer in body or goods except for a distinct breach of law established in the ordinary courts of the land."[29] This is what the Supreme Court of the United States recognizes as "the difference in security of judicial over administrative process."[30] However, the demand for judicial process has not prevented the establishment of administrative commissions subject to some form of judicial control. Administrative justice has been fitted into the governmental system of the United States — but without that independence or finality which characterizes the traditional arms of state. The "rule of law" has been restated to require judicial control of administrative action: ". . . Every citizen is entitled . . . to call into question in such a court the legality of any act done by an administrative official."[31]

It is partly the desire for check and balance to prevent unauthorized or arbitrary action and partly the desire for a judicially developed body of law or judicially controlled administration of government that underlies the judicial apexing of the field of public

discussion of the treatment in European countries see: von Hippel, *Die Verschiebung der Machtverhältnisse im Alten und Neuen Deutschland, Dargestellt an der Lehre Montesquieu's, und die Praktische Bedeutung dieses Prinzips fur die Juristische Konstruktion*, 43 Rechtsgeleerd Magazijn 59, 85–89 (1924).

[26] Dicey, *Law of the Constitution* (8 ed., 1927), pp. xxxvii–xlviii, 179–409. But see: Dicey, *Development of Administrative Law in England*, 31 Law Q. Rev. 148 (1915); Hewart, *The New Despotism* (1929), pp. 23–36.

[27] Dickinson, *Administrative Justice and the Supremacy of Law* (1927), particularly Ch. II.

[28] Pound, *Justice According to Law*, 13 Col. L. Rev. 696 (1913), 14 Id. 1, 103 (1914).

[29] Dicey, *Law of the Constitution* (8 ed., 1927), pp. 183–184.

[30] Crowell *v.* Benson, 52 S. Ct. 285, 296 (1932).

[31] Dickinson, *Administrative Justice and the Supremacy of Law* (1927), p. 35.

administration. This was the crucial issue in the debates on the Hepburn Act which vitalized the Interstate Commerce Commission. In the United States there is no completely separate or dual administration of justice — no autonomous administrative system; instead, the exercise of administrative powers is subject to judicial supervision under principles which the courts themselves have developed in recent years. "... The course of development has been to displace or push back the purely common law [control of administrative officials by mandamus or certiorari] and to build up forms of relief which, while not organized into an entirely separate jurisdiction as in France or Germany, yet likewise constitute a special body of administrative law." [32]

Protection of Private Rights. The traditional function of the courts in the United States, standing between the people and their government and officials, is the protection of private rights.[33] But so far as the Federal Trade and Interstate Commerce Commissions are concerned, the maintenance of substantive rights is infrequently mentioned in the course of review of administrative determinations.[34] By subjecting the commissions to a scrutiny more

[32] Freund, *Historical Survey of American Administrative Law* in *Growth of American Administrative Law* (1923), pp. 12–13.

[33] Here again a natural law flavor persists. It has been said that in the forum of the courts "the individual may assert his rights; there the government must accept definition of its authority. There the individual may challenge the legality of governmental action and have it adjudged by the test of fundamental principles, and that test the government must abide. . . ." Woodrow Wilson, *Constitutional Government in the United States* (1911), p. 142.

Some writers make authority over private rights the tender spot in administrative law: "What we cannot say of administrative power in general [that it is permissible with proper personnel] we can say of discretionary administrative power over individual rights, namely that it is undesirable per se and should be avoided as far as may be, for discretion is unstandardized power and to lodge in an official such power over person or property is hardly conformable to the 'Rule of Law.'" Freund, *Historical Survey* in *Growth of American Administrative Law* (1923), pp. 22–23. And in the land where the "rights of Englishmen" were put forward by the courts as champions against the royal power, it is now urged that this function of the courts is no less important as a protection against the popular executive. Hewart, *The New Despotism* (1929), Ch. VII.

[34] Compare: "Courts are constantly called upon to consider deprivation of 'liberty' or 'property' in the light of changing economic conditions. . . . 'Due process,' 'liberty of contract,' and 'property rights' are somewhat relative terms, incapable of accurate, precise and lasting definition. . . . If, as petitioner's counsel concedes, the section is free from 'constitutional objection,'

or less in accordance with recently developed principles and by rendering decision in terms of statutory authority and evidence, "due process of law" and "private rights" have almost disappeared from the language of the decisions. It is not that the judges who test legislation in terms of private rights are any less vigilant in the censorship of administrative orders (the contrary is to be expected); there are more subtle ways of reaching the same result — chiefly through "interpretation." The commissions have been held down to a procedure and scope of authority which makes abstract consideration of validity of their orders unnecessary. So far as the due process clause remains, it is to be seen in the judicial prohibition of "arbitrary and capricious" action,[35] and the requirement of orderly process.

if 'the powers and activities of its ministerial agency' (the Federal Trade Commission) are properly 'circumscribed,' the query arises, To what circle should such powers be confined? We are still dealing with words of general meaning, and make no progress." Swift & Co. *v.* Federal Trade Commission, 8 F. (2d) 595, 598 (1925), *on appeal* 272 U. S. 554. "A hearing is granted before the Commission, and ultimate review by the Circuit Court of Appeals is provided; therefore there is no denial of due process." Chamber of Commerce of Minneapolis *v.* Federal Trade Commission, 280 Fed. 45, 48 (1922). "The right of review to determine whether the findings of the commission are based upon substantial evidence or whether they are arbitrary, oppressive, and therefore in excess of its powers, and whether the order made is responsive to and justified by such findings, satisfies the requirement of due process. There is no ground in a case of this nature to say that the petitioners did not have, or were denied, a full and sufficient hearing." Arkansas Wholesale Grocers' Ass'n *v.* Federal Trade Commission, 18 F.(2d) 866, 871 (1927), *certiorari denied* 275 U. S. 533.

Where the courts have used private rights as the mode of decision, regulation is either made difficult or nullified. For example, the "right to sell" made the regulation of resale price maintenance by the Federal Trade Commission ineffective. But compare: Brown, *The Right to Refuse to Sell*, 25 Yale L. J. 194 (1916).

[35] Compare: Louisiana U. P. B. Ry. Co. *v.* United States, 257 U. S. 114, 116–117 (1921); United States *v.* New River Co., 265 U. S. 533, 538, 542 (1924); United States *v.* Chicago etc. R. Co., 282 U. S. 311, 324, 331 (1931).

There are those who identify this language with the natural law of political and legal thought in other centuries. See, for example: Haines, *Revival of Natural Law Concepts* (1930), particularly pp. 232–234. But there is a difference. "If, however, we can attribute to law the epithet 'natural,' it is, as we have said, in a different sense from that which formerly attached to the expression 'natural law.' That expression then meant that nature had imprinted in us, as one of the very elements of reason, certain principles of which all the articles of the code were only the application. The same expression ought to mean today that law springs from the relations of fact which exist between

Interpretation of Statutory Authority. More often stressed by publicists than even the protection of private rights is the demand that administrative agencies be held within the scope of authority granted them by the legislature — the "jurisdiction" and "intra vires" of the common law. Although administration must necessarily include interpretation of the law, it is ordinarily assumed that final determinations of the limits of authority of an administrative body "of course cannot be left for that body to determine for itself." [36] It is the attempt to do away with this third party arbiter that has caused great outcry in England recently.[37] In the United States this function of the judicial arm of the state is taken for granted. "The point is," said Mr. Justice Cardozo, "that this power of interpretation must be lodged somewhere, and the custom of the constitution has lodged it in the judges." [38]

A study of the relations of courts to administrative agencies

things. . . . It is no longer in texts or in systems derived from reason that we must look for the source of law. . . ." Vander Eycken, *Methode positive de l'interpretation juridique*, p. 401, Sec. 239. Quoted in Cardozo, *Nature of the Judicial Process* (1921), p. 122.

". . . History gave us nothing more than a doctrine of holding the ministers and agents of the Crown to the legal limits of their authority, refusal to give effect to royal assumption of the powers of Parliament, and an assertion of judicial limitations upon legislative power. The interpretation of the limits imposed upon the federal and state governments by constitutional provisions for due process of law, as securing against arbitrary and unreasonable exercise of powers, is derived not from the historical materials of Anglo-American public law, but from an ideal of political action in the commonwealths of the new world." Pound, *The Ideal Element in American Judicial Decisions*, 45 Harv. L. Rev. 136, 141 (1931).

[36] Dickinson, *Administrative Justice and the Supremacy of Law* (1927), p. 235.

[37] See: Allen, *Bureaucracy Triumphant* (1931), particularly p. 62 et seq.; Hewart, *The New Despotism* (1929); Marriott, *The Crisis of English Liberty* (1930), pp. 1–18. And for an article following the same lines of criticism in the United States see: Burgess, *Recent Efforts to Immunize Commission Orders against Judicial Review*, 55 A. B. A. Rep. (1930).

[38] Cardozo, *Nature of the Judicial Process* (1921), p. 135. And compare: "And without having recourse to any of the elementary writers, or to the popular conventions of Europe, we have a most commanding authority in the sense of the American people, that the right to interpret laws does, and ought to belong exclusively to the courts of justice." Kent, C., in Dash *v.* Van Kleek, 7 Johns. 477, 509 (1811). "Obviously, if the executive could determine its own competence, it would, in fact, be the master of the legal imperatives by which it lives. By entrusting the decision of such disputes to a body outside the executive, an independent assessment of validity can be obtained." Laski, *Introduction to Politics* (1931), p. 62.

would be incomplete without careful consideration of this interpretative function of the courts for, as often as not, decisions are put upon the ground of *ultra vires* whereas another court or another judge would confine review to the evidence and reach the same result. The interpretation of authority in reviewing administrative orders does not proceed *in vacuo* but is made in view of a concrete situation presented in the record. On a comparatively broad interpretation of legislative policy, the Interstate Commerce Commission is sustained in the courts, while the orders of the Federal Trade Commission — subjected to abstract analysis of evidence with the purposes of the statutes almost entirely ignored — are easily rejected by the courts.

The position of the courts with respect to legislation and administration — the judicial function in outlining the scope of administrative authority — is customarily justified upon various grounds. In addition to the almost universal insistence upon a disinterested interpreter of statutes, there is a deep-seated demand for a check upon what is conceived to be the zeal,[39] or the specialized nature of the task,[40] of administrative officers and agencies. But the interpretative function of the courts in connection with general delegations of authority may, and often does, become a means of judicial limitation upon administrative, and consequently upon

[39] However, this idea is so stressed that the result often amounts to zeal to restrain proper administration. The Commerce Court displayed something of this tendency. Compare: "Let us not think of the bureaucrat as an octopus ever reaching his tentacles for more and more absolute powers. He is both efficient and disinterested; we are proud of our Judges in England, and we have as good reason to be proud of our Civil Service. But it is exactly from the executive officer's efficiency and zeal that we must save ourselves — and him. His business is to get things done. He knows best what is to be done and the most convenient means of doing it; he is the expert, with special means of knowledge at his command; and when principles of law are put in his way, he is apt to be impatient of them as mere pedantic obstructions." Allen, *Bureaucracy Triumphant* (1931), p. 59.

[40] ". . . The essential difference between the task of adjudication and the task of governmental administration" is said to be the consideration which makes it necessary for the courts to pass upon administrative rules. "The function of an administrative body is to get something done, not to adjudicate controversies nor to mark out and delimit rights. . . . It must seek a practical solution of one case rather than a rule for all cases; and this requires that its determinations . . . must be subject ultimately to the check of an adjudicating body primarily interested in general rules of delimitation between opposing rights." Dickinson, *Administrative Justice and the Supremacy of Law* (1927), p. 235. And see Allen, *Bureaucracy Triumphant* (1931), p. 60.

legislative, authority. Judicial exposition of the "intent" of the legislature,[41] except within very wide limits, is no satisfactory explanation of the limitations imposed by the courts upon either the Interstate Commerce Commission or the Federal Trade Commission. Under another conception, which is quite generally implied in the language of the decisions, the substance of the law is complete and requires no more than judicial technique for perfect application; to whatever extent this may be true in some fields of the law,[42] the delimitation of the scope of broadly delegated authority is by no means comparable.

However, one who reads the masterly opinion of Mr. Justice Brandeis in the *New England Divisions Case*[43] cannot fail to be impressed with the interpretative function of the courts. Definite interpretation of the limits of authority adds to the statement of the law or public policy and, unlike treatment on doctrine or minute scrutiny of evidence, may be corrected by further legislation. So far as the Interstate Commerce Commission is concerned, a vigorous legislative policy and judges keenly aware of the problems of railroad regulation have for the most part moved the courts to abandon a meticulous search for statutory authority. Any other method of interpretation is unsuited to the nature of the statutes.

The Nature of the Statutes. The character of the legislation under which the commissions operate and the legislative commands or prohibitions which they administer are variously described as "standard," "discretion," or "delegated authority."[44] Academic

[41] Compare: Gray, *The Nature and Sources of the Law* (1909), Secs. 370–399. Authoritative judicial exposition of the intent of the law-maker is understandable as of the time when the common law judges sat in the legislative councils. See: Plucknett, *Statutes and their Interpretation in the Fourteenth Century* (1922), pp. 49–50. For recent discussions see: Radin, *Statutory Interpretation,* 43 Harv. L. Rev. 863 (1930); Landis, *Note on "Statutory Interpretation,"* *ibid.* 886.

[42] For a discussion see: Cardozo, *The Nature of the Judicial Process* (1921), Lect. III.

[43] 261 U. S. 184 (1923). See also the opinion of Chief Justice Taft in Wisconsin Railroad Commission *v.* Chicago etc. R. Co., 257 U. S. 563 (1922).

[44] The present form of delegated power in the United States has been described as "if not a grant of law-making power, at least a power of filling in details, a power of making rules, a power of giving definite content to legal standards. . . ." Pound, *Administrative Application of Legal Standards,* 44 A. B. A. Rep. 445, 446 (1919). "In framing standards the law seeks neither to generalize by eliminating the circumstances nor to particularize by including them; instead, the law seeks to formulate the general expectation of society as

discussion centers in the distinction or relation of this type of legislation to strict rules. The term "standard" partly describes the nature of the statutes.[45] Like the standards in the common law, the general phrases of the Interstate Commerce Act, the Clayton Act, and the Federal Trade Commission Act cannot and should not be crystallized into strict rule.[46] The standards ordinarily administered by trial courts or by juries under the supervision of

to how individuals will act in the course of their undertakings, and thus to guide the common sense or expert intuition of jury or commission when called on to judge of particular conduct under particular circumstances. . . . These standards are devised to guide the triers of fact or the commission in applying to each unique set of circumstances their common sense resulting from their experience." Pound, *ibid.* 456–457. And see: Pound, *Introduction to the Philosophy of Law* (1922), p. 120.

[45] It may be quite proper to compare the phrase "unfair methods of competition" with other general expressions. For example: ". . . The phrase [unfair methods of competition] is no more indefinite than 'due process of law.' . . . If the expression 'unfair methods of competition' is too uncertain for use, then under the same condemnation would fall the innumerable statutes which predicate rights and prohibitions upon 'unsound mind,' 'undue influence,' 'unfaithfulness,' 'unfair use,' 'unfit for cultivation,' 'unreasonable rate,' 'unjust discrimination,' and the like. . . . Congress declares the public policy, fixes the general principles that are to control, and charges an administrative body with the duty of ascertaining within particular fields from time to time the facts which bring into play the principles established by Congress." Sears, Roebuck & Co. *v.* Federal Trade Commission, 258 Fed. 307, 311 (1919). However, it does not follow that, because the statutes contain general terms, the duty of filling out the details must necessarily fall upon the courts.

[46] Crystallization, or the development of strict rules in the field of regulation of trade and transportation, is to be avoided because, once certain situations are labelled as within the rules, all others tend to become accepted as lawful and then changing conditions or adroit maneuvering go unchallenged. Growth of the law is checked. "The refusal of Congress to list the methods of competition included in the term 'unfair' was undoubtedly wise if for no other reason than that it leaves the Trade Commission free to extend the scope of the law to meet the inventive genius of certain types of business men as rapidly as the courts will support it." Seager and Gulick, *Trust and Corporation Problems* (1929), p. 424.

The tendency to crystallize the law has often been noted in the field of the common law itself. See: Pound, *Justice According to Law*, 13 Col. L. Rev. 696, 699 and n. 14 (1913). There is no safeguard against atrophy save clear understanding of the forms of the statement of the law and its application: "Some parts of the administration of justice obstinately resist the attempt to reduce them completely to the domain of law." *Ibid.* 699. "Experience is pointing, if not to a true proportion between [rule and discretion], at least to a partitioning of the field of judicial activity between them, and . . . the problem is gradually settling down to one of the respective fields of two necessary

judges are subject to judicial exposition and limitation — the expert on the bench controls administration by the lay jury. However, when courts expound the precise meanings of the Interstate Commerce Act, the Clayton Act, or the Federal Trade Commission Act, they do violence to the conception and nature of delegated legislative power. These standards, if such they may be called, are not the materials of common law administration of justice; nor is it that the legislature had a definite legal order in mind — rather, authority has been granted to the administrative agency to work out the problem thus specified.[47]

Nevertheless, because of this very character of the Federal Trade Commission Act the courts assume complete authority.[48] If, as is the case with the Federal Trade Commission Act, it is for the courts "ultimately to determine as a matter of law" what the standard "unfair methods of competition" means, then the courts are either exercising the delegated authority or, by fiction, convert a general

elements in the judicial administration of justice." *Ibid.* 700. The general problem of legal science is "not to discover the fundamental principles or ultimate conceptions from which a complete and perfect body of rules may be deduced, but to define rightly the respective provinces of these two elements in the administration of justice and to give to each its proper development in that province." *Ibid.* 705.

[47] "The striking recourse to administrative powers in recent federal economic legislation (Interstate Commerce Commission, Federal Trade Commission, Shipping Board) is due to . . . the inability of the legislature to formulate standards sufficiently definite for private guidance." Freund, *Administrative Powers over Persons and Property* (1928), p. 29. And compare: Dickinson, *Administrative Justice and the Supremacy of Law* (1927), p. 315 et seq. "If administrative action is fettered by minute requirements imposed by the legislature . . . the opportunities for impending litigation will leave vast activities to the mercy of the cunning, selfish and avaricious and the means designed for protection will defeat their own purpose." Charles E. Hughes, *Some Observations*, New York Times, June 22, 1920, p. 11. Compare the discussion in: Freund, *Historical Survey* in *Growth of American Administrative Law* (1923), p. 38 et seq.

[48] Compare an example of the ordinary statement found in the decisions: "The statute does not define the term 'unfair methods of competition,' therefore the question is one for the ultimate determination of the courts as are the phrases 'unsound mind,' 'undue influence,' 'unfair use,' 'due process of law,' found in many other statutes." L. B. Silver Co. *v.* Federal Trade Commission, 289 Fed. 985, 990 (1923). Such statements ignore the province of administrative tribunals and disregard the difference between constitutional standards, such as "due process of law," — which are the peculiar province of the courts, — and legislative standards — which have been entrusted to administrative tribunals.

expression or specification of delegated power into substantive law. Although the problem has been delegated to a specialized tribunal, the courts of law have set themselves in the place of the administrators, which means to many people that the purpose of the entire scheme is set aside — the classical politics and economics of judges prevail in full.[49] There are different reasons for this treatment of the so-called standards in the trade commission acts — the failure to recognize the nature of the legislation may be due to the desire to reduce the law to rules or to reluctance to permit a general delegation of authority.

Administrative Authority. A more candid recognition of the nature of the statutes appears when the authority of the commissions is described as "discretion." [50] Although discretion is nothing new and not even desirable in all fields of the common law itself,[51]

[49] The courts expressly link together the judicial power to determine what is "unfair competition" with common law content — the customary judicial precedents. Compare the leading decision of the Supreme Court: "It is for the courts, not the commission, ultimately to determine as a matter of law what [the words 'unfair methods of competition'] shall include. They are clearly inapplicable to practices never heretofore regarded as opposed to good morals because characterized by deception, bad faith, fraud or oppression, or as against public policy because of their dangerous tendency unduly to hinder competition or create monopoly." Federal Trade Commission *v.* Gratz, 253 U. S. 421, 427 (1920). And also: "From this absence of [legislative definition] it is reasonable to infer that it was in the mind of Congress that, as unfair competition had long been a subject of judicial scrutiny, determination, and was involved in remedial suits at law for damages and of injunctive suits in equity to prevent continuance, the definition and ascertainment of what constituted unfair competition was a legal question which the law could determine. Indeed, in the nature of things, it was impossible to describe and define in advance just what constituted unfair competition, and in the final analysis it became a question of law, after the facts were ascertained, whether such facts constitute unfair competition in business, for the test of fairness, as of fraud, is the application by the law of moral standards to the actions of men." Curtis Publishing Co. *v.* Federal Trade Commission, 270 Fed. 881, 908 (1921), *affirmed* 260 U. S. 568.

[50] For a general discussion see Dickinson, *Judicial Control of Administrative Discretion*, 22 Am. Pol. Sci. Rev. 275 (1928).

[51] "In no legal system, however minute and detailed its body of rules, is justice administered wholly by rule, without any recourse to the will of the judge and his personal sense of what should be done to achieve justice in the cause before him." Pound, *Justice According to Law*, 13 Col. L. Rev. 696–697 (1913). "In general the sociological jurists stand for what has been called equitable application of law; that is, they conceive of the legal rule as a general guide to the judge, leading him toward the just result, but insist that within wide limits he should be free to deal with the individual case, so as to meet the

it was nearly twenty years before any real discretion in the Interstate Commerce Commission was recognized, and even today discretion in the Federal Trade Commission is hardly mentioned.[52] At the same time the regulation of interstate transportation has not been reduced to the application of a body of rules or adherence to precedent.[53]

Without more than touching on the much debated subject of rule and discretion, it may be noted that there are two aspects of the problem which directly concern the administration of both the Interstate Commerce Act and the Federal Trade Commission Act. In the first place, if there is to be any measure of delegated authority in the commissions, some discretion — some freedom from interference by other branches of government — must be left them. The margin, of course, depends upon the nature of the subject matter and the terms of the legislative charter. Of course, the field cannot be divided at one stroke or by formula. The nearest approach to this treatment is to be found in the categories of "questions of fact" and "legislative functions" which have been developed by the courts as the field of discretion allowed the Interstate Commerce Commission. But the demarcation is not absolute, the courts intrude upon what has previously been classified as discretionary, and as a matter of practice the field of discretion is restricted beyond any meaning to be gleaned from the language often used.

In the second place — or perhaps to put the same thing in another way — there is not and cannot be a fixed line between rule and discretion. Rules are abstractions.[54] They may, conceivably,

demands of justice between the parties and accord with the general reason of ordinary men." Pound, *Scope and Purpose of Sociological Jurisprudence*, 25 Harv. L. Rev. 489, 515 (1912).

[52] In fact, the only place where discretion in the trade commission has been mentioned is in the admission or exclusion of evidence. ". . . The weight of authority is that the acceptance or exclusion of such testimony is a matter of discretion." Federal Trade Commission *v.* Good Grape Co., 45 F. (2d) 70, 72 (1930). However, the courts refuse to be bound by the evidence admitted. *Infra*, p. 29 et seq.

[53] For a discussion see: Sharfman, *The Interstate Commerce Commission* (1931), II, 367–384.

[54] We have "the orthodox nineteenth-century theory of a group of legal conceptions, derived by strict logical analysis from the body of rules that make up the legal tradition, and of subsuming particular states of fact under these conceptions by a purely logical process. . . . But in truth the legal theory expresses only an ideal to which the legal order was never able actually to con-

be formulated and applied to any state of fact. Orders of the Interstate Commerce Commission have been invalidated by the formulation of abstract rules and assumption of particular states of fact although the actual evidence does not approach even in terms the subject matter assumed by the rule.[55] Every portion of the records upon which the Federal Trade Commission has made orders has been treated under rules — as "matters of law" — to the complete exclusion of administrative discretion. However, it must be admitted that — despite the abstractions which rules involve and the nature of the subject matter — when the trade regulation legislation was pending there was demand for a body of law, to be administered through a commission or otherwise, which would be certain and ascertainable in advance of litigation.[56] Today there is a demand for advance opinions.[57] And yet, although the judiciary has excluded administrative discretion in the regulation of competition, the courts themselves have developed no body of rules.[58]

form and from which it has been constantly compelled to depart. For human interests will assert themselves continually in new ways and significant institutions of every-day life often arise extra-legally and produce their most important results independent of or even against the law." Pound, *Administrative Application of Legal Standards*, 44 A. B. A. Rep. 445, 453 (1919). And there are those who deny that rules are effective at all: "In the actual thinking of actual lawyers and actual judges there is usually no such compartmenting into rules and non-rules. . . . Such a division may sometimes be useful, but is often harmful to clear thinking about the judicial process." Frank, *Are Judges Human*, 80 U. Pa. L. Rev. 17, 21 (1931).

55 A flagrant example of hypothetical application of rule may be seen in the majority opinion overruling the Interstate Commerce Commission in United States *v.* Chicago etc. R. Co., 282 U. S. 311 (1931).

56 Henderson, *The Federal Trade Commission* (1924), p. 17; Butler, *The Supreme Issue of 1912*, pp. 18–19.

57 "In no field of the law is a measure of certainty more needed than in that which governs the business practices now under the jurisdiction of the federal trade commission; the Commission was established to relieve business enterprise from the uncertainties with which court decisions had enveloped the Sherman Act; . . ." Dickinson, *Administrative Justice and the Supremacy of Law* (1927), p. 250. Compare the practice of the Attorney General in "approving" combinations under the anti-trust laws. These materials are collected in Frankfurter and Katz, *Cases on Federal Jurisdiction* (1931), pp. 101–105. But advance opinions are not given by the Federal Trade Commission. See: Annual Report of the Federal Trade Commission, 1916, p. 13; Clark, *The Federal Trust Policy* (1931), p. 183.

58 See, for example: American Tobacco Co. *v.* Federal Trade Commission, 274 U. S. 543 (1927); *infra*, pp. 72–73.

III. Division of Functions

Partly the recognition that there must be some area for the exercise of administrative discretion [59] and partly the quest for some solving rule has led to legislative and judicial delimitation of the respective spheres of administrative and judicial action. But, so far as rules have been developed, at most this tendency has achieved only scattered and not always consistent categories which are now disappearing from the decisions on review of the orders of the Federal Trade Commission and the Interstate Commerce Commission.

Legislative and Judicial. Borrowing terminology from the doctrine of separation of powers, a classification of the functions of administrative agencies has been partly developed in terms of "legislative" and "judicial" duties of the Interstate Commerce Commission according as administrative decisions are left to the discretion of the commission or subject to judicial review. As a formula this is no less foredoomed to failure than the tripartite

[59] "If the right of judicial review is not to some degree limited, the courts will have purely administrative duties imposed on them and they will be encroaching on the legislative power when they are forced to deal with regulatory matters. The judiciary does not exercise any supervisory authority over the acts of the legislative or executive branches of government. . . . When the supervisory power of the courts has been extended to matters of executive and legislative decision and discretion, the courts have been given a place of preeminence which our scheme of constitutional government never contemplated." C. Pound, *Constitutional Aspects of Administrative Law* in *Growth of American Administrative Law* (1923), pp. 122–123.

The division of functions between administrative agencies and courts is often discussed in terms of rule and discretion. See, for example: Freund, *Substitution of Rule for Discretion in Public Law*, 9 Am. Pol. Sci. Rev. 666 (1915); *Rule and Discretion*, Note 33 Harv. L. Rev. 972 (1920). Other discussions proceed in terms of administrative "finality." For example: Albertsworth, *Judicial Review of Administrative Action by the Supreme Court*, 35 Harv. L. Rev. 127 (1921); Dickinson, *Administrative Justice and the Supremacy of Law* (1927), pp. 39–75; Freund, *Administrative Powers over Persons and Property* (1928), pp. 285–299; Grimm, *Administrative Determinations*, 3 St. Louis L. Rev. 140 (1919); Hankin, *Conclusiveness of the Federal Trade Commission Findings as to Facts*, 23 Mich. L. Rev. 233, 233–237 (1925); Powell, *Conclusiveness of Administrative Determinations in the Federal Government*, 1 Am. Pol. Sci. Rev. 583 (1907); Tennant, *Administrative Finality*, 6 Can. Bar Rev. 497 (1928); Tollefson, *Administrative Finality*, 29 Mich. L. Rev. 839 (1931); Isaacs, *Judicial Review of Administrative Findings*, 30 Yale L. J. 781 (1921).

division of governmental functions.[60] At most, the term "legislative" serves to describe subject matter which the courts leave to the discretion of administrative agencies.

Law and Fact. The one functional distinction between the spheres of the courts and the commissions which persists in professional writing and the opinions of the judges is the description of some determinations as "questions of fact" and others as "matters of law." The traditional description of the division of duties between judge and jury, phrased to give a "plausible ring of rationality" [61] to legal thinking, is taken over into administrative law and applied to the division of function between courts and administrative agencies.[62] Much qualified, it runs through the opinions reviewing orders of the Interstate Commerce Commission, and because the words are used in the Federal Trade Commission Act the opinions enforcing or rejecting orders of the commission are replete with reference and discussion.

So far as the orders of the Interstate Commerce Commission are concerned, the courts are left to work out their own principles of control,[63] but in providing for judicial review and enforcement of the orders of the Federal Trade Commission there was a legislative attempt to fix a functional division of authority between the commission and the courts. President Wilson recommended the com-

[60] For an extended discussion see: Dickinson, *Administrative Justice and the Supremacy of Law* (1927), pp. 15–25.

[61] See: Pound, *Administrative Application of Legal Standards*, 44 A. B. A. Rep. 445, 462 (1919).

[62] For this and other analogies see: Dickinson, *Administrative Justice and the Supremacy of Law* (1927), p. 154 et seq. and particularly the materials collected in n. 81, p. 154. For materials on the controverted subject of law and fact in connection with the application of legal standards see: *ibid.*, n. 21, p. 315. On the relation of judge and jury compare: "The judges have always answered a multitude of questions of ultimate fact which forms part of the issue. It is true that this is often disguised by calling them questions of law." Thayer, *Preliminary Treatise on Evidence* (1898), p. 202. And, of course, juries answer questions of law. *Ibid.*, p. 253 et seq. ". . . The legal profession did not strive . . . to construct a purely technical apparatus for conducting trials, but built up its administration of justice as a compromise between the professional element of the Bench on one side, and the popular element of the jury on the other. The first was supposed to deal exclusively with the *law* in the cases, while the latter was called up originally for a verdict as to the *facts* of the trial." Vinogradoff, *Introduction to Historical Jurisprudence* (1920), pp. 7–8.

[63] Except reparation orders and valuation orders which are by statute to be given *prima facie* effect in the courts.

mission "as a clearing house for the facts," [64] and Congress provided that the judgment of the commission on the facts was to be conclusive but matters of law were reviewable in the courts. Although determinations of fact by the trade commission are made conclusive, abstract consideration of the evidence and the treatment of each part of the record as some form of "question of law" has been the means for substitution of the judgment of courts for the decisions of the commissioners. And on the other hand, while the courts are unrestrained in working out the scope of review of Interstate Commerce Commission orders, judicial scrutiny has been sparing and proceeds upon the broad basis of legislative policy and the necessities of each case. "Fact" has served as the label for a category of determinations of the Interstate Commerce Commission which the courts leave almost entirely to the discretion of the administrative body. It is apparent that the differences in statutory provisions in no way explain the dissimilarities in the judicial treatment of the orders of these commissions.[65]

"The delusive simplicity of the distinctions between questions of law and questions of fact has been found a will-of-the-wisp by travellers approaching it from several directions." [66] So far as the experience of the Interstate Commerce and Federal Trade Commissions discloses, the distinction between "law" and "fact" neither makes for consistency nor provides a workable separation.[67]

[64] Special Address to Congress, January 20, 1914, *Messages and Papers of the Presidents*, XVII, 7916; Cong. Rec., Vol. 51, 1963. Compare: "Law is . . . subsequent to the facts. . . . Law follows them; it does not precede or predict or invent them." Wilson, *Law and the Facts*, 5 Am. Pol. Sci. Rev. 1, 2 (1911).

[65] Compare: "Courts may generally be relied upon to interpret statutory provisions in such manner that reviewing powers which they deem essential to private right are not unduly curtailed, and they are apt to ignore refinements of drafting which appear to stand in the way of their power." Freund, *Historical Survey* in *Growth of American Administrative Law* (1923), p. 35.

[66] Isaacs, *The Law and the Facts*, 22 Col. L. Rev. 1 (1922). Thayer's chapter on the province of judge and jury (*Preliminary Treatise on Evidence*, Ch. V) is apparently the basis of much of the current thought on this subject. Compare: "The familiar maxim that questions of law are for the [court] and questions of fact for the [jury], with its popular and embarrassing implication that there is some logical table of affinity which prevents the coupling of law and common sense in intimate union, is as arid as it is neat." Fifoot, *English Law and its Background* (1932), p. 18. There is an essay in strikingly modern tone in 2 Edinburgh Law Journal 144 (1837).

[67] The same determinations are variously labelled "law" or "fact," and even the theoretical separation becomes mixed. Compare: Congress has the power "to authorize an administrative commission to determine . . . pro-

The differentiation may be useful in some instances, but it has in no measure kept the courts and commissions apart. Facts are the materials out of which rules of law are fashioned — principles or rules of law "are merely the legal relations of . . . facts expressed in general words." [68] Consequently, the agency which controls the rules may dispose of the facts as it will.[69] Every "fact" found by the Federal Trade Commission is treated as a matter of "law" in the courts.[70] Even Mr. Justice Brandeis — to whom much of the non-interference of the federal courts with the regulation of interstate transportation must be ascribed — by the turn of a sentence converts a "question of fact" into a "question of law." [71]

visionally the mixed question of law and fact whether . . . methods are unfair." National Harness Manufacturers Ass'n *v.* Federal Trade Commission, 268 Fed. 705, 707 (1920).

[68] ". . . Legal principles have no separate existence from the actual conduct and circumstances of men, that is, the facts of particular cases; but that they are merely the legal relations of such facts expressed in general words. . . ." *Law and Fact*, 2 Edinburgh Law Journal, 144, 148 (1837).

[69] ". . . The judges," says Thayer in speaking of law and fact in jury trials, "are . . . forever advancing . . . on the theoretical province of the legislator and the juryman." *Preliminary Treatise on Evidence* (1898), p. 208. And of course the converse is true — every question may be viewed as one of fact: "All inquiries into the truth, the reality, the actuality of things, are inquiries into the fact about them. . . . But this, it may be said, is a portentous sort of definition; it is turning every question into a question of fact. That is true, so far as any question asks about the existence, the reality, the truth of something. But, obviously, in actual legal use the term has other limitations." *Ibid.*, pp. 191–192.

[70] Compare two fairly representative opinions: "The facts as found by the commission, being supported by testimony are conclusive; but the effect of them is a question of law, to be expressed in a conclusion of law. . . ." Beech-Nut Packing Co. *v.* Federal Trade Commission, 264 Fed. 885, 889 (1920), *reversed* 257 U. S. 441. "Whatever may be the exact meaning of the phrase 'unfair methods of competition,' it is now settled that it is for the courts and not the Commission to determine as a matter of law what is and what is not included in the phrase. This rule is not voided by stating as a finding of fact what is a mere conclusion of law." National Biscuit Co. *v.* Federal Trade Commission, 299 Fed. 733, 738 (1924), *certiorari denied* 266 U. S. 613.

Even where the courts protest that the questions are solely interpretation of the statutes, they review the evidence and accept and reject evidence. This was done, for example, in both courts in Federal Trade Commission *v.* Gratz, 258 Fed. 314 (1919), 253 U. S. 421 (1920).

[71] ". . . A finding that the discrimination is unjust is ordinarily a finding of fact. . . . But the question presented here is whether the discrimination found can be held in law to be attributable to the appellants, and whether they can be required to cancel existing joint rates, unless it is removed. No finding made

The jury analogy or other analogies drawn from the common law system [72] are unsuited to the problem of judicial review of administrative action. The judge in controlling a jury is directing laymen and is "not a mere moderator but is the governor of the trial"; referees, auditors, masters in chancery and the like are the agents of the court and "are always subject to the direction of the court and their reports are essentially advisory." [73] But the commission and the courts are separately constituted and independent bodies composed of specialists in their respective fields. Here is the vital distinction.[74] When the courts do more than hold the commis-

by the Commission can prevent the review of such questions." Central R. Co. *v.* United States, 257 U. S. 247, 256–257 (1921).

[72] Compare an opinion on review of an order of the Federal Trade Commission: "While it was the exclusive right of a jury in a case at law to find the facts in any given case, it still remained the duty of the trial judge, before entering judgment, to decide whether from those facts the injury of unfair competition in business could be lawfully inferred. So also, when the case was in equity, while it was the province of the judge to find the facts, it also was his duty, and as well the duty of a reviewing court, to decide whether, upon those facts so found, the injury of unfair competition in business existed. Presumably, with this recognized existing jurisdiction of federal courts over cases of unfair business competition in mind, Congress passed the Trade Commission Act. . . . When Congress invoked an exercise of supervisory power on the part of [the] courts over the action of the Trade Commission, and enacted that this supervisory power should be exercised before the orders of the Trade Commission could be enforced, it would seem to follow that the supervisory powers which the court was meant and intended to exercise were the usual powers exercised in the usual way by those courts when exercising their power to review, and while the act provided that the findings of fact made by the Commission were final and conclusive, it still remained the duty of the supervising court to determine the same legal questions which a supervising court had in reviewing actions of the trial court, namely, whether under all the facts found by the Trade Commission a case of unfair business competition was established." ". . . When Congress, in invoking such reviewing and supervisory power, said 'the court . . . shall have jurisdiction of the proceeding and of the question determined therein, and shall have power to make and enter *upon the pleadings, testimony and proceedings* set forth in such transcript, a decree affirming, modifying or setting aside the order of the Commission' it was using language which aptly described the customary jurisdiction and power theretofore exercised by Circuit Courts of Appeals in reviewing cases of alleged unfair business competition." Curtis Publishing Co. *v.* Federal Trade Commission, 270 Fed. 881, 908–910 (1921), *affirmed* 260 U. S. 568.

[73] Chief Justice Hughes in Crowell *v.* Benson, 52 S. Ct. 285, 296 (1932).

[74] "Here we come to an impasse in the development of administrative law under our constitutional system. . . ." Rosenberry, *Administrative Law and the Constitution.* 23 Am. Pol. Sci. Rev. 32, 42 (1929).

sioners to the outlines of their authority or demand the existence of evidence which justifies the exercise of that authority, then the legal expert interferes with the administrative specialists who comprise the personnel of the Interstate Commerce Commission and the Federal Trade Commission. Ordinarily the jury is dealing with matters of common knowledge and accepted significance; the commissions are presumably developing public regulation in a new and intricate field. However, even juries may accept or reject evidence and draw inferences, but the Federal Trade Commission may do neither.

IV. The Evidence

If administrative agencies are to be allowed to develop their own system, "law" and "fact" in the field of judicial control of administration must remain only names of parts of the process whereby courts examine the scope of administrative authority and determine whether the disputed situation falls within that authority. "Law" and "fact" in this field are simply the formal links in legal thinking which connect authority with evidence to justify the exercise of that authority. Rules of law must be formulated for no other purpose than to express the judicial estimation of the limits of delegated authority — a process of outlining the scope of the statutes under which administrative agencies operate; the courts ought not intervene to lay down what the judiciary believes the proper rule for the particular case or for all similar cases, for to do so is to usurp the task of administrators who act under broadly delegated authority.[75] Similarly, judicial review of the administrative ascertainment of facts should involve no more than an inquiry into the sufficiency of the evidence to bring the matter within the range of administrative competence (that is, there must be sufficient evidence to identify the particular subject matter with the statutory authority of the administrative tribunal). But the judicial eye looks further into the record to find whether or not there is sufficient evidence upon which a decision may be based, and here bench and administration come in conflict. When courts

[75] But compare: ". . . Where the ground of difference between court and fact-finding body can be isolated and expressed as a general proposition applicable beyond the particular case to all similar cases, the court, if it holds the proposition of sound law, must enforce it by overruling the administrative determination." Dickinson, *Administrative Justice and the Supremacy of Law* (1927), p. 168.

investigate the propriety of inferences drawn from the cumulated bits of evidence in the record, they tend to reduce administrative tribunals to mere magistracies for the conduct of hearings preliminary to judicial consideration. However, although the determination of the facts is admittedly *the* function of the administrative commissions, experience has shown that on judicial examination of the evidence upon which administrative action is predicated the courts frequently oust administrative judgment and substitute therefor the opinions of judges.

Although rules on the admissibility of evidence are not binding on the commissions, all that is in the record does not have probative force.[76] The courts still determine whether "evidence" is sufficient "in law" to establish a particular "fact." Between the record of the evidence and the conclusions to be drawn therefrom is a crucial zone.[77] In reviewing the orders of the Interstate Commerce Commission the courts have come to accept the conclusions of the commission — even to the extent of making administrative conclusions of law (though labelled "ultimate facts") *prima facie* evidence in jury trials.[78]

But in reviewing the orders of the Federal Trade Commission the courts have generally indulged extended inquiry into the abstract nature of proof.[79] Physical facts, relationships, circumstances, acts, mental states, opinion, "other facts,"[80] "negative

[76] On the general subject of rules of evidence in administrative tribunals see: Wigmore, *Administrative Board Rules*, 17 Ill. L. Rev. 263 (1922); Ross, *Applicability of Rules of Evidence in Proceedings before Workmen's Compensation Commissions*, 36 Harv. L. Rev. 263 (1923); Wigmore, *Evidence* (2 ed., 1923), p. 27.

[77] The difficulty in the relation of courts to administrative agencies "is enhanced by the peculiar character of administrative findings of fact. The dispute usually does not turn upon the truth or falsity of the facts established by the commission, but upon the truth or falsity of its conclusions, i. e. either the completeness of the facts to serve as a basis of judgment, or their interpretation and effect. These conclusions must in the nature of things be largely matters of opinion, and the difference between law and fact becomes obscure." Freund, *Historical Survey* in *Growth of American Administrative Law* (1923), p. 32.

[78] Reparation orders. See: Meeker & Co. *v.* Lehigh Valley R. Co., 236 U.S. 412 (1915).

[79] For example: Raladam Co. *v.* Federal Trade Commission, 42 F.(2d) 430 (1930), affirmed on other grounds 283 U. S. 643.

[80] Compare: "In the language of the statute, we think the 'findings of the Commission as to the facts are supported by testimony,' so far as they go. But there are other facts thoroughly proven, admitted at bar, and aiding discus-

acts" [81] — all have received searching attention. Between the evidence and its legal effect the courts run the length and breadth of the legal theory of knowledge — findings, facts, conclusions,[82] inferences,[83] and ultimate facts [84] are terms freely used.[85] When the evidence does not conform to common law requirements the courts are suspicious.[86] Although the exercise of delegated authority of Congress does not and cannot "depend upon the absolute existence in reality of any fact," [87] this is exactly what the courts purport to seek in determining whether or not there is evidence to support an order of the Federal Trade Commission. The source of this difficulty is the failure of the courts to accept or, perhaps,

sion." Standard Oil Co. of N. Y. *v.* Federal Trade Commission, 273 Fed. 478, 480 (1921).

[81] "To these conclusions there should be added certain negative acts, which may be of importance and which are according to the undisputed proofs." Toledo Pipe-Threading Machine Co. *v.* Federal Trade Commission, 11 F.(2d) 337, 339 (1926).

[82] "While these findings are attacked as prejudicial, incomplete, and in some instances unsupported by any evidence, we are persuaded that they should be accepted as the basis of action on the part of this court. . . . Omission has purposely been made of certain findings, more properly called conclusions." Q. R. S. Music Co. *v.* Federal Trade Commission, 12 F.(2d) 730, 732 (1926).

[83] "The controversy turns on the inferences properly to be drawn from the facts. . . ." Thatcher Mfg. Co. *v.* Federal Trade Commission, 5 F.(2d) 615, 616 (1925), *affirmed in part* 272 U. S. 554. See also: Wholesale Grocers' Ass'n *v.* Federal Trade Commission, 277 Fed. 657, 662 (1922).

[84] Misrepresentation, for example, is held to be "an ultimate fact that may be definitely established by the evidence." Procter & Gamble Co. *v.* Federal Trade Commission, 11 F.(2d) 47, 48 (1926), *certiorari denied* 273 U. S. 718.

[85] "The Commission's findings . . . often confound a finding (i. e. a statement of some proved fact) with a conclusion (i. e. an inference drawn from the facts proved). . . ." Eastman Kodak Co. *v.* Federal Trade Commission, 7 F.(2d) 994, 995 (1925), *affirmed* 274 U. S. 619.

[86] ". . . We must inquire whether the Commission's findings of fact are supported by evidence, and this inquiry includes an ascertainment of what kind of evidence, or evidence so-called, the fact-findings rest upon. If by evidence is meant testimonial matter legally competent, relevant, pertinent, and material, this record contains very little of that kind." John Bene & Sons *v.* Federal Trade Commission, 299 Fed. 468, 469 (1924). "Ordinarily the admission of incompetent testimony cannot be assigned as error in a proceeding of this kind, because the court is only concerned with the question whether there is any competent testimony to support the findings of the commission; but, inasmuch as the objection here interposed goes to a considerable part of the testimony admitted and considered by the commission, we deem it proper to consider it briefly." Hills Bros. *v.* Federal Trade Commission, 9 F.(2d) 481, 484 (1926).

[87] Mr. Justice Brandeis, dissenting, in Crowell *v.* Benson, 52 S. Ct. 285, 306 (1932).

to appreciate the matters to be proved; without purpose in view — or at least without open discussion in the opinions — the evidence is adrift.[88]

At first the Supreme Court held that in all but very clear cases the determinations on the evidence should be left to the Federal Trade Commission. "... As the statute grants jurisdiction to make and enter, upon the pleadings, testimony and proceedings, a decree affirming, modifying, or setting aside an order, the court must also have power to examine the whole record and ascertain for itself the issues presented, and whether there are material facts not reported by the commission. If there be substantial evidence relating to such facts from which different conclusions reasonably may be drawn, the matter may be and ordinarily, we think, should be remanded to the commission — the primary fact-finding body — with direction to make additional findings; but if, from all the circumstances, it clearly appears that, in the interest of justice, the controversy should be decided without further delay, the court has full power to do so." Two justices, however, felt this statement might bear "the construction that the court has discretion to sum up the evidence *pro* and *con* on issues undecided by the commission, and make itself the fact-finding body" whereas they thought it was of high importance that the courts "scrupulously comply with the evident intention of Congress that the federal commission be made the fact-finding body, and that the court should in its rulings preserve the board's character as such, and not interject its views of the facts where there is any conflict in the evidence." [89] Nevertheless, this "doubt" and cautionary concurring opinion has not stayed actual practice. From the beginning the courts have determined the weight of the evidence and have substituted their judgment for the conclusions of the commissioners.[90] While on one

[88] Compare: "Evidence is always a relative term. It signifies a relation between two facts, the ... proposition to be proved, and the ... material evidencing the proposition. The former is necessarily hypothetical; the latter is brought forward as a reality for the purpose of convincing the tribunal that the former is also a reality. No correct and sure comprehension of the nature of any evidential question can ever be had unless this double or relative aspect of it is distinctly pictured in each instance." Wigmore, *Principles of Judicial Proof* (2 ed., 1931), p. 8.

[89] Curtis Publishing Co. *v.* Federal Trade Commission, 260 U. S. 568, 580, 583 (1923); and see also the opinion in the lower court, 270 Fed. 881, 911–912.

[90] "The result ... is that practically all that is left to the commission to determine conclusively are mere questions of physical fact and even as to findings involving chiefly such questions, the courts in some cases have felt free to

occasion the Supreme Court announced — perhaps unintentionally — that "the weight to be given to the facts and circumstances . . . as well as the inferences reasonably to be drawn from them is for the Commission," [91] this rule (which had not been followed) was later repudiated by a divided court.[92]

The "statements of facts" in the opinions of the courts are simply the conclusions of the court from the evidence in the record. Dissenting opinions bring out the differences of judgment on the evidence even between judges. Of course no one conceives that the translation of evidence into either facts or law can be made a matter of mechanical legal science. The point is, however, that this is precisely the function of the administrative specialist. When the courts interpret the evidence, any given result may be reached without doing violence to the customary rules of law.

The plausible nature of the distinction between law and fact is illustrated by the advocacy of such a division of function in England [93] and in the literature of political science.[94] However, separation of functions into "fact-finding" and "law-making" does not explain the relations of the courts to the Federal Trade Commission and the Interstate Commerce Commission. With a clearly developed and judicially recognized authority, the Interstate Commerce Commission operates as an authoritative agency for

go back of the findings of the commission to see what conclusions could reasonably be drawn from the testimony and if in their judgment the commission has erred, the courts are apt to conclude that the findings are not supported by the evidence." Tollefson, *Judicial Review of the Decisions of the Federal Trade Commission*, 4 Wis. L. Rev. 257, 297 (1927).

Examples of judicial revaluation of the evidence have already been cited. See also: Philip Carey Mfg. Co. *v.* Federal Trade Commission, 29 F.(2d) 49 (1928), and B. S. Pearsall Butter Co. *v.* Federal Trade Commission, 292 Fed. 720 (1923).

There are some statements in the lower courts to a contrary effect: Moir *v.* Federal Trade Commission, 12 F.(2d) 22, 25 (1926); Ayer *v.* Federal Trade Commission, 15 F.(2d) 274, 276 (1926); Chamber of Commerce etc. *v.* Federal Trade Commission, 280 Fed. 45, 48 (1922); Indiana etc. Co. *v.* Federal Trade Commission, 26 F.(2d) 340, 341 (1928). But at times the courts are quite frank: "In our judgment (this practice) cannot deceive the actual purchaser. . . ." Ostermoor & Co. *v.* Federal Trade Commission, 16 F.(2d) 962.

[91] Pacific States Paper Trade Ass'n *v.* Federal Trade Commission, 273 U. S. 52, 63 (1927).

[92] International Shoe Co. *v.* Federal Trade Commission, 280 U. S. 291 (1930).

[93] Port, *Administrative Law* (1929), 294; Allen, *Bureaucracy Triumphant* (1931), 99.

[94] See *supra*, n. 64.

the regulation of transportation. The Federal Trade Commission has foundered in the attempt to justify before the courts its proceedings toward ends which are not judicially recognized. With much discussion of principle and doctrine and liberal use of the legal terminology of proof, the federal courts have dealt freely with the orders of the trade commission.[95] Orders of the Interstate Commerce Commission, on the other hand, are sustained without doctrinal mechanics or minute scrutiny of the evidence.

V. Conclusion

It is apparent that — while there are several formal approaches to the review of a particular administrative order such as authority, procedure, evidence, and so on — there is no formula which separates the work of the courts from that of the commissions nor which explains the different judicial treatment of the two administrative bodies. Rules and doctrines operate in the abstract with generous assumptions of fact, but the interpretation of the statutes — the delimitation of administrative authority — and the test of conclusions drawn from the evidence are likewise points at which administrative orders are vulnerable at the hands of the courts.

As between the two theories of judicial relation to administrative agencies — that which admits of but one system of justice with the ultimate authority in all particulars in the courts and that theory which recognizes a dual system — the practice of the courts, broadly speaking, follows the first for the trade commission and the second for the commerce commission. But since in neither field do the courts surrender their veto power, particular theories of judicial relation are shifting and obscure. The character of the judicial process is nowhere better stated than in the often quoted words of Mr. Justice Harlan:

> The courts have rarely, if ever, felt themselves so restrained by technical rules that they could not find some remedy, consistent with the law, for acts, whether done by government or by individual persons, that violated . . . justice or were hostile to the . . . principles devised for the protection of the essential rights of property.[96]

---

[95] But compare an earlier estimate: "The conclusiveness of findings of fact must . . . be pronounced a serious defect of the Federal Trade Commission law." Freund, *Shifting Theories of Control*, 7 A. B. A. J. 656, 657 (1921).

[96] Monongahela B. Co. *v.* United States, 216 U. S. 177, 195 (1910). See also: Tollefson, *Administrative Finality*, 29 Mich. L. Rev. 839, 839–840 (1931).

"As the courts undertake to define judicial power when no exact and perfect,

This view has been carried out more fully in connection with the trade commission than with the commerce commission:

> If there be substantial evidence . . . , the matter may be and ordinarily, we think, should be remanded to the [Federal Trade] commission . . . , but if, from all the circumstances, it clearly appears that, in the interest of justice, the controversy should be decided without further delay, the court has full power to do so.[97]

The demand for a formal check upon administrative action by further resort to some regularly constituted tribunal seems firmly rooted in political thinking.[98] Stripped of desire for con-

inclusive and exclusive definition of general application seems possible . . . , and as they also say that they have power to exercise or to refuse to exercise it . . . , much confusion arises as to the nature and proper limitation of judicial review." C. Pound, *Constitutional Aspects of Administrative Law* in *Growth of American Administrative Law* (1923), pp. 123–124.

[97] Curtis Publishing Co. *v.* Federal Trade Commission, 260 U. S. 568, 580 (1923).

[98] "In the estimation of English-speaking people generally, a right of review is no less sacred than the right to be heard in the first instance." Rosenberry, *Administrative Law and the Constitution*, 23 Am. Pol. Sci. Rev. 32, 41 (1929). In the literature there is constant demand or assumption that arbitrary action is to be avoided only by a regularly constituted and formal control and that, further, only in this way may jurisdictional lines be preserved. In contrast with this type of statement, however, is the extent to which judicial control has actually been developed.

However, there is another side. No governmental agency takes reversal at the hands of a second easily. The very existence of a possible veto has great effect, and when such power is used liberally it results in inaction, excessive caution or subterfuge. "When it is urged that harm will follow if the decisions of the boards are made final and without appeal to the courts on matters within their jurisdiction, it might be replied that the decisions of the court in matters within their jurisdiction are final; that perfection does not attach exclusively to the courts; that injustice may take place in any tribunal; that finality might as well be made an incident of the proper exercise of legislative or executive power as of the proper exercise of judicial power and that administrative boards may have been too much restricted by insistence upon enforcement of rights through individual initiative, by judicial forms, — the plaintiff and defendant theory of procedure, — which make administrative orders the result of trial rather than of investigation." C. Pound, *Constitutional Aspects of Administrative Law* in *Growth of American Administrative Law* (1923), p. 127.

The demand for *judicial* review is put upon the basis that administrators are, by the nature of their tasks, not fitted for the development of a body of law and that judicial review provides the "growing point" in the law. Dickinson, *Administrative Justice and the Supremacy of Law* (1927), pp. 203 et seq., 234–235. But this view, though much qualified, posits the development of a body of rules as the purpose of law. Compare: "Almost the whole energy of our ju-

formity to the traditional administration of law, there is still an insistence upon dual authority as a stabilizing or cautionary

dicial system is employed in working out a consistent, logical, minutely precise body of precedents. The important part of our system is not the trial judge who dispenses justice to litigants but the judge of the appellate court who uses the litigation as a means of developing the law; and we judge the system by the output of written opinions and not by the actual results *inter partes* in concrete cases. But the life of the law is in its enforcement." Pound, *Scope and Purpose of Sociological Jurisprudence*, 25 Harv. L. Rev. 489, 514 (1912). The Congressional idea in creating the Federal Trade Commission was to provide an agency which would "build up a body of information and of administrative law" so that "gradually standards [would] be established that [would] be accepted and . . . constitute our code of business morals." Senator Newlands, Cong. Rec., Vol. 51, 11083. But neither the courts nor the commission have developed a body of rules or principles, and so far as the Interstate Commerce Commission is concerned the law has been formulated by the commission with the consent of the courts. The commerce commission has developed rules — crystallized the "standards" — which in the case of the long-and-short-haul clause have been incorporated into the statute. See: Vanderblue, *The Long and Short Haul Clause since 1910*, 36 Harv. L. Rev. 426 (1923), and the amendatory legislation of 1920 (the Transportation Act), Sec. 406, 41 Stat. 456, 480. Some of the judicial decisions are given without opinion; others are based on interpretations of particular situations in a field which is so changing that precedents do not become fixed; and the tendency of the courts to examine the specific determinations of the commissions rather than the scope of their authority is a method of avoiding statement of the law. Furthermore, a body of rules does not necessarily fix the law because this very "growing point" enables the courts through interpretation of the facts and formulation of new rules to avoid precedent.

Finally, admitting the necessity of some reviewing agency, one administrative tribunal might be controlled by another and an autonomous administrative system developed. Compare the statement of a state supreme court judge who sees the solution in some form of specialized appellate tribunal: "One of the most persuasive arguments against a too generous employment of the right to a judicial review is the fact that courts are not equipped to review findings of fact in many technical fields. . . . On the other hand, an unintelligent, improperly equipped administrative body, ignorant of fundamental legal principles, may by its findings and orders do such great injustice that one who suffers therefrom ought, according to the conceptions of justice which obtain among Anglo-American peoples, to be entitled to have them reviewed. Here we come to an impasse in the development of administrative law under our constitutional system. . . ." Rosenberry, *op. cit.*, p. 44. Specialized appellate tribunals are not unknown in the present federal government, and something like it was attempted with the establishment of the Commerce Court. "The need for a coherent system of administrative law, for uniformity and despatch in adjudication, for the subtle skill required in judges called upon to synthesize the public and private claims peculiarly involved in administrative litigation, these and kindred considerations will have to be balanced against the tradi-

force.[99] However, the partnership of differently constituted and traditionally opposed institutions of government in the business of public administration inevitably leads to friction. Whatever division of function is urged, there still remains in the courts a power

tional hold of a single system of courts, giving a generalized professional aptitude to its judges and bringing to the review of administrative conduct a technique and a temperament trained in litigations between private individuals." Frankfurter and Landis, *The Business of the Supreme Court* (1927), pp. 184–186. The creation of a separate body of law outside the field of courts of justice "might be no more radical than that which took place when the Court of Chancery developed the principles of equity to mitigate the harshness and severity of the medieval common law. . . ." C. Pound, *Constitutional Aspects* in *Growth of American Administrative Law* (1923), pp. 130–131. "There is really nothing in the French division of jurisdiction more repugnant to English notions than in the division of our own jurisdiction into Common Law and Equity. Both, in the course of time, have become merely matter of machinery." Allen, *Bureaucracy Triumphant* (1931), p. 54. "There is no reason why the administrative law of the future should not be regularized and developed as part of the ordinary legal system of the land." *Ibid.*, pp. 98–99. There are examples of transition from administrative agencies into courts in the "legislative" courts established by Congress. See: Ex Parte Bakelite Corporation, 279 U. S. 438 (1929); Katz, *Federal Legislative Courts*, 43 Harv. L. Rev. 894 (1930).

"It may well be that some of the principles of Administrative Law are foreign to those of our Common Law, but it can be urged that new circumstances have arisen for which the Common Law does not adequately provide and cannot conveniently be made to provide remedies." "It is to . . . new situations that it is suggested that Administrative Law can properly and under proper safeguards be applied. It is no use trying to defeat it by an appeal to the traditional prejudice against bureaucracy. Some new method must be devised either by adapting old law to modern situations or creating a new code to deal with them." Lord Justice Sankey, *Foreword* to Port's *Administrative Law* (1929).

[99] "The whole question of appeal from administrative tribunals urgently calls for consideration. Not only is the right of appeal vital to the litigant, but the mere existence of it is a powerful stimulus to efficiency and care in the tribunal of first instance — a fact which, in my submission, far outweighs the argument that the existence of an appellate court makes the first trial a mere formal preliminary to a fuller hearing." Allen, *Bureaucracy Triumphant* (1931), p. 66. Compare: "It is complained that the decisions of the board are final and without appeal. So are the decisions of the courts in matters within their jurisdiction. There must be a final tribunal somewhere for deciding every question in the world. Injustice may take place in all tribunals. All human institutions are imperfect — courts as well as commissions and legislatures. Whatever tribunal has jurisdiction, its decisions are final and conclusive unless an appeal is given therefrom. The important question always is, what is the lawful tribunal for the particular case? In my judgment, in the present case, the proper

to keep administration within the bounds of authority, but the judicial interpretation of the general phrases of statutes delegating authority to administrative agencies tends to limit both legislative and administrative power and the judicial examination of evidence impinges upon the function of the commissions to an even greater extent.[100] Difficulties arise from the fact that on final consideration by the more venerable arm of the government the whole proceeding is examined. The power to develop a particular part of the record into rules and to interpret the evidence vests the courts with complete control. To what effect the courts have exercised their power over the Federal Trade Commission and the Interstate Commerce Commission must next be examined.

tribunal was the legislature, or the board of commissioners which it created for the purpose." Mr. Justice Bradley, dissenting, in Chicago, Milwaukee & St. Paul Ry. Co. *v.* Minnesota, 134 U. S. 418, 465 (1890). And see the remarks of Mr. Justice Holmes in a tax case: "The Board was created for the purpose of using its judgment and its knowledge. . . . Within its jurisdiction, except . . . in the case of fraud or a clearly shown adoption of wrong principles, it is the ultimate guardian of certain rights. The State has confided those rights to its protection and has trusted to its honor and capacity as it confides the protection of other social relations to the courts of law. Somewhere there must be an end." Chicago, B. & Q. Ry. Co. *v.* Babcock, 204 U. S. 585, 598 (1907).

[100] Compare: "As interpretation on the one side runs into lawmaking and so the judicial function runs into the legislative function, on the other side interpretation runs into application and so the judicial function runs into the administrative or executive." Pound, *Introduction to the Philosophy of Law* (1922), p. 108.

CHAPTER III

THE FEDERAL TRADE COMMISSION IN THE COURTS

I. Political and Legislative History

The regulation of trade at common law and the events leading to the establishment of the Federal Trade Commission have been thoroughly sifted elsewhere — in fact, no administrative agency in the United States has merited so extensive a literature as the trade commission.[1] Advocated by both major parties in the presidential campaign, the commission was established in 1914. Its purpose was to provide teeth for the laws through a permanent

[1] For example: Blaisdell, *The Federal Trade Commission* (1932); Butler and Lynde, *The Federal Trade Commission* (1915); Clark, *The Federal Trust Policy* (1931), pp. 165–187; Curtis, *The Trusts and Economic Control* (1931); Daish, *The Federal Trade Commission,* 24 Yale L. J. 43 (1914); Davies, *Trust Laws and Unfair Competition* (Dept. of Comm., Bureau of Corporations, 1915); Davies, *The Federal Trade Commission* in *Growth of American Administrative Law* (1923), and 18 Fla. S. B. A. 93 (1925); Durand, *The Trust Problem* (1915), Ch. V; Fayne, *The Federal Trade Commission: The Development of the Law Which Led to Its Establishment,* 9 Am. Pol. Sci. Rev. 57 (1915); Hankin, *Functions of the Federal Trade Commission,* 6 Ill. L. Q. 183, 183–184 (1924); Harland and McCandless, *The Federal Trade Commission* (1916); Haycroft, *Attempts of Congress to Promote Free Competition,* 8 Nat. U. L. Rev. 39 (1928); Henderson, *The Federal Trade Commission* (1924), Ch. I; Holt, *The Federal Trade Commission* (1922); Jones, *The Trust Problem in the United States* (1921), Ch. XV; Jones, *Historical Development of the Law of Business Competition,* 35 Yale L. J. 905, 36 Id. 42, 207 (1926), 36 Id. 351 (1927); Montague, *Anti-Trust Laws and the Federal Trade Commission: 1914–1926,* 27 Col. L. Rev. 650, 13 A. B. A. J. 328 (1927); Rublee, *The Original Plan and Early History of the Federal Trade Commission,* Proc. Acad. Pol. Sci., xi, 666 (1924–1926); Seager and Gulick, *Trust and Corporation Problems* (1929); *Public Regulation of Competitive Practices* (Nat. Ind. Conf. Bd., 1925); *Statutes and Decisions Pertaining to the Federal Trade Commission* (1930), n., p. 2.

In addition to the material noted there are other articles devoted to jurisdiction and judicial review of the commission's orders: Hankin, *Jurisdiction of the Federal Trade Commission,* 12 Calif. L. Rev. 179 (1924); Hankin, *Judicial Review of Federal Trade Commission's Orders,* 6 Ill. L. Q. 264 (1924); Hankin, *Conclusiveness of the Federal Trade Commission's Findings as to Facts,* 23 Mich. L. Rev. 233 (1925); Levy, *A Decade of the Federal Trade Commission,* 11 Va. L. Rev. 21, 111 (1924), 169, 372 (1925); Tollefson, *Judicial Review of the Decisions of the Federal Trade Commission,* 4 Wis. L. Rev. 257 (1927).

and specialized body of administrators. It superseded the former Bureau of Corporations which had been set up as an investigative division of the Department of Commerce and Labor.[2] The new commission of five members was to supply a speedy, preventive, and expert administration of the law which was felt to be lacking under the former system. However, the legislative history of the statutes which the commission is commanded to enforce, so far as their substantive provisions are concerned, discloses only vague purpose and sharp disagreement on detail.[3] The legislative statement of the relations of the commission to the courts has not been changed since the creation of the commission, nor have the powers of the commission been altered except for the extension of its authority to include foreign trade[4] and the transfer of some of its powers to other governmental agencies.[5] Accordingly, with the original legislation in mind, the development and present state of judicial relations with the commission are to be discovered in the decisions and opinions of the courts reviewing, enforcing, or refusing to enforce the orders of the commission.

II. The Statutes

Statutory Provisions. The duties given the Federal Trade Commission fall into two classes — regulatory and investigative.[6] The

[2] Compare: ". . . The great value to the American people of the Interstate Commerce Commission has been largely because of its independent power and authority. The dignity of the proposed [federal trade] commission and the respect in which its performance of its duties will be held by the people will also be largely because of its independent power and authority." Report of the House Committee (1914), 63d Cong., 2 Sess., No. 533, p. 3.

[3] See, for example: Henderson, *The Federal Trade Commission* (1924), Ch. I.

[4] Export Trade Act, April 10, 1918, 40 Stat. 516.

[5] Packers and Stockyards Act, August 15, 1921, 42 Stat. 159. See: Veeder, *The Federal Trade Commission and the Packers*, 15 Ill. L. Rev. 485 (1921); and possibly also: *Grain Futures Act*, 42 Stat. 998 (1922). (See Chamber of Commerce of Minneapolis *v.* Federal Trade Commission, 13 F. (2d) 673.) *Tariff Act* of 1916 as amended in 1922 and 1930, 39 Stat. 795, 42 Stat. 943, was repealed by the Act of June 17, 1930, 46 Stat. 696, and by Section 703 unfair methods of competition in importation of articles or in their sale are declared unlawful; the Tariff Commission is authorized to investigate and the President to execute the provision. *Capper-Volstead Act*, 42 Stat. 388 (1922), agricultural associations; for an account of the legislative history with references and the distrust of the Federal Trade Commission see: Seager and Gulick, *Trust and Corporation Problems* (1929), pp. 443–444.

[6] The investigative function and absorption of the Bureau of Corporations were parts of the Federal Trade Commission project. Report of Senate Com-

investigative duties are clearly distinguished in the act from the power to regulate competition, but the former are not the principal concern in this study. The statutes fixing the regulatory powers and duties of the commission are brief. The powers of the commission are stated in two acts, and on only five sections of these are the regulatory orders of the commission based.

The Clayton Act vested authority in the commission to prohibit four types of commercial practice.[7] Section 2 is aimed at the elimination of price discrimination which injures or destroys the business of a competitor. Section 3 declares unlawful lease or sale of goods on condition that the lessee or purchaser not use or deal in the goods of a competitor of the seller or lessor. Section 7 prohibits a corporation from acquiring the whole or any part of the stock or other share capital of a competing corporation. And Section 8 prohibits any one person from serving as a director in two or more competing corporations of certain size. These prohibitions are dependent upon the existence of interstate commerce in each instance and upon the tendency of any particular practice to substantially lessen or restrain competition or create monopoly (in the case of Section 8, where an "elimination of competition by agreement between them would violate any of the provisions of any of the anti-trust acts").

The fifth, and broadest, grant of authority to the commission is the single sentence of the Federal Trade Commission Act which declares that "unfair methods of competition in commerce are hereby declared unlawful." [8] On the meaning of the phrase "unfair *methods* of competition" there were differences of opinion in the Senate debates, although the Senate committee reported that "the term 'unfair competition' has a legal significance which can

mittee, 63d Cong., 2 Sess., No. 597, pp. 11–12. Randolph, *Inquisitorial Power Conferred by the Trade Commission Bill*, 23 Yale L. J. 672 (1914). The investigative powers of the commission, as interpreted by the courts, are inadequate. This is the one phase of its work in which the commission has persistently requested legislation. See *infra*, p. 182 n. 41, and compare the discussions in Seager and Gulick, *op. cit.*, pp. 467–472, 546–547; Keezer and May, *The Public Control of Business* (1930), pp. 88 et seq., 241; Handler, *Constitutionality of Investigations by the Federal Trade Commission*, 28 Col. L. Rev. 708, 905 (1928).

A comparative study of the investigative powers of the Interstate Commerce Commission and the Federal Trade Commission would be fruitful, but space does not permit. It should be noted that specific orders in the various fields of regulation have often been preceded by general investigations.

[7] 38 Stat. 730 (1914).

[8] 38 Stat. 717, September 26, 1914, Sec. 5.

be enforced by the Commission and the courts, and that it is no more difficult to determine what is unfair competition than it is to determine what is a reasonable rate or what is unjust discrimination." [9] The struggle to "interpret" these words is illustrated in those opinions which stress — without very clear reason — the fact that the phrase "unfair competition" was changed to "unfair methods of competition" before final passage. The prohibition of this section, of course, is limited to practices used in interstate commerce. The development of a further limitation — that the matter be "to the interest of the public" — will be discussed presently.

As a "delegation of authority" these enactments confer broad powers [10] even though as a statement of law for specific instances they are vague.[11] How far-reaching the powers of the commission are to be depends upon the action of the commission as limited by the courts.[12]

After procedure before the commission and issuance of an order prohibiting a specific practice,[13] the matter may be taken to a federal circuit court of appeals either by the commission to enforce

[9] Report of Senate Committee, 63d Cong., 2 Sess., No. 597, p. 13.

[10] Compare the statement of a writer in 1915 after summarizing the powers stated in the acts: "Verily, a colossus stands astride the business World." Gallagher, *The Federal Trade Commission*, 10 Ill. L. Rev. 31, 42.

[11] Early attempts at interpretation will illustrate: Needham, *The Federal Trade Commission*, 16 Col. L. Rev. 175 (1916); Stevens, *Unfair Competition*, 29 Pol. Sci. Q. 282 (1916); Haines, *Efforts to Define Unfair Competition*, 29 Yale L. J. 1 (1919); Rogers, *Unfair Competition*, 17 Mich. L. Rev. 490 (1919); Carrington, *Unfair Competition*, 7 Va. L. Rev. 361 (1921); Paul, *Unfair Competition and Its Late Developments*, 6 St. Louis L. Rev. 73 (1921).

[12] There is an excellent discussion of this problem on the basis of the statutory provisions with a remarkable intimation of what was to happen a decade later in Kerr, *The Trade Commission and the Courts*, 9 Ill. L. Rev. 338 (1914).

[13] While this study concerns only judicial review of the orders of the commission, it is important to bear in mind the stages through which matters have passed before coming to the attention of the courts. After the matter is brought to the attention of the commission, there is a preliminary investigation to determine whether the commission has jurisdiction, an investigation into the facts, an examination of the record by a commissioner who makes recommendations to the full commission, the issuance of a complaint, and answer by the respondent, taking of testimony or stipulation of facts in lieu thereof, filing of briefs and oral argument before the full commission, and finally the decision of the commission. Later there was added a preliminary review of the record by a "board of review" consisting of five lawyers from the commission's staff, including an informal hearing of the parties (see Ann. Rep., 1925, pp. 65, 111; 1927, p. 2) before the matter is finally considered by the full commission.

its order or by the party against whom the order is directed to have the order set aside. Appeal from the decisions of the intermediate federal courts lies within the discretion of the United States Supreme Court, and the Supreme Court's refusal to review is an affirmance of the lower court's decision. The record of the investigation by the commission, together with the findings of fact and conclusions of law made by the commission, are transmitted to the enforcing or reviewing court which, by the Federal Trade Commission Act, is given "jurisdiction of the proceeding and the question determined therein" and has authority "to make and enter upon the pleadings, testimony, and proceedings set forth . . . a decree affirming, modifying, or setting aside the order of the commission" although "the findings of the commission as to the facts, if supported by testimony," are "conclusive."

The commission's first years were taken up with the formulation of policy and then with war work. The law of trade regulation was carefully studied.[14] Cooperation with industry, which had been so much stressed while legislation was pending, was sought but without particular success.[15] The resources and facilities of the commission were used in the conduct of the war from 1917 to 1919.[16] It was not until 1919 that the first order of the commission in the regulation of competition was brought to a test in the courts, and it was not until 1920 that the commission was able to report that its work had "reached a point where through final disposition of a large number of cases, it was possible for the Commission's orders and the law under which it works to become the subject of review in the courts." [17]

III. The Course of Judicial Control (by Fiscal Years)

1919–1920: The Gratz Case. The first decision on review of an order of the Federal Trade Commission was handed down by the Circuit Court of Appeals for the Seventh Circuit on August 29,

[14] Davies, *Trust Laws* (1915); see also: Ann. Rep., 1916, pp. 6, 26–27.

[15] Compare: Ann. Rep., 1916, p. 15.

[16] See: Executive Order, June 15, 1917, *Messages and Papers of the Presidents*, XVIII, 8366 at 8370; Ann. Rep., 1917, p. 3; 1918, pp. 1–8, 9–27, 42–52; 1919, pp. 3, 17–43, 97–99. However, regulatory activities were not entirely suspended: Ann. Rep., 1918, pp. 53–84; 1919, pp. 45–87.

[17] Ann. Rep., 1920, p. 7. (The annual reports of the commission cover the period from July 1 to June 30.)

1919.[18] After investigation and hearing, the commission had ordered a mail order merchandising company to cease false and misleading advertising as to its own wares and misrepresentations of the merchandise sold by its competitors. The company was also directed to cease selling a staple at less than cost on condition that the purchaser simultaneously take other merchandise at prices which gave the company a profit on the transaction without letting the customer know the facts. To the contention of the company that the Federal Trade Commission Act — the prohibition of unfair methods of competition — was void for indefiniteness unless limited to previously existing common-law definitions, the court replied that the words "unfair methods of competition" were like numerous legal standards such as "due process of law," or "unjust discrimination." The statute was interpreted to mean that the commissioners were to "exercise their common sense, as informed by their knowledge of the general idea of unfair trade at common law, and stop those trade practices that have a capacity or a tendency to injure competitors . . . quite irrespective of whether the specific practices in question have yet been denounced in common-law cases." The court found no lack of process under the Constitution since a day in court was specifically provided wherein "the same principles and tests that have been applied under the common law" or statutes involving similar general expressions would prevail. Having touched upon the common law, the legal conception of standards, and the doctrine of supremacy of law, the court next considered the question of delegation of legislative and judicial power and found that necessity, practice, and the nature of judicial and legislative functions permitted this type of administration. The court determined, however, that the requirement that the company desist from selling below cost (the use of "leaders" on condition that other merchandise be purchased at the same time) was improper only when advertised to mislead purchasers or injure competitors; the order of the commission was, therefore, modified in this particular. The company contended that it had already abandoned the practices and that hence the order of the commission should be vacated, but the court answered that it was for the commission to determine "the real nature of the

[18] Sears, Roebuck & Co. *v.* Federal Trade Commission, 258 Fed. 307. An earlier proceeding in the form of a petition to vacate an interlocutory order of the commission had been dismissed on August 16, 1918, as premature. Federal Trade Commission *v.* Nulomoline Co., 254 Fed. 988.

petitioner's attitude" and that the company could not attack the order of the commission and at the same time claim that it had abandoned the objectionable practice. One of the three judges, however, thought that there had been no unfairness toward competitors (although the company had admitted that its advertisements were unfair and unjust), that this past instance did not afford "remotest cause to believe there would be a repetition," and that the matter was not of public interest as required by the statute and therefore not within the jurisdiction of the commission. It is noteworthy that in this first case were presented most of the problems which continue to vex the commission for the next ten years.

Relying upon this initial success, there is a definitely buoyant attitude in the commission's report to Congress on the year's work: "... Upon the creation of the Commission it was empowered to leave the shores defined by the common law, and taking the knowledge of those decisions with it, to embark on an uncharted sea, using common sense plus the common law for its compass."[19] However, the commission was not entirely unaware that court decisions on pending appeals would become "the legal corner stones that will clarify the general principles, defining what is unfair competition."[20]

This first decision was followed, six months later, by three decisions of the Circuit Court of Appeals for the Second Circuit reversing the commission.[21] On June 7, 1920, the Supreme Court of the United States gave its first decision on review of an order of the commission.[22] This is the outstanding decision on the relation of the courts and the commission.

The commission found that a firm engaged in the distribution of steel ties used in binding bales of cotton (which firm was found to have a dominating and controlling position through its relation with the manufacturer of the ties) refused to sell the product unless at the same time purchasers took a proportionate amount of bagging to be used with the ties. The commission ordered the dis-

[19] Ann. Rep., 1919, p. 45.

[20] Idem, p. 46.

[21] Beech-Nut Packing Co. *v.* Federal Trade Commission, 264 Fed. 885 (resale price maintenance); New Jersey Asbestos Co. *v.* Federal Trade Commission, 264 Fed. 509 (commercial bribery); Ward Baking Co. *v.* Federal Trade Commission, 264 Fed. 330 (sales practice). February 26, 1920.

[22] Federal Trade Commission *v.* Gratz, 253 U. S. 421, *affirming* 258 Fed. 314.

continuance of this method of forcing sales. A circuit court of appeals reversed the order of the commission. Although the lower court said there was "testimony to support the findings of fact," nevertheless the court did inquire into the evidence and adopted the firm's defense — that the practice had been adopted to prevent private parties securing a corner in the market at a time when there was a shortage in ties. According to the established rule in appellate courts, the tribunal which hears evidence is entitled to reject any part thereof, but here the court accepts certain evidence and rejects findings of the commission.

The commission appealed to the Supreme Court. There the reversal of the commission was sustained on the ground that the complaint "was wholly insufficient to charge respondents with practicing 'unfair methods of competition in commerce' within the fair intendment of those words." Having reversed the commission on a point of pleading, the court refused to "discuss conflicting views concerning validity and meaning of the act creating the commission or the effect of the evidence presented." Delegation of authority to the commission was denied: "The words 'unfair method of competition' are not defined by statute and their exact meaning is in dispute. It is for the courts, not the commission, ultimately to determine as a matter of law what they include." And the act was construed as no change in the previous state of the law. The words "unfair methods of competition," said the court, "are clearly inapplicable to practices never heretofore regarded as opposed to good morals because characterized by deception, bad faith, fraud or oppression, or as against public policy because of their dangerous tendency unduly to hinder competition or create monopoly. The act was certainly not intended to fetter free and fair competition as commonly understood and practiced by honorable opponents in trade." Despite the present liberal rules of pleading in other fields of the law both in interpretation of pleadings and direct and implied amendments, unless the original complaint issued by the commission contains every allegation deemed necessary by the courts, an order issued is "improvident and, when challenged, will be annulled by the court." A vigorous dissenting opinion pointed out that the decision of the majority was contrary to established practice in pleading, that there was sufficient evidence upon which the commission could reasonably find unfair competition, and that on the facts — which the lower court had found sufficiently supported by evidence —

the order of the commission should be sustained, and the judicial interpretation of the powers of the commission was protested.[23]

The report of the commission to Congress after this decision was handed down contains a hopefully strained interpretation of legal developments: "These decisions go far toward furnishing a workable interpretation of the [Federal Trade Commission Act, Section 5]. The decisions in other cases now pending, one in the Supreme Court, will doubtless throw further light on its construction and remove much of the doubt respecting the general principles which must govern its administration." [24] But three years later the commission informed Congress that this opinion, in limiting the commission to matters previously regarded as opposed to good morals or against public policy, "tended to restrict the jurisdiction of the commission to precedents established under the common law and judicial decisions" the result of which affected adversely "the ready development of the law of business practices under the commission's rulings." At the same time, borrowing from the dissenting opinion, the commission reported that the decision contained "a second denial . . . when the court attached to the commission's procedure a rule of pleading comparable in its strictness to that governing a criminal indictment." [25]

1920–1921: Proceedings to Restrain Investigations. The next legal developments were two attempts, by application to the courts for injunctions, to halt inquiries begun by the commission.[26] A firm sought to stop an investigation of alleged commercial bribery. The court sustained the act as constitutional and determined that

[23] For the purposes of this comparative study, the following remarks from the dissenting opinion are directly in point: "In leaving to the Commission the determination of the question whether the method of competition pursued in a particular case was unfair, Congress followed the precedent which it had set a quarter of a century earlier, when by the Act to Regulate Commerce it conferred upon the Interstate Commerce Commission power to determine whether a preference or advantage given to a shipper or locality fell within the prohibition of an undue or unreasonable preference or advantage."

[24] Ann. Rep., 1920, p. 48.

[25] Ann. Rep., 1923, p. 7.

[26] Ann. Rep., 1921, p. 24: "A new development of the year . . . was the attempt, in two instances, to have courts of equity enjoin the Commission from hearing and determining the charges stated in complaints issued by it, . . . in both instances the attempt failed. . . ." A previous attempt to halt investigation was dismissed as premature. Federal Trade Commission *v.* Nulomoline Co., 254 Fed. 988 (1918).

injunctive relief was improper and that the jurisdiction of the circuit courts of appeals *after* the completion of proceedings by the commission was the only remedy. "In all of the proceedings, whether before the commission or the court, the amplest provision is made for notice to and full hearing of all parties interested, and for this court . . . to anticipate by injunction the action of the commission, and the judgment of the court charged under the law with the review thereof, would be clearly an usurpation of authority." [27] The second attempt took place in the courts of the District of Columbia, but the court refused to halt the investigation into resale price maintenance and tying contracts. An attempted appeal was dismissed.[28]

These decisions avoided further complication in the procedure under the act and enabled the commission to complete investigation before its work could be attacked in the courts. Nevertheless, in later years attempts will again be made to stop proceedings before the commission issues its order or makes findings.

Also, during this fiscal year, in proceedings in the intermediate federal courts the commission's orders were upheld in one instance,[29] reversed in several,[30] and petitions for review of other orders were filed and pending in different circuit courts of appeals. The commission appealed all cases of reversal in the lower courts; the forthcoming decisions of the highest court in these appeals establish the first final pronouncements on the law of unfair competition administered under the Federal Trade Commission Act.

1921–1922: Restricted Administration. The decisions of the United States Supreme Court during the fiscal year 1921–1922

[27] T. C. Hurst & Son *v.* Federal Trade Commission, 268 Fed. 874 (Oct. 20, 1920).

[28] Supreme Court, District of Columbia, no opinion, August 12, 1921. Ann. Rep., 1921, pp. 26–27; 1922, pp. 20–21.

[29] National Harness Mfrs. Asso. *v.* F. T. C., 268 Fed. 705 (Dec. 7, 1920) (concerted action to prevent competitors from securing supplies).

[30] Curtis Publishing Co. *v.* F. T. C., 270 Fed. 881 (Mar. 2, 1921); Fruit Growers' Express *v.* F. T. C., 274 Fed. 205 (June 16, 1921) (appeal to Supreme Court dismissed on stipulation, 261 U. S. 629); Standard Oil Co. *v.* F. T. C., 273 Fed. 478 (May 11, 1921); Winstead Hosiery Co. *v.* F. T. C., 272 Fed. 957 (Apr. 13, 1921).

Proceedings for review of one order were dismissed on stipulation of counsel. Standard Oil Co. *v.* F. T. C. 271 Fed. 1023 (Jan. 11, 1921).

are, therefore, the beginnings of the line of decisions which became those "legal corner stones" anticipated by the commission in 1919. The first of these cases involved resale price maintenance, a practice which had been declared unlawful under the Sherman Act and which the Federal Trade Commission now sought to enforce under the broad provision of Section 5 of the Federal Trade Commission Act. A manufacturer had been directed to cease the practice of maintaining retail prices — particularly by cooperative action or by refusal to supply retailers who would not sell the product at prescribed prices only. A circuit court of appeals, relying upon an opinion of the Supreme Court which appeared to distinguish between agreements to maintain prices and price maintenance attained in other ways, reversed the commission. The Supreme Court, however, determined that the precedents under the Sherman Act were material only so far as they declare "public policy" and that the essential agreement, combination, or conspiracy might be "implied from a course of dealing or other circumstances." The system of listing retailers as "undesirable" or "price cutters" and methods of securing information as to the resale prices were held within the prohibition of the statute, and the commission was sustained.[31] Three justices dissented on the ground that resale price fixing did not have "a dangerous tendency unduly to hinder competition," a view that has since received practical recognition. A fourth justice dissented on the ground that since there were no contracts fixing resale prices, the company was free to deal as it wished.

Although the Supreme Court was sharply divided, resale price maintenance was established as a method of unfair competition and became one of the chief activities of the commission. However, enforcement is made difficult and the state of the law on the point is unsatisfactory owing to the attempt of the Supreme Court to steer a course between the "right not to sell" for any or no reason and methods of securing information as to price cutters. As one writer has put it: "A system of price maintenance, enforced by a policy of refusing to sell to price cutters, is permitted, but modern business methods may not be used to make it effective."[32]

Another point deserves mention. Regardless of the significance of the change made in this particular case, the Supreme Court

[31] Beech-Nut Packing Co. *v.* F. T. C., 257 U. S. 441 (Jan. 3, 1922), *reversing* 264 Fed. 885.

[32] Henderson, *The Federal Trade Commission* (1924), p. 299.

modified the broad order of the commission to prohibit the specific practices shown (of obtaining information on price cutters) plus "other equivalent *cooperative* means of accomplishing the maintenance of prices." The Supreme Court furnished a precedent for revising the orders of the commission which the circuit courts of appeals freely exercised in later years. On the basis of this decision the Supreme Court directed the commission to modify another order.[33]

The Supreme Court next, by refusing to review decisions of a circuit court of appeals, sustained the annulment of two orders of the commission respecting commercial bribery in the form of percentages on purchases. Although the supplies were transported into the state and sold to shipping companies, the orders were reversed on the ground that no interstate commerce was involved, and although the supplies were later used on the seas, no foreign commerce was involved.[34]

The authority of the federal government to regulate general trade practices as well as carriers is, of course, based upon the commerce clause of the constitution. The courts and the commission may differ on the interpretation of the constitution, but since the courts have preempted the field in the course of constitutional development until the matter has become a judicial question (although the regulation of trade and commerce in its present aspects may be entirely dissociated from the traditional problem of state's rights) it may seem out of place to suggest that an administrative difference of opinion be entitled to consideration.

Just as the Supreme Court, in reversing a circuit court of appeals and sustaining an order of the commission, had established resale price maintenance as a form of unfair competition, another case with the same judicial history confirmed the commission in its efforts to stamp out fraudulent advertising and misbranding of merchandise. The commission directed a manufacturer to cease advertising and labelling clothing as "wool," "merino," or "worsted" which was only part wool. The manufacturer ad-

[33] Mishawaka Woolen Mfg. Co. *v.* F. T. C., 283 Fed. 1022 (Sept. 13, 1922), *certiorari denied* 260 U. S. 748, the court "assuming that the commission will modify its order accordingly."

[34] Winslow et al. *v.* F. T. C., 277 Fed. 206 (Nov. 1, 1924), *certiorari denied* 258 U. S. 618.

mitted that the products, though so advertised and labelled, were not composed wholly of wool but asserted that these products were made "to meet the varying demands of the trade" and that the trade practice had been "followed by all the manufacturers engaged therein." The agreed statement of facts also recited that large quantities of similar wearing apparel imported from foreign countries were similarly labelled and sold in competition with the goods of the manufacturer now ordered to desist. The lower court reversed the order on the ground that the commission was not "a censor of commercial morals generally" and could only act in a matter of public interest, and that — assuming that some consumers were misled or deliberately deceived — "the result is in no way connected with unfair competition, but is like any other misdescription or misbranding of products." The commission then took the case to the Supreme Court, where the lower court was reversed and the commission sustained.[35] The opinion of the Supreme Court, unlike that of the lower court, emphasized the facts which misled the buying public, found undoubted support in the evidence, and found further that even buyers for retailers as well as the public were deceived by the labels. As to the defense that this was the general trade practice, the court found the matter one of public interest and that the practice was an unfair method of competition against manufacturers who might brand their product truthfully. General indulgence in a practice, it was held, does not make it fair, and the deception of the buying public is sufficient even though retailers are not misled. Furnishing another with the means of consummating a fraud, said the court, has "long been a part of the law of unfair competition." Although the opinion sets store on unfairness to a possible "truthful" manufacturer, this seems no more a matter of unfair competition than resale price maintenance in the previous case. Nevertheless, deception of the public is stressed rather than unfair competition, the opinion is written by one of the four dissenting justices in the former case, and only one justice dissented.

To summarize: During this fiscal year the Supreme Court established the power of the commission over resale price maintenance and false or misleading advertising or misbranding. In addition, there were a number of decisions in the circuit courts of appeals,

[35] Winstead Hosiery Co. *v.* F. T. C., 258 U. S. 483 (Apr. 24, 1922), *reversing* 272 Fed. 957.

in four of which the commission's orders were reversed [36] and in four of which its orders were sustained.[37] Another circuit court of appeals refused to interfere with a pending investigation.[38] At the close of the fiscal year the commission reported that "the notable feature of the year for the commission was the development of the law of unfair competition as exemplified by those decisions in the courts which further established and defined the powers of the commission." [39]

1922–1923: Administration Further Restricted. Within the following twelve months, however, the commission was reversed by the decision or with the approval of the Supreme Court in three items of trade regulation of first importance. By these decisions the commission's attempts to regulate two new features of trade practice were set aside.

Merchandising arrangements conditioned upon the exclusion of products of competitors had long been regarded as unfair competition, and Congress in the Clayton Act prohibited a lease, sale, or contract "on condition, agreement, or understanding" not to deal in the commodities of competitors of the lessor or sellers when the effect was "to substantially lessen competition or tend to create monopoly in any line of commerce." The first judicial test of this trade practice occurred in connection with an order of the commission directed against an exclusive dealing device in the form of a distribution system.[40] A large magazine-publishing company had built up a system whereby its agents marketed and distributed magazines through local schoolboys. The point of objection was the insistence of the company that its agents distribute no other magazines through the local organizations. This, the commission

[36] Canfield Oil Co. *v.* F. T. C. (and) Five Other Cases, 274 Fed. 571 (July 1, 1921); Kinney-Rome Co. *v.* F. T. C., 275 Fed. 665 (Sept. 8, 1921); Raymond Bros.-Clark Co. *v.* F. T. C., 280 Fed. 529 (May 8, 1922); Sinclair Refining Co. *v.* F. T. C., 276 Fed. 686 (Sept. 8, 1921).

[37] Aluminum Co. of America *v.* F. T. C., 284 Fed. 401 (June 1, 1922); Royal Baking Powder Co. *v.* F. T. C., 281 Fed. 744 (May 1, 1922); Western Sugar Refinery et al. *v.* F. T. C., 275 Fed. 725 (Oct. 10, 1921); Wholesale Grocers Ass'n *v.* F. T. C., 277 Fed. 657 (Jan. 6, 1922).

[38] Chamber of Commerce of Minneapolis *v.* F. T. C., 280 Fed. 45 (Mar. 27, 1922).

[39] Ann. Rep., 1922, p. 2.

[40] Curtis Publishing Co. *v.* F. T. C., 260 U. S. 568 (Jan. 8, 1923), *affirming* 270 Fed. 881 (Mar. 2, 1921).

determined, was unfair competition. The company took the matter to a circuit court of appeals which reversed the order of the commission. The lower court reviewed the evidence extensively, entered into a full discussion of doctrine, and based decision upon its view of the evidence. The company had asserted, by way of defense, that certain powerful competitors were seeking to make use of the distribution system which had been built up over a period of years at considerable expense. The court found that the agreements with the local persons who received the magazines and handled them through the schoolboys were "agencies" and not "contracts of sale," therefore not within the Clayton Act. The court also found that the company did not have a monopoly on the means of distribution.

The commission appealed to the Supreme Court, but there the reversal of the commission was approved. The opinion of the Supreme Court follows the general outline of the opinion of the lower court. The evidence to the effect that this distributing system was built up by the company, that it required exclusive agents to train and superintend the boys and otherwise handle the distribution of magazines, that only part of these agents had previously been engaged in dealing with periodicals of other publishers, and that the company had no intent to engage in an unfair method of competition was stressed. The contracts were held "agencies" and not "sales," thereby removing difficulties under the Clayton Act. Instead of assuming (as would ordinarily be done on review of a jury verdict) that the evidence supporting facts not found by the commission had been rejected, the court reconsidered the whole case and declared that the agreements "were made without unlawful motive, and in the orderly course of an expanding business." ". . . The commission has not found all the material facts; but, considering those which it has found, and the necessary effect of the evidence, the order to desist is clearly wrong, and should be set aside without further delay." The industry and diligence of the company were held so commendable that the result did not constitute an unfair method of competition in spite of "insuperable . . . difficulties which rivals must face." The justices had some difficulty in stating the power and duty of the courts in reviewing the record, but the court was unanimous in concluding that the evidence so clearly showed no unfair method of competition that reversal of the order was warranted without returning the case to the commission for further findings.

The distinction between "sale" and "agency" is technical[41] and conducive to evasion of the act, and the courts have variously interpreted these arrangements.[42] Then too, it is difficult to understand the judicial emphasis on lack of motive; if the effect is to lessen competition or create monopoly, this should suffice and, in fact, is sometimes held sufficient.[43] The commission commented specially in its report to Congress.[44] The case presents clearly differences of judgment — the commission believed the arrangement in effect impaired competition but the court stressed the business acumen of the company and found nothing illegal.

Tying or exclusive contracts in another form came before the Supreme Court in connection with the review of a number of orders of the commission directed against gasoline manufacturers. In proceedings against some thirty refiners and wholesalers the commission had condemned and ordered the discontinuance of the practice of leasing underground tanks and pumps to retail dealers at nominal prices upon condition that the equipment be used only with gasoline supplied by the lessor. Many of the companies sought review of the orders in the circuit courts of appeals and in each of these cases the orders of the commission were reversed.[45]

[41] Compare the remark of President Wilson: "We have created, in the Federal Trade Commission, a means of inquiry and . . . to remove the barriers of misunderstanding and of a too technical interpretation of the law." Acceptance of Renomination to the Presidency, September 2, 1916, *Messages and Papers of the Presidents*, XVIII, 8149 at 8158.

[42] For example: "Because the petitioners are making the new form of so-called 'agency contracts,' it cannot be argued that they have discontinued the methods found by the commission to be offensive. . . . We regard this new form of contract as an effort to modify the form, and not the substance, of the petitioners' business methods." Butterick Co. *v.* F. T. C., 4 F.(2d) 910 (Jan. 5, 1925).

[43] See, for example: Aluminum Co. of America *v.* F. T. C., 284 Fed. 401 (June 1, 1922) (acquisition of stock of competitor: "We have to do only with the 'effect' of the transaction."), *certiorari denied* 261 U. S. 616.

[44] ". . . The Supreme Court held that notwithstanding the findings of the commission were not disturbed by the Circuit Court of Appeals, the circuit court or the Supreme Court could find additional facts upon their own motion and reverse the commission's order. . . . The law creating the commission states that the findings of the commission . . . if supported by the testimony shall be conclusive." Ann. Rep., 1923, p. 7.

[45] Standard Oil Co. *v.* F. T. C., 273 Fed. 478 (May 11, 1921); Canfield Oil Co. *v.* F. T. C., 274 Fed. 571 (July 1, 1921); Sinclair Refining Co. *v.* F. T. C., 276 Fed. 686 (Sept. 8, 1921); Standard Oil Company *v.* F. T. C., 282 Fed. 81 (July 14, 1922). In the Supreme Court, 261 U. S. 463 (Apr. 9, 1923).

With more or less doctrinal discussion and with considerable inquiry into the nature of monopoly and unfair methods of competition, the intermediate federal courts concluded that, as a matter of law, this was not an unfair method of competition. In the last decision, however, the dissenting judge pointed out that the practical effect was to tend toward monopoly and that the practice enabled gasoline wholesalers to obtain effective control of whole territories since the individual retailer could not, or was inclined not to, use more than one pump and hence used the gasoline of only one manufacturer.

The commission took the cases to the Supreme Court, where the lower courts were sustained and the commission reversed. The Supreme Court found that the contracts did not "undertake to limit the lessee's right to use or deal in the goods of a competitor," that the contract was not "properly described by the complaint," and that it was "not within the letter of the Clayton Act." To the contention of the commission that the practical effect — in as much as the retailers generally had only one set of equipment — was to confine dealers to the products of a single lessor, the court gave an abstract answer — "the lessee is free to buy wherever he chooses; he may accept and use as many pumps as he wishes, and may discontinue any or all of them." As to possible violation of the prohibition against unfair methods of competition, the court found nothing "opposed to good morals because characterized by deception, bad faith, fraud or oppression" but on the contrary found that the companies were "vitally interested" in a safe method of handling the highly inflammable product, assuring the public of the genuineness of the brand, with no intention to acquire monopoly and without the probable effect of tending to unduly lessen competition. The court thought that the practice "promoted the public convenience by inducing many small dealers to enter the business and put gasoline on sale at the crossroads."

Here again the judgment of the trade commissioners is contrary to that of the judges, and the judges substitute their opinion for that of the commission. Nor was the law clarified. Fraud, bad faith, and deception had been insisted upon in some of the circuit courts of appeals as a necessary element of unfair methods of competition; the commission looked forward to the decision of the Supreme Court, but the opinion does not specifically treat the point.[46]

[46] Ann. Rep., 1922, pp. 23–24.

Acquisition of stock or other share capital of a competitor, the effect of which substantially lessens competition, is prohibited by the Clayton Act. The career of this section before the courts — in both the interpretation and administration — is perhaps the most illuminating of the phases of federal anti-trust law administered by the Federal Trade Commission.

In the first case to reach the Supreme Court an order of the commission issued under the authority of this portion of the Clayton Act came before the Circuit Court of Appeals for the Third Circuit, and on June 1, 1922, the commission was sustained.[47] The dominant manufacturer of aluminum had absorbed what was virtually its only competitor, and the commission had ordered the company to divest itself of this acquisition. The company then sought reversal of the order on the ground that the smaller concern had been in serious financial difficulties and was on the road to bankruptcy when saved by the merger, that the transaction had assisted in the prosecution of the war, and that it was not the stock of a competitor that had been acquired but of an entirely new corporation (which had been formed for the purposes of the transaction). The circuit court of appeals, however, determined that the effect of the transaction, regardless of its form, was to substantially lessen competition. The defenses, the court felt, "have to do with the motive for the transaction. We have to do only with the 'effect' of the transaction; and with its effect only as it may 'substantially lessen competition . . . or restrain commerce, . . . or tend to create a monopoly.'" One judge, dissenting, believed the defenses of the company should have been accepted. The Supreme Court refused to review the decision.

The notable feature of this decision is the emphasis on the effect of the transaction rather than its form. But the success of the commission in this instance was only temporary. The lesser manufacturing company suspended operations, became insolvent, and was indebted to the dominant company for over half a million dollars. The dominant company then sought to bring suit and take the plant of the lesser company in satisfaction of the obligation. The commission felt that this violated all that had been done and sought to have the court modify the original decree to prevent the acquisition of physical assets of the insolvent company. The commission asserted that the insolvency and indebtedness were simply

[47] Aluminum Co. of America *v.* F. T. C., 284 Fed. 401, *certiorari denied* 261 U. S. 616 (Feb. 26, 1923).

a device to circumvent the operation of the original order of the commission, but the court determined otherwise, and the acquisition of the plant by the dominant company was permitted.[48]

The second section of the Clayton Act prohibits direct or indirect discrimination in prices between different purchasers of commodities where the effect would lessen competition substantially or tend to create monopoly. The first judicial test of this question occurred on review of an order of the commission prohibiting a manufacturer from discriminating in prices between wholesalers and those who distributed directly to the buying public.[49] Certain retailers had organized a buying corporation, but the manufacturer refused to allow this corporation regular wholesaler's prices. The commission based its order to desist upon both the specific provision of the Clayton Act and the general provision of the Federal Trade Commission Act. The circuit court of appeals first examined the complaint against the company and found that it alleged no monopoly, deception, fraud or bad faith, and that it had alleged nothing from which injury to the public could be concluded. The court then interpreted the Clayton Act as prohibiting practices which lessened competition between retailers but not practices which reduced competition between those who bought from a manufacturer. The court found authority in the legislative history of the Clayton Act for the proposition that the act was designed to prevent price cutting in certain localities destructive of the business of competitors. The objection to this argument is obvious — the legislative motive ought not operate to limit the general application of legislation to the single, dramatized instance which had furnished the impetus for legislation. The further argument of the court — that since the manufacturer could sell or refuse to sell to whom it chose, it could therefore discriminate between wholesalers and retailers — if carried to logical conclusions would make all discriminations permissible. The court felt that there was a legitimate discrimination between wholesalers and retailers, and that retailers who formed their own wholesale or buying corporation were, nevertheless, retailers. The Supreme Court, in refusing to review the lower court, affirmed the reversal of the commission's order.

[48] Aluminum Co. of America *v.* F. T. C., 299 Fed. 361 (June 24, 1924).

[49] Mennen Co. *v.* F. T. C., 288 Fed. 774 (Mar. 13, 1923), *certiorari denied* 262 U. S. 759 (June 11, 1923).

The effect of the decision is to maintain the present distribution system. Certainly there is question whether the trade regulation laws are to be used for the modification of the present method of marketing manufactured products. However, retail associations have ground for complaint when discriminated against in favor of "old line" wholesalers, and as a matter of competition, regional monopoly in the distribution of products (by wholesalers) may reasonably come within the scope of the statutes. The commission in its report to Congress, specially commented on, but did not criticize, the interpretation of the law established by the decision.[50]

These reversals at the hands of the Supreme Court were hardly counteracted by the success of the commission in the lower courts.[51] The annual report to Congress, so far as legal developments are concerned, is noncommittal: "While the law administered by the commission has been subject to review by the courts in relatively few cases, a number of important decisions have been rendered which have materially affected the commission's work." [52]

1923–1924: The Public Interest Requirement. The following year an order of the commission respecting imitation of a competitor's trade name and trade mark was sustained and an order respecting interference with a competitor's purchases was reversed with the approval of the Supreme Court.

One of the well-recognized methods of unfair competition is the imitation of a competitor's name and trade labels. The authority of the Federal Trade Commission over such practices is to be found in the broad provision of Section 5 of the Federal Trade Commis-

[50] Ann. Rep., 1923, pp. 42–43.

[51] The commission's appeal to the Supreme Court in one instance of reversal in a circuit court of appeals was dismissed on stipulation of the parties. Fruit Growers' Express *v.* F. T. C., 261 U. S. 629 (Apr. 9, 1923). In another instance an application for review in the Supreme Court was dismissed on the understanding that the order of the commission would be modified to conform to a prior decision of the Supreme Court. Mishawaka Woolen Mfg. Co. *v.* F. T. C., 283 Fed. 1022 (Sept. 13, 1922). In addition to the other decisions of the lower courts discussed in the text, there were the following: Guaranty Veterinary Co. *v.* F. T. C., 285 Fed. 853 (Nov. 6, 1922); Juvenile Shoe Co. *v.* F. T. C., 289 Fed. 57 (May 14, 1923); L. B. Silver Co. *v.* F. T. C., 289 Fed. 985 (Feb. 16, 1923); Southern Hardware Jobbers' Ass'n *v.* F. T. C., 290 Fed. 773 (June 13, 1923). In all of these cases the orders of the commission were affirmed or modified.

[52] Ann. Rep., 1923, p. 6.

sion Act prohibiting "unfair methods of competition." A case of this sort in connection with an order of the commission first came before the Supreme Court in the fall of 1923. The commission had ordered a manufacturer to cease imitating the name and trade mark of an established company. The matter was taken to a circuit court of appeals where, after a brief discussion of the evidence, the order of the commission was upheld and enforcement granted notwithstanding the claim of the petitioner that it had ceased the objectionable practices.[53] The Supreme Court refused to review the decision.

Cases of this sort are so strongly characterized by fraud and unfairness that they call for little comment in the courts. The orders of the commission are ordinarily sustained except in those instances which the courts feel are so trivial that commission action is not warranted.

The next test of the commission's authority at the hands of the Supreme Court occurred in connection with an order prohibiting a wholesale concern from interfering with the efforts of a retail stores system to purchase commodities directly from the manufacturer. The wholesale concern sought to prevent a chain store organization from securing supplies directly from the manufacturer by threatening to cease dealings with the manufacturer unless this business was handled through the wholesale concern. A circuit court of appeals thought there was no unfair method of competition since there had been no combined action or conspiracy to prevent the chain stores securing commodities, and held that "so far as petitioner itself is concerned, it had the positive and lawful right to select any particular merchandise which it wished to purchase, and to select any person or corporation from whom it might wish to make its purchase. . . . Any incidental result which might occur by reason of petitioner exercising a lawful right cannot be charged against petitioner as an unfair method of competition." Here again the decision proceeds on the abstract "right" to buy or refuse to deal "for any reason . . . or for no reason at all" regardless of effect. The lower court reversed the order of the commission, in which decision the Supreme Court concurred.[54] The

[53] Juvenile Shoe Co. *v.* F. T. C., 289 Fed. 57 (May 14, 1923), *certiorari denied* 263 U. S. 705 (Oct. 15, 1923).

[54] Raymond Bros.-Clark Co. *v.* F. T. C., 280 Fed. 529 (May 8, 1922), *affirmed* 263 U. S. 565 (Jan. 7, 1924).

opinion of the Supreme Court follows closely the outline of the opinion of the lower court; the language of the circuit court of appeals was approved, some quotations were taken from earlier Supreme Court decisions, and some materials were added from decisions under the Sherman Act to the effect that one could deal with whom he chose. The lack of any element of conspiracy, noted by the lower court, was emphasized.

The curious result is that, whereas a combination cannot indulge in this practice, a single company whose business covers six western states may rightfully do the same thing. The tendency of courts to permit all but concerted action is marked in the decisions in this field. Here a single large concern is permitted to bring pressure upon smaller competitors to force them to deal with it.

In the lower federal courts during this fiscal year the commission was sustained in one instance,[55] reversed in three cases,[56] the enforcement of an order previously approved in part was refused in one proceeding,[57] one case was withdrawn,[58] and another dismissed.[59] Some twelve petitions for review of orders were pending. The only comment by the commission is that "the law of unfair competition is being developed with resulting clarity in the channels of trade. . . ." [60]

There had been comment that the commission was concerning itself with cases of a comparatively petty nature. One of the three recommendations contained in an intensive study of the commission under the Commonwealth Fund was that the commission "exercise greater discretion in selecting those cases which involve questions of public importance." [61] The commission itself had been aware that it was not a court for the settlement of private disputes

[55] Fox Film Corp. *v.* F. T. C., 296 Fed. 353 (Jan. 7, 1924).

[56] John Bene & Sons *v.* F. T. C., 299 Fed. 468 (May 8, 1924); B. S. Pearsall Butter Co. *v.* F. T. C., 292 Fed. 720 (July 19, 1923); National Biscuit Co. *v.* F. T. C., 299 Fed. 733 (May 5, 1924).

[57] L. B. Silver Co. *v.* F. T. C., 292 Fed. 752 (Oct. 16, 1923).

[58] United Typothetae etc. *v.* F. T. C., no opinion.

[59] Occidental Oil Corp. *v.* F. T. C., no opinion.

[60] Ann. Rep., 1924, p. 1.

[61] Henderson, *The Federal Trade Commission*, p. 337 et seq. ". . . The Commission is handling too many cases, and . . . it should exercise a greater discretion in selecting those cases which involve questions of public importance. It does not seem necessary that public funds be employed to prosecute cases involving controversies between private parties, where a full and adequate remedy can be obtained in a court. . . . The same comment applies to other

but was given authority to act primarily on behalf of the public and only secondarily for the redress of private wrongs.[62] Although the commission maintained that the existence of public interest was a matter within its discretion, the courts dealt with "public interest" from various angles. On March 17, 1925, the commission announced that it would not "entertain proceedings of alleged unfair practices where the alleged violation of law is a purely private controversy redressable in the courts except where [the] practices substantially tend to suppress competition. . . ." [63]

However, neither the declaration nor any change of attitude on the part of the commission affected the matter. Congress had provided that the commission undertake proceedings if "it shall appear *to the commission* that a proceeding by it in respect thereof would be to the interest of the public." [64] On principle, the commission — in more intimate contact with the field of regulation — should be allowed to lay out its own work and determine what practices should be tackled first as well as what matters were better left to private litigation or too trivial for formal action. The courts, however, make "public interest" a jurisdictional requirement — without which the orders of the commission are invalid — and take to themselves the determination of the existence of "public interest." The casual words of legislative draftsmen,[65] or at most words which seem to have been directed to the discretion of the commission, are often distorted in application.

1924–1925: Lull in Development. The first of the decisions confirmed by the Supreme Court during the next fiscal year in-

cases . . . involving trivial or merely technical offenses, in which the public interest is not always easy to discern. . . .

"It should not be forgotten that the Federal Trade Commission was organized primarily to deal with the trust problem, the problem of monopoly and restraint of trade. All other matters are incidental, and it is therefore doubly important that time should not be wasted upon petty squabbles and dishonesties."

[62] Ann. Rep., 1922, p. 35.

[63] Ann. Rep., 1925, p. 111; *Rules of Practice and Procedure and Statements of Policy* (1925), p. 12; and see: Ann. Rep., 1927, p. 2.

[64] The public interest proviso applies only to the prohibition of unfair methods of competition; it "was omitted from the Clayton Act, presumably because such violations would *per se* be of interest to the public, as distinguished from an unfair method of competition, which might involve only a private injury." Ann. Rep., 1916, p. 5.

[65] For a convenient discussion of difference of opinion in the Senate debates see: Henderson, *The Federal Trade Commission* (1924), pp. 35–36.

volves a curious application of the public interest clause. The commission ordered two wholesale companies to cease discriminating in prices by means of discounts between chain stores and individual retail stores. The wholesale companies had a schedule of discounts according to the value of monthly purchases. The chain stores by purchasing as a system secured larger discounts than the individual and independent retailers, and the latter were not allowed to secure the same advantage by pooling their interests and combining their orders. The commission sought to correct the discrimination and disadvantage of the independent retailer by ordering the wholesalers (1) to base chain store discounts upon the quantity delivered to each store, treating each branch of the chain as a separate purchaser, or (2) allow separate and individual purchasers to pool their purchases for the purpose of securing discounts. The court reversed the orders of the commission on the ground that discounts were proper under the Clayton Act, that chain store systems must be considered as a unit (when so considered, of course, there is no discrimination), that "the discount plan was designed for the individual dealer as well as for the large chain store owner," that "it is the right of a merchant engaged in private business freely to exercise his own independent discretion as to the parties with whom he will deal," that the injury was immaterial because it came after the retailer has the commodities "and is disposing of them at retail," that the practice was not prejudicial to the public, and that it was improper to order the wholesaler to allow the discounts to pooled orders because "by pooling purchases the retail customers . . . would afford no service in the sale of the . . . product to the consumers beyond that which each furnishes individually."[66] The court concluded that this was a practice "which is recognized by manufacturers . . . and is inoffensive to good business morals. . . . While the chain store owner may handle more . . . this is but the result of healthy competition. A manufacturer . . . cannot be expected to adopt a uniform policy that is appropriate to meet the small buyer and the large buyer. There is no discrimination between the large buyer, such as the owner of a chain store, and a grocer owning but one store." The Supreme Court refused to review the decision.

The remarks of the court to the effect that the practice is not injurious to the public is particularly open to objection since it

[66] National Biscuit Co. *v.* F. T. C., 299 Fed. 733 (May 5, 1924), *certiorari denied* 266 U. S. 613 (Oct. 20, 1924).

seems to demand the showing of direct damage to the buying public rather than regard the more general public interest or public policy in the maintenance of competition. Certainly the public interest requirement ought not be so particularized. On the substantive point the decision of the court is interesting because the circumstances are something new — chain stores are a comparatively recent development in merchandising. Of course, the matter could not have been within the "intent" of Congress. But the court will not allow the commission to regulate the new development, nor will the court permit the independent retailer to combine for the purpose of meeting the new form of competition.

During this same fiscal year the Supreme Court also refused to review the decision of a circuit court of appeals in which an order of the commission directing a group of manufacturers to cease practices for maintaining resale prices and prohibiting retailers from dealing in the product manufactured by competitors was sustained.[67] In the lower courts the commission's orders were affirmed in four instances,[68] modified in four,[69] and reversed in three;[70] there were also nine proceedings pending. The commis-

[67] There was first an attempt to prevent the commission from proceeding with the investigation. *Supra*, n. 28. Then, after the commission had issued its order, some of the manufacturers took the matter to a circuit court of appeals. The manufacturers claimed that the practices were not unfair because they were used by the trade generally, that competition was in fact fostered, and that because of its unique character the industry was to be distinguished from those situations in which the practice had previously been condemned. These defenses were abruptly dismissed by the court. As to the further defense that the industry had substituted a new form of contract which was one of agency rather than sale (which device had been successful in a previous Supreme Court case), the court found that the new form of contract was "an effort to modify the form and not the substance, of petitioners' business methods." The manufacturers were also unsuccessful in their attempt to delay enforcement of the decree. Butterick Co. et al. *v.* F. T. C., 4 F.(2d) 910 (Jan. 5, 1925), *certiorari denied* 267 U. S. 602 (Mar. 16, 1925).

[68] Oppenheim, Oberndorf & Co. *v.* F. T. C., 5 F.(2d) 574 (Apr. 14, 1925); F. T. C. *v.* Pure Silk Hosiery Mills, 3 F.(2d) 105 (Dec. 8, 1924), see: Ann. Rep., 1925, pp. 53–54; Swift & Co. *v.* F. T. C., 8 F.(2d) 595 (Feb. 16, 1925); the *Butterick Case* (4 F.(2d) 910) is discussed in the text.

[69] Eastman Kodak Co. *v.* F. T. C., 7 F.(2d) 994 (May 18, 1925); F. T. C. *v.* Thatcher Mfg. Co., 5 F.(2d) 615 (Apr. 16, 1925); Western Meat Co. *v.* F. T. C., 1 F.(2d) 95 (Sept. 2, 1924); Pacific States Paper Trade Ass'n *v.* F. T. C., 4 F.(2d) 457 (Feb. 9, 1925).

[70] Chicago Portrait Co. *v.* F. T. C., 4 F.(2d) 759 (Dec. 23, 1924); Heuser *v.* F. T. C., 4 F.(2d) 632 (Mar. 2, 1925); John C. Winston *v.* F. T. C., 3 F.(2d) 961 (Feb. 27, 1925).

sion attempted to secure enforcement of one of its orders through the Court of Appeals of the District of Columbia but the court held that it was without jurisdiction.[71]

1925–1926: Indifferent Success in Administration. At this point the development of the regulatory function of the commission is poised. While the authority of the commission in connection with specific instances of resale price maintenance, false advertising and misbranding, acquisition of stock of competitors, and imitation of competitors' trade names had been sustained after tests in the lower courts and the Supreme Court, the commission had been denied authority to develop a new law of unfair competition and in each case the courts either reversed the commission or stood ready to refuse to enforce any order with which they did not agree. This state of affairs was not unnoticed by those who looked critically at the results, and yet hope was expressed for future development.[72]

During the following fiscal year, however, the commission met with no success before the Supreme Court in its efforts to suppress misrepresentation in merchandising,[73] although it was sustained in

[71] F. T. C. *v.* Klesner, 6 F.(2d) 701 (June 1, 1925).

[72] Compare: "Even today . . . the commission is frequently having to change its conception, as a result of reversals of its orders by the courts on review. . . . It is probable that the organization has not met with any more serious handicaps, resulting from judicial review, than is usually incidental to the formative period of most such bodies." Davies, *The Federal Trade Commission* in *The Growth of American Administrative Law* (1923), p. 86. "Indeed, a search of the opinions . . . does not reveal a single case in which it can be said with assurance that the findings of the Commission have in any way affected the decision of the court. . . . Despite the dicta of the Supreme Court, I venture the opinion that the matter is not yet foreclosed. . . ." Henderson, *The Federal Trade Commission* (1924), pp. 336–337. And see: Stevens, *What Has the Federal Trade Commission Accomplished?* 15 Am. Econ. Rev. 625–651 (1925).

[73] On October 12, 1925, the Supreme Court approved two reversals of the commission by refusing to review decisions of lower federal courts. These cases involved representations or devices calculated, so the commission determined, to mislead purchasers into believing they were securing price reductions. The first involved the practice of giving "checks" which purported to entitle the holder to "reductions" in the prices and also the practice of holding "drawings" to secure special prices. The commission ordered the company to cease the practice, but the Circuit Court of Appeals for the Seventh Circuit, admitting that the methods were "false" and "unworthy," reversed the commission on the ground that it had not been shown that the public was injured; one judge dissented. The Supreme Court refused to review the decision.

one proceeding involving resale price maintenance. The opinion of the lower court in the latter case [74] is notable on the point of public interest, and marks the first instance wherein a court has left a matter, although qualifiedly, to the discretion of the commission: "An examination of the statute shows very clearly that the question whether a proceeding by the commission . . . would be to the interest of the public . . . is committed to the discretion of the commission, is to be determined by the commission before proceedings are instituted, and is not thereafter a subject of controversy either before the commission or before the court, except in so far as the question of public interest is necessarily involved in the merits of the case, and, if the commission finds that the method of competition in question is prohibited by the act, no other or further finding on the question of public interest is required." In

Chicago Portrait Company *v.* F. T. C., 4 F.(2d) 759 (Dec. 23, 1924), *certiorari denied* 269 U. S. 556 (Oct. 12, 1925). Here, again, a court demands the showing of specific injuries to purchasers — saying, "there is no evidence or finding that any purchaser was dissatisfied" and "there is nothing to show that any one was deceived or misled" — although the court admits that the methods were false.

In the second case the commission found that sales literature misled the purchaser into believing that he was receiving a set of books free by subscribing to an "encyclopedic" service, whereas in fact the price was that regularly charged for both. The commission ordered the company to cease the practice, but the Circuit Court of Appeals for the Third Circuit believed that the practice as modified by the company was no longer misleading. The Supreme Court refused to review the decision. John C. Winston Co. *v.* F. T. C., 3 F.(2d) 961 (Feb. 27, 1925), *certiorari denied* 269 U. S. 555 (Oct. 12, 1925). In this case it must be admitted that the matter was trivial and the modified practice could hardly mislead the ordinary urban citizen; nevertheless the court substitutes its judgment for that of the commission. That a respondent may more or less modify a practice, after the commission has ordered it to cease, and then attack the original order is hardly consistent with speedy and effective regulation. The commission thought these practices were "highly deceptive." Ann. Rep., 1925, pp. 54–55.

[74] This case involved the attempt of a manufacturer to fix minimum resale prices. The policy was carried out through bulletins, advertisements in trade journals, and by the manufacturer's salesmen. The manufacturer refused to sell to retailers who failed to comply. The commission's order to desist was approved by a circuit court of appeals. The court found that the evidence was sufficient and properly admitted, dismissed the argument that others were engaged in the same practice, and found that while a simple refusal to sell was not unlawful yet methods of supervising the sales of retailers were unlawful. The Supreme Court sustained the decision by refusing to review. Hills Bros. *v.* F. T. C., 9 F.(2d) 481 (Jan. 4, 1926), *certiorari denied* 270 U. S. 662 (Apr. 12, 1926).

addition to these decisions, there were of course a number of proceedings in the lower federal courts; these cases with two exceptions dealt with resale price maintenance.[75] However, the decisions during this period are overshadowed by the important and far-reaching decisions that shortly followed.

1926–1927: Regulation of Monopoly Denied; the Clayton Act Ineffectual. The decisions of the Supreme Court during the fiscal year 1926–1927 were of such consequence that the year marks a definite turning point in the work of the Federal Trade Commission. The legal developments for the period center in the judicial treatment of orders issued by the commission to prevent monopoly or restraint of competition through acquisition of stock or assets of competitors. Substantial diminution of competition by acquisition of stock or other share capital of a competitor is prohibited by the Clayton Act and the commission is given authority to enforce the provision. One instance of such enforcement had been successfully carried to the Supreme Court in 1923, although the lower court thereafter so modified the decision as to nullify the original order.[76] Now a series of cases, almost all of which concerned the meatpacking industry, came before the Supreme Court after varying treatment at the hands of circuit courts of appeals.

In the first of these decisions the Circuit Court of Appeals for the Ninth Circuit affirmed the order of the commission requiring a large manufacturing company to divest itself of the stock of competitors, the acquisition of which — in the judgment of the commission — eliminated competition in a large section of the country, but the court later granted the company a rehearing and modified its judgment to permit the company to keep the physical assets of the competitor acquired by means of the stock and also to permit the company to dispose of the shares to its officers, agents, or employees.[77] The judge who had written the original opinion ob-

[75] Moir *v.* F. T. C., 12 F.(2d) 22 (order affirmed, Mar. 29, 1926); Q. R. S. Music Co. *v.* F. T. C., 12 F.(2d) 730 (order affirmed, Apr. 9, 1926); F. T. C. *v.* Advance Paint Co. (dismissed without prejudice to entry of modified order; no opinion); Procter & Gamble Co. *v.* F. T. C., 11 F.(2d) 47 (order modified, Apr. 7, 1926); Toledo Pipe-Threading Machine Co. *v.* F. T. C., 11 F.(2d) 337 (order modified, Mar. 13, 1926); American Tobacco Co. *v.* F. T. C., 9 F.(2d) 570 (order reversed, Oct. 20, 1925). Seventeen other proceedings were pending (Ann. Rep., 1926, pp. 25–45).

[76] *Supra*, p. 56 et seq.

[77] Western Meat Co. *v.* F. T. C., 1 F.(2d) 95 (Sept. 2, 1914), 4 F.(2d) 223 (Feb. 17, 1925).

jected to the modification: "It is . . . in effect leaving the theretofore active and substantial competition between the parties entirely eliminated, with the return of stock worth only the paper on which it is printed." In the second case, the transactions to secure a monopoly through acquisition of patent rights were complicated but the commission found that they "were an artifice and subterfuge." The circuit court of appeals (Third Circuit) sustained the commission.[78] As to the contention that the commission could only order divestiture of the "stock" of the competitors and not of physical assets, the court said: "In effecting the remedy . . . the Commission must meet the situation as the offending corporation has made it. If it created the situation so as to defeat the statute, the offending party cannot be heard to say that thereby the Commission is helpless and the law unenforceable." And as to the contention that it would be a practical impossibility to separate the properties: "Nor do the acts of the offending corporation in commingling the assets of the corporation whose stock it has acquired in violation of the statute with assets of its own raise a legal barrier against remedying an evil which the law was expressly enacted to prevent." The court found, however, that the acquisition of one of the smaller competitors was not objectionable because it had previously begun to give up its interest in the industry and that at the time of acquisition its competition "was so inconsiderable that the lessening of competition thereby was not substantial." One judge dissented, believing that the defenses of the company should be accepted. In the third case, the Circuit Court of Appeals for the Seventh Circuit affirmed the order of the commission and refused the company a rehearing.[79] The opinion dealt with the construction and constitutionality of the act, and rejected the defense of the company — that it had purchased the stock merely as an investment. The opinion concluded with a word of regret: ". . . Delay in instituting proceedings of the character here under review, frequently works an unnecessary hardship to the aggrieved party. Certainly a limitation of time should be fixed, by statutory enactment or otherwise, during which these proceedings must be instituted. The purchasing company would not then (as appears was done in the case before us) invest vast sums of money enlarging and improving the acquired property before [the commission] took steps to restore the status of the companies."

[78] F. T. C. *v.* Thatcher Mfg. Co., 5 F.(2d) 615 (Apr. 16, 1925).
[79] Swift & Co. *v.* F. T. C., 8 F.(2d) 595 (Feb. 16, 1925).

The Supreme Court, however, found it unnecessary to wait for legislation to remove any possible hardship imposed upon manufacturers by orders directing them to give up property acquired — as the commission believed — in violation of the statute. The section was construed to permit the commission to order divestiture of stock but not to order divestiture of physical assets of competitors unless the commission had acted *before* the properties were merged.[80] "The act has no application to ownership of a competitor's property and business obtained prior to any action by the Commission, even though this was brought about through stock unlawfully held." But as to the first case, where the company had acquired the physical properties after the commission had ordered divestiture of the stock, the court said: "The purpose which the lawmakers entertained might be wholly defeated if the stock could be further used for securing the competitor's property [that is, before finally disposing of the stock]. And the same result would follow a transfer to one controlled by or acting for the [company]." In short, the court held that the act prohibited the acquisition of stock of competitors and also the use of that stock to acquire the physical properties of competitors *provided* the commission had taken action before the physical properties had been acquired. The court intimated, however, that there might still be a remedy under the Sherman Act: "If purchase of property has produced an unlawful status, a remedy is provided through the courts." Four justices dissented; they saw no reason why the commission should be without authority merely because "the company succeeded in securing the assets of the controlled corporation before the Commission instituted a proceeding." On the basis of this decision another proceeding was dismissed.[81]

These decisions establish a "race for priority" — the commission must discover impending business mergers and take action before there is an acquisition of the assets of competitors. Although the first comment by the commission is noncommittal,[82] in later years these decisions are referred to as "practically nullifying" the statute.[83]

The decisions just noted under the Clayton Act were shortly

[80] 272 U. S. 554 (Nov. 23, 1926).

[81] Armour & Co. See: Ann. Rep., 1925, p. 42; 1926, pp. 39–40; 1927, p. 76.

[82] Ann. Rep., 1926, pp. 1–2.

[83] Ann. Rep., 1929, pp. 6–7, 59–60. The commission made a special report on investigation of stock acquisitions.

taken as controlling in a somewhat similar order under the broad provision of the Federal Trade Commission Act. This case involved the manufacturer of almost all motion picture film used in the country. When users of film began to purchase foreign-made products, the company purchased and established extensive laboratories for developing film. It threatened then to operate these laboratories unless existing laboratories used the company's product exclusively. The trade promptly agreed to use only the company's "raw" film. After investigation, the commission ordered the company to cease this practice and ordered it to divest itself of the property held as a threat. The company then carried the matter to the Circuit Court of Appeals for the Second Circuit, which court modified the order of the commission to prohibit action "in agreement" but reversed the order so far as it required divestiture of the property.[84] The opinion of the court bristles with quotation marks in ridicule of the facts reported by the commission. The monopoly of the company was approved because it "was the first American manufacturer, had pushed its trade with skill, and made what is still regarded as the best raw film anywhere obtainable." (It may be noted that the court does not hesitate to draw its own conclusions — that the company had developed by "skill" and that it made "the best raw film anywhere obtainable.") The court then proceeded to misstate the order of the commission — as though the commission had determined that the manufacturer had "no legal right to embark on the new business of finishing his own raw material." The court held that there was "nothing unfair in the company going into the business of making pictures." The suggestion of innocent purpose is hardly justified. The company had not gone "into the business of making pictures" nor had it prepared "to compete in the picture making art" except so far as necessary to use the possibility as a threat. On review the Supreme Court pointed out that the lower court had rendered its decision "without referring specifically to the purpose for which the [company] acquired and maintained the three laboratories." But then the Supreme Court itself proceeded to disregard the purpose of the arrangement and, referring to the previous decisions under the Clayton Act — just discussed — said: "So here, the Commission had no authority to require that the Company divest itself of the ownership of the laboratories which it had acquired

[84] Eastman Kodak Co. *v.* F. T. C., 7 F.(2d) 994 (May 18, 1925), *affirmed* 274 U. S. 619 (May 31, 1927).

prior to any action by the Commission." Two justices dissented on the ground that the decisions under the Clayton Act were not material, that the limitation upon the powers of the commission was unjustified, that while "superficial examination might suggest that the [company's] course of conduct involves nothing more than the innocuous process of extending its business to include an allied trade" here it is "fairly inferable from the stipulated facts that there was no intention of permanent expansion," and that "that part of the order which still stands, forbidding the agreement for the suppression of competition, is futile if the [company] may retain the laboratories as a threat to compel the manufacturers . . . to do that which they could not lawfully agree to do."

The abstract right to hold property is sustained notwithstanding the purpose or use to which the property is put and even though the purpose or effect be to render ineffective the trade regulation act.

As a result of these four decisions the commission was moved to report specially on "The Present Status of the Clayton Act as Administered by the Federal Trade Commission." [85] However, the report criticizes the courts only inferentially in listing the decisions and explaining the grounds asserted by the courts in their opinions. No legislation is recommended. Evidently the commission finds itself in a dilemma — the Clayton Act has been severely restricted and yet the commission must not be represented as without substantial powers to justify its continued existence.

Of the section declaring it unlawful for any corporation engaged in interstate commerce to acquire part or the whole of the stock or share capital of another such corporation where the effect would be to substantially lessen competition, it is said: "So far as the commission is concerned, it is a question whether the effectiveness of the act to fulfill the purpose of Congress has not been materially lessened by these decisions. While this is true, it should not be concluded that the deterrent effect of the law is entirely nullified." On the prohibition of price discrimination, the report simply lists the adverse judgments in the three cases that came before the courts. The several decisions on tying contracts were enumerated — four setting aside the orders of the commission and two sustaining the commission. There were no decisions on the provision prohibiting common directors in competitive corporations; the commission remarked that "the few cases arising under this part of the statute are probably due to the fact that its requirements

[85] Ann. Rep., 1927, pp. 13–17.

can readily be met and the desired results obtained by other means." [86]

The courts in denying effect to the Clayton Act have, at the same time, refused to make use of the English common law and American legal tradition against monopoly — although these same materials have been applied by the courts in working out the American law of corporations.[87] This very refusal of the judiciary to develop either the legislative or traditional materials strengthens the case for administrative justice.

In the meantime the Supreme Court disposed of four other orders of the commission. A seemingly futile order regarding misbranding of soap was sustained.[88] Next the Supreme Court reversed the decision of a circuit court of appeals and sustained an order of the commission respecting price fixing by an association of paper products wholesalers.[89] The opinion of the Supreme Court in this

[86] See also: Ann. Rep., 1916, p. 3. And compare: "The Clayton Act has not succeeded in preventing the control of a maximum of capital with a minimum of investment, although it has made merging-for-merging's sake more difficult and less profitable. It can always be avoided, however, . . . by the purchase of assets instead of the purchase of stock." Fortune, II, No. 3, p. 96.

[87] See Henderson, *The Position of Foreign Corporations in American Constitutional Law* (1918), pp. 19–21.

[88] The first of these cases involved an order of the commission directing a manufacturer to cease misbranding products by making false representations as to content. The lower court held that the amount of the ingredient necessary (naphtha in soap) was "an ultimate fact to be established by evidence" and not a mere matter of opinion as the company contended. The commission was sustained and the Supreme Court refused to interfere. Procter & Gamble Co. *v.* F. T. C., 11 F.(2d) 47 (Apr. 7, 1926), *certiorari denied* 273 U. S. 718 (Oct. 25, 1926). The lower court found that the ingredient was "volatile" and that if products "do not speedily reach the consumer a large but indeterminate amount . . . will escape by evaporation." The commission was directed to modify its order to specify the amount to be used at time of manufacture rather than the content at time of sale to consumer. The commission investigated for several years before issuing a final order. Ann. Rep., 1929, p. 102; 1928, p. 65. On the face of it, the entire proceeding appears futile — to require that an ingredient be used in manufacture which is likely, or certain, to disappear through evaporation before reaching the consumer is a gesture. The order might well have been reversed or the manufacturer directed to cease labelling the product as including the ingredient. At any rate, it is difficult to see how the ordinary purchaser could have been misled since, if the ingredient is apt to evaporate, the consumer has probably never known its benefits.

[89] The association had been directed by the commission to cease price fixing. A circuit court of appeals sustained the order of the commission except so far as it forbade the discussion which tended to or did fix prices (the court saying

case contains language on the scope of judicial review strikingly different from that of previous decisions: "The validity of the inference or conclusion drawn by the Commission and of this part of the order depends upon the proper estimation of the facts. . . . The weight to be given to the facts and circumstances admitted as well as the inferences reasonably to be drawn from them is for the Commission." Had this view been followed, the remainder of this narrative would read differently. However, when later one of the lower courts relied upon this pronouncement, it was reversed by the Supreme Court — the majority reverting to the doctrine of the Curtis Case and the minority maintaining the rule here announced.[90]

Next, in two cases the scant powers of the commission in the field of resale price maintenance were, for all practical purposes, revoked. In the first of these the Supreme Court refused to review the decision of a circuit court of appeals in which the opinion of the Supreme Court in the leading case on the subject was distinguished, the findings of the commission were rejected, and the powers of the commission limited to cases of fraud.[91] The difficulties here, as in all instances of regulation of price maintenance, are due to the distinction originally laid down by the Supreme Court reconciling decisions under the Sherman Act and the powers of the commission under the legislation of 1914 — briefly this, that whereas one might sell to whom he chose, yet he might not actively investigate the resale prices of retailers of his products. From the beginning efforts to regulate this matter have not eliminated the practice but only forced the manufacturer to use other means than the few prohibited. The second case involved price maintenance in combination and by a single manufacturer.[92] A circuit court of appeals,

that it was not "the purpose of the statutes to reduce trade organizations to the status of mere social clubs"), and except so far as the order forbade the members from agreeing upon and publishing a joint price list. The commission, believing that this modification destroyed the effect of the order, carried the case to the Supreme Court. Pacific States Paper Trade Ass'n et al. *v.* F. T. C., 4 F.(2d) 457 (Feb. 9, 1925), *reversed in part* 273 U. S. 52 (Jan. 3, 1927).

[90] *Infra*, p. 85 et seq.

[91] Harriet Hubbard Ayer Co. *v.* F. T. C., 15 F.(2d) 274 (Nov. 1, 1926), *certiorari denied* 273 U. S. 759 (Mar. 14, 1927). This particular court had uniformly insisted that the trade commission statute made unlawful only those practices amounting to fraud; this interpretation was repeated with the further statement that the commission was without power "to regulate trade policy."

[92] American Tobacco Co. *v.* F. T. C., 9 F.(2d) 570 (Oct. 20, 1925), 274 U. S. 543 (May 31, 1927).

quoting extensively from the *dissenting* opinion of the Supreme Court justices in the leading case on resale price maintenance and approving the dissenting opinion of one of the trade commissioners, accepted the defense of the company and found that the practices were directed toward securing a fair profit for its jobbers and preventing a demoralized condition in the trade. Whereas the lower court and the parties agreed that the case involved not only unlawful combination but also price maintenance by the single manufacturer, the Supreme Court in its opinion viewed the case as solely a matter of agreement or combination. The circuit court of appeals and the Supreme Court were considering different things — one spoke of resale price maintenance in all forms and the other of concerted action, yet the lower court was affirmed and the commission reversed. Furthermore — notwithstanding the statutory provision making the determinations of the commission final on questions of fact if supported by evidence — the Supreme Court opinion states that "proper decision of the controversy depends upon a question of fact," and then refuses to interfere with the decision of the lower court because the conclusions depend "on appreciation of circumstances which admit of different interpretations"! In short, the Supreme Court in effect recognizes that the function of the commission has been usurped by the lower federal court and then on that very ground refuses to intervene. The opinions add nothing to the judicial literature on the subject; the opinion of the Supreme Court is less than a column in length — it sustains the lower court, whose opinion is characterized as "of uncertain intendment and . . . not satisfactory as an exposition of the law." The effort of the commission to secure an interpretation of the statutes on points about which the various circuit courts of appeals were in conflict was unsuccessful.[93] By this time resale price maintenance on the part of a single manufacturer or jobber, just as acquisition of stock of competitors, becomes an ineffective item of trade regulation. In later years the orders of the commission on this subject are whittled down or reversed.[94] Shortly, false advertising and misbranding of merchandise will be the only phase of trade practice in which the commission makes any real effort toward regulation through the courts.

1927–1928: New Problems in Enforcement; the Changed Function

[93] Ann. Rep., 1927, p. 69.

[94] See, for example: Cream of Wheat Co. *v.* F. T. C., 14 F.(2d) 40 (July 26, 1926).

of the Commission. Review of the commission's orders brings questions of conspiracy and the imitation of a competitor's trade name and labels before the Supreme Court during the next fiscal year. On April 5, 1927, the Circuit Court of Appeals for the Eighth Circuit sustained an order of the commission directing a wholesale grocers' association to cease practices which through confederated action sought to confine the distribution of products to "regular channels" — that is, through wholesalers — and to prevent dealers from securing products directly from the producers or manufacturers. The evidence was clear, and the court unanimously sustained the action of the commission. The association took the matter to the Supreme Court, where, by refusal to review the decision of the lower court, the order of the commission was sustained.[95] Although the courts displayed no hesitancy in sustaining this order, it should be noted that cases involving the maintenance of the "regular" distribution system — manufacturer, wholesaler, and retailer — have not met with the same success when the practices are those of a single wholesaler instead of an association. Concerted action (called "conspiracy" when found illegal) even before the creation of the trade commission had been more vigorously regulated than the actions of single corporations or individuals.

The next matter to reach the Supreme Court brings out a new problem — judicial procedure for the enforcement of commission orders. The Circuit Court of Appeals for the Second Circuit sustained an order of the commission, but the commission was directed to determine whether the order had been disobeyed before the court would consider granting enforcement.[96] One judge even

[95] Arkansas Wholesale Grocers' Ass'n *v.* F. T. C., 18 F.(2d) 866 (Apr. 5, 1927), *certiorari denied* 275 U. S. 533 (Oct. 17, 1927).

[96] The order of the commission directed a manufacturer to cease imitation of the trade name of a competitor's product. The lower federal court found that there had in fact been an imitation and that there was sufficient evidence that this was misleading, that the company had misrepresented its product as "registered" and copyrighted, that it was a matter of public interest, and that the statutes were constitutional. The Supreme Court refused to review the decision. Thereafter, in accordance with the direction of the lower court, the commission investigated the alleged violation and found that there had been literal compliance with the order; the court then dismissed the application for enforcement but left standing the decision as to the validity of the order. F. T. C. *v.* Balme, 23 F.(2d) 615 (Jan. 9, 1928), *certiorari denied* 277 U. S. 598 (May 21, 1928). See also: Ann. Rep., 1929, p. 103 (application for enforcement dismissed May 16, 1929).

went so far as to protest determining the validity of the order at all until disobedience had been shown. As against devious possibilities in procedure suggested by counsel opposing the orders of the commission, the commission contended that the question of violation of its orders was not subject to judicial scrutiny but that, upon the affirmance of an order, enforcement should be granted as a matter of course.[97]

The decision in this case moved the commission to report specially on the problem of enforcement of orders. The report for the period includes a section on the "vexatious problem and procedure in the enforcement of orders directed against unfair methods of competition."[98] The statute provides that, if the order of the commission is not obeyed, the commission "may apply to the circuit court of appeals . . . for the enforcement of its order" and that the court "shall have jurisdiction of the proceedings . . . and shall have power to . . . enter . . . a decree affirming, modifying, or setting aside the order of the commission."

The propriety of granting enforcement, irrespective of violation of the commission's orders, had been a point in the very first opinion on review of an order, August 29, 1919.[99] There, answering the contention that the objectionable practices had been abandoned, the court said that it was for the commission to determine "the real nature of the petitioner's attitude" and that there was no assurance in sight that "if it could shake [the commission's] hand from its shoulder, it would not continue its former course." This view had been followed in some courts,[100] but others — following the established equity practice in injunction proceedings — laid down the rule that enforcement would not be granted where the practice had ceased "long before the bill was filed and there is no reason to apprehend its renewal."[101] On October 22, 1926, the Circuit Court of Appeals for the Seventh Circuit determined that the commission must first prove that its order had been violated before the court would consider the validity of the findings and order.[102] In short, before penalties could be imposed, the commis-

[97] Ann. Rep., 1928, p. 77. [98] *Ibid.*, pp. 77–79.

[99] Sears, Roebuck & Co. *v.* F. T. C., 258 Fed. 307.

[100] Juvenile Shoe Co. *v.* F. T. C., 289 Fed. 57 (1923), *certiorari denied* 263 U. S. 705; Fox Film Corp. *v.* F. T. C., 296 Fed. 353 (1924); Moir *v.* F. T. C., 12 F.(2d) 22 (1926).

[101] L. B. Silver Co. *v.* F. T. C., 292 Fed. 752 (1923); Butterick Co. *v.* F. T. C., 4 F.(2d) 910 (1925).

[102] F. T. C. *v.* Standard Education Society, 14 F.(2d) 947 (1926).

sion must prove (1) a violation of its order, then (2) the validity of its order, and finally (3) violations of the order as affirmed by decree of court in the previous proceeding.[103] The ground is covered three times before an offender is subject to punishment — all this in addition to the numerous examinations and hearings before the original order of the commission is entered.

Now, in the case which had just reached the Supreme Court, the Circuit Court of Appeals for the Second Circuit determined that on application of the commission for the enforcement of its order the court would first determine whether the order was valid, but would not enter a decree of enforcement — instead, the court after affirming the order directed the commission to take evidence to determine whether the order had been violated and return the evidence and findings to the court before enforcement of the decree would be granted.[104] As to this decision, comparing it to the decision of the Seventh Circuit, the commission reported: "The advantage of the procedure adopted by the second circuit over that required by the seventh circuit is that the commission may secure a decision with respect to the validity of its order before being called upon to prove that it has been violated. If the order is held invalid, time will not have been wasted in taking testimony with respect to its violation. However, even under the ruling of the second circuit, if we interpret it correctly, after an order of the commission is found valid, a decree of enforcement will evidently not issue without proof of the violation of the commission's order. After such a decree is obtained, a violation of the decree is undoubtedly punishable as contempt. Here again it seems necessary to prove twice a violation of law to get an order of enforcement and to prove still a third violation to inflict punishment." And the commission went on to say of the general situation:

> It will be seen that the effect of these decisions has been to make the procedure for securing obedience to the statute very cumbersome, tedious, and expensive. It is difficult to conceive that Congress intended to prescribe such a procedure. The statute shows on its face an attempt to make its enforcement speedy and direct. The procedure before the commission is as informal and direct as is consistent with due process of law. The act provides for a review of the proceedings by the circuit courts of appeals instead of by the district courts, as is the case with the Interstate Commerce Commission act and other acts, shortening the process through the

---

[103] Ann. Rep., 1928, p. 78.

[104] F. T. C. *v.* Balme, 23 F.(2d) 615 (1928), *certiorari denied* 277 U. S. 598 (1928).

courts by one step. The section also provides that the decision of the circuit court of appeals shall be final, except that the Supreme Court may review the judgment of the circuit court of appeals on certiorari. An appeal as a matter of right from the judgment of the circuit court of appeals is not provided for. Finally, the section provides that the circuit court of appeals shall expedite cases arising under it in every way. These provisions manifest the legislative intent to secure a speedy and inexpensive compliance with the commission's valid orders. [105]

Some of these decisions enable those who oppose the orders of the commission to postpone, by means of the several stages of procedure, enforcement and subjection to the coercion of the law. Violators of the commission's orders secure a further chance without penalty. Although the case has been fully examined and an order issued, the commission is forced to exercise continued diligence to discover and be able to prove subsequent violations of its orders. Yet this continues to be a vexed question.[106]

In the lower federal courts during these last two fiscal years (1926–1927, 1927–1928) in other proceedings the commission was affirmed in four instances,[107] orders were modified in two instances,[108] reversed in three cases,[109] four proceedings were dismissed,[110] some intermediate action was taken in three cases,[111] and there were further proceedings in previously decided cases — details and new problems of enforcement [112] — while other cases were pending.

[105] Ann. Rep., 1928, pp. 78–79.

[106] Arkansas Wholesale Grocers' Ass'n *v.* F. T. C., 18 F.(2d) 866 (1927); F. T. C. *v.* Baltimore Paint & Color Works, 41 F.(2d) 474 (1930).

[107] Indiana Quartered Oak Co. *v.* F. T. C., 26 F.(2d) 340 (May 14, 1928); J. W. Kobi Co. *v.* F. T. C., 23 F.(2d) 41 (Dec. 12, 1927); Louis Leavitt *v.* F. T. C., 16 F.(2d) 1019 (Dec. 9, 1926); Sea Island Thread Co. *v.* F. T. C., 22 F.(2d) 1019 (Nov. 23, 1927).

[108] Cream of Wheat Co. *v.* F. T. C., 14 F.(2d) 40 (July 26, 1926); Chamber of Commerce of Minneapolis *v.* F. T. C., 13 F.(2d) 673 (July 13, 1926).

[109] F. T. C. *v.* Klesner, 25 F.(2d) 524 (Apr. 2, 1928); Ostermoor & Co. *v.* F. T. C., 15 F.(2d) 692 (Jan. 10, 1927); Utah-Idaho Sugar Co. *v.* F. T. C., 22 F.(2d) 122 (Oct. 21, 1927).

[110] Armour & Co. *v.* F. T. C.; F. T. C. *v.* Dobe; F. T. C. *v.* Ajax Rope Co.; Jones Hardware Co. *v.* F. T. C.

[111] Klesner *v.* F. T. C., 6 F.(2d) 701 (June 1, 1925), *reversed* 274 U. S. 145 (Apr. 18, 1927); Royal Baking Powder Co. *v.* F. T. C.; F. T. C. *v.* Standard Education Society, 14 F.(2d) 947 (Oct. 22, 1926).

[112] Procter & Gamble Co. *v.* F. T. C., 11 F.(2d) 47 (Jan. 5, 1926), *certiorari denied* 273 U. S. 718 (Oct. 25, 1926); F. T. C. *v.* Pure Silk Hosiery Mills, 3 F. (2d) 105 (Dec. 8, 1924); Western Meat Co. *v.* F. T. C., 1 F. (2d) 95

A change in emphasis upon the various functions of the commission now becomes pronounced. The commission began its work with a careful preliminary consideration of the legal aspects of trade regulation. The World War seriously interrupted its regular activities. After the war the first years of the commission's work centered about the development of a law of unfair competition and the enforcement of the Clayton Act. The commission entered upon this activity under the impression that it was "empowered to leave the shores defined by the common law" and develop regulatory practice to fit the conditions which had called forth the creation of the commission.[113] But the first pronouncement of the Supreme Court of the United States began a line of decisions which restricted the operation of the legislation of 1914 and reduced the Federal Trade Commission to the role of public prosecutor.

The annual reports of the commission for the first years of its active regulation stressed the development of a law of unfair competition by means of investigation, issuance of orders to cease and desist, and enforcement through the federal courts. This emphasis on legal development is shown by the introductions, summaries, and special sections in the reports to Congress for 1920, 1921, 1922, 1923, and 1924.[114] Beginning with the report for the year 1925 the investigative work of the commission is stressed,[115] and in 1927 the commission announced "new conceptions of the part of the Federal Trade Commission . . . in the commercial life of the Nation" and emphasized "a new constructive agency known as the trade practice division," "cooperation with business," and the settlement of minor cases "by stipulation."[116] Investigations authorized by Congress were again the outstanding feature reported in 1928,[117] and in 1929 the "major activities" for the fiscal year are reported as the "continuation of the investigation of power and gas utilities," "holding of 31 trade practice conferences," "continuation of the investigation of chain store systems," "campaign against fraudulent and misleading advertising," "continuation of the investigation of resale price maintenance," and the "investigation

(Sept. 2, 1924); 272 U. S. 554 (Nov. 23, 1926); F. T. C. *v.* Standard Education Society, 14 F.(2d) 947 (Oct. 22, 1926).

113 Ann. Rep., 1919, p. 45.

114 Ann. Rep., 1920, pp. 1, 43–62; 1921, pp. 5–9, 24–37; 1922, pp. 1–8, 19–39; 1923, pp. 1–15, 28–60; 1924, pp. 1–3, 10–64.

115 See particularly the reports for 1925, pp. 1–2, 1926, p. 1.

116 Ann. Rep., 1927, particularly at p. 1.

117 Ann. Rep., 1928, pp. vii–ix.

of the newsprint industry."[118] Only two of these items — false advertising and price maintenance — involved enforced orders of the commission.

The original policy of authoritative regulation changed to a policy of investigation and publicity (reminiscent of the former Corporation Commission which the Federal Trade Commission superseded) and a policy of trade practice conferences, the latter being described as "the commission's chief contribution to self-government of industry"[119] and further described as a procedure permitting "an industry to make its own rules of business conduct — to establish its own law merchant, in cooperation with the commission."[120] Investigation and publicity, while high-sounding, are a definite reversion to the conception of commission function in the earlier stage of public regulation which was, at least ostensibly, repudiated by the creation of commissions with power to enforce orders.[120a] Public opinion and accepted morality are substituted for the coercive power of the state. In line with these developments is the growing practice of settling matters by agreement — a system of arbitration and conciliation rather than regulation.[121] It is

[118] Ann. Rep., 1929, p. 8.

[119] Ann. Rep., 1929, p. 9. For the development of trade practice conferences, originally called "trade practice submittals," see: Ann. Rep., 1921, pp. 32–33; 1923, pp. 17, 75–80; 1924, pp. 65–73, 1925, pp. 67–80; 1926, pp. 47–54, 166–169; 1927, pp. 7–12, 213–224; 1928, pp. 5–16, 186; 1929, pp. 9–10, 15, 30–54; 1930, pp. 38–46; 1931, pp. 6, 107–110.

[120] Ann. Rep., 1927, p. 1. See also: *Trade Practice Conferences* (1929).

[120a] But compare: ". . . The strength and vigor of the industrial and commercial system by which modern wealth is produced and distributed springs from spontaneous enterprise and free competition. Coercive regulation is an anomaly in such a system, and only within minimum limits can it be maintained without undermining the whole organization by attacking the primary motives upon which reliance is placed. Only a system of administrative regulation which permits and encourages business voluntarily to purge itself of abuses and unfair practices inimical to its own sustained prosperity can in the end accomplish its fundamental purpose. Relentless persecution and pitiless publicity should be reserved for proven malefactors. Investigation, conference, negotiation, and warning should be the most characteristic methods of Federal Trade Commission procedure." *Public Regulation of Competitive Practices* (National Industrial Conference Board, 1925), pp. 229–230.

[121] Ann. Rep., 1927, pp. 1–2; 1930, p. 58. "Stipulations in which various individuals and companies agreed to cease and desist from unlawful practices charged were approved and accepted by the commission during the fiscal year in 165 cases. . . . During the five and one-half years in which the stipulation system had been in effect, as of June 30, 1931, a total of 837 stipulations had been approved and accepted by the commission." Ann. Rep., 1931, p. 43.

not too much to say that the restraining hand of the judiciary was an important factor in turning the attention of the commission to activities other than trade regulation through orders enforceable only in the courts.[122]

1928–1929: False Advertising and Misbranding. However, there are still some orders to defend, — almost all involving false advertising or misbranding of products, — and there are proceedings from previous years to conclude. During the fiscal year 1928–1929 in the field of false advertising and misbranding the commission was engaged in twenty proceedings before the circuit courts of appeals and one before the Supreme Court.[123] There were also proceedings before the circuit courts of appeals respecting two orders directing divestiture of stock of competitors,[124] and one order prohibiting espionage upon and misrepresentation of a competitor.[125] One pending proceeding concerned unfair competition in distribution of products.[126] It is worthy of note that on Jan-

Stipulations listed: Ann. Rep., 1926, pp. 154–165; 1927, pp. 178–212; 1928, pp. 182–185; 1929, pp. 217–221; 1930, pp. 220–232; 1931, pp. 201–217. See also the volumes of Federal Trade Commission Decisions.

[122] But compare an estimate of the role of the courts in this connection made in 1925: *Public Regulation of Competitive Practices* (Natl. Ind. Conf. Bd.).

[123] Bradley *v.* F. T. C., 31 F.(2d) 569 (Mar. 18, 1929) and F. T. C. *v.* Powe, 35 F.(2d) 1017 (June 28, 1929) — both affirmed the commission. Further proceedings in connection with orders previously affirmed: Procter & Gamble Co. *v.* F. T. C., 11 F.(2d) 47 (Jan. 5, 1926), 273 U. S. 717 (Oct. 25, 1926; see: Ann. Rep., 1929, p. 102); F. T. C. *v.* Balme, 23 F.(2d) 615 (Jan. 9, 1928), *certiorari denied* 277 U. S. 598 (May 21, 1928) (Ann. Rep., 1929, p. 103). In other cases no final action was taken and they remained pending. Ann. Rep., 1929, pp. 92–107.

In the case which reached the Supreme Court the Circuit Court of Appeals for the Second Circuit had affirmed the order of the commission after finding the evidence sufficient and the matter one of public interest, although one of the three judges "reluctantly" concurred in the opinion. The party affected took the case to the Supreme Court, which refused to review the decision of the lower court and thereby left the commission's order affirmed. Indiana Quartered Oak Co. *v.* F. T. C., 26 F.(2d) 340 (May 14, 1928), *certiorari denied* 278 U. S. 623 (Oct. 15, 1928). As a result of this decision and in accordance with stipulations previously entered five decrees of enforcement were entered in several circuit courts of appeals against five other firms. Ann. Rep., 1929, pp. 103–104.

[124] International Shoe Co. *v.* F. T. C., 29 F.(2d) 518 (Nov. 27, 1928); Western Meat Co. *v.* F. T. C., 33 F.(2d) 824 (June 24, 1929).

[125] Philip Carey Mfg. Co. *v.* F. T. C., 29 F.(2d) 49 (Nov. 12, 1928).

[126] F. T. C. *v.* Paramount Famous-Lasky Corporation (see: Ann. Rep., 1929, p. 92).

uary 17, 1929, occurred the first instance in which a court enforced an order of the commission by punishment for disobedience.[127]

The report of the commission for this period notes as the major activities: continuation of investigations regarding power and gas utilities ("their financial structure and publicity enterprises"), chain store systems, newsprint paper industry, and resale price maintenance; the holding of thirty-one trade practice conferences; and the campaign against fraudulent and misleading advertising.[128] The last of these is the only item of regulation enforced by orders through the courts, and the burden of this phase of the commission's work now devolves upon a board consisting of three of the commission's attorneys; [129] furthermore, the regulation appears to be conciliatory rather than authoritative.[130] Also, resale price maintenance — formerly an important item of litigation and regulation — is now the subject of "an inquiry into general business phases and not necessarily related to individual complaints." [131]

July 1, 1929–December 31, 1930: Restriction of Administration Confirmed. The final period of the decade 1920–1930 saw the conclusion of years of proceedings in three cases and the final disposition of two others by the Supreme Court. In the lower courts, five orders of the commission were affirmed,[132] four were modi-

[127] Louis Leavitt *v.* F. T. C., 16 F.(2d) 1019 (see: Ann. Rep., 1929, p. 96).

[128] Ann. Rep., 1929, p. 8.

[129] "Creation of the special board of investigation to handle cases of fraudulent advertising was partly a result of the commission's having on file a large number of applications for complaint. . . . The Board . . . was given general power to investigate, hold informal hearings, and make reports and recommendations to the commission." Ann. Rep., 1929, pp. 10–11. See also: Ann. Rep., 1929, pp. 55–56; 1930, pp. 55–57; 1931, pp. 111–113.

[130] "In all cases where the advertisers agree to revise their advertising representations the board negotiates . . . the necessary stipulations. . . . In a few cases where it appears impossible or impractical to negotiate stipulations . . . the board recommends prosecution of proceedings. . . ." Ann. Rep., 1931, pp. 112–113.

[131] Ann. Rep., 1929, p. 11. See also: 1928, p. 37; 1930, pp. 7, 36; 1931, pp. 5, 28–31. "Proposed legislation would give American manufacturers the right, if they choose to use it, of fixing and maintaining resale prices for their identified products." Ann. Rep., 1929, p. 69.

[132] In addition to the Kay case, discussed presently in the text, there were: F. T. C. *v.* Baltimore Paint & Color Works, 41 F.(2d) 474 (June 10, 1930); F. T. C. *v.* Grand Rapids Varnish Co. 41 F.(2d) 996 (Oct. 8, 1929); Lighthouse Rug Co. *v.* F. T. C., 35 F.(2d) 163 (Oct. 25, 1929); Masland Duraleather Co. *v.* F. T. C., 34 F.(2d) 733 (Sept. 18, 1929).

fied,[133] three were reversed,[134] five proceedings were dismissed on agreement between the parties,[135] and thirteen other proceedings were pending in the various circuit courts of appeals.[136] Of these thirty proceedings, twenty involved false advertising or misbranding.

After reaching the Supreme Court for the second time, one long-drawn-out litigation over an order of the commission directing divestiture of stock of a competitor was finally dismissed on agreement of the parties.[137] Another litigation, pending since the early

[133] Bayuk Cigars Inc. *v.* F. T. C. (Circuit Court of Appeals, Third Circuit, June 14, 1930; Nov. 5, 1930); F. T. C. *v.* Cassoff, 38 F.(2d) 790 (Feb. 17, 1930); F. T. C. *v.* Good Grape Co., 45 F.(2d) 70 (Nov. 10, 1930); N. Flugelman & Co. *v.* F. T. C., 37 F.(2d) 59 (Jan. 6, 1930).

[134] In addition to the Raladam case discussed presently in the text: Berkeley & Gay Furniture Co. *v.* F. T. C., 42 F.(2d) 427 (July 2, 1930); F. T. C. *v.* American Snuff Co., 38 F.(2d) 547 (Mar. 24, 1930).

[135] Four involving misrepresentation, one involving acquisition of assets of a competitor. See: Ann. Rep., 1930.

[136] Including cases only to January 1, 1931.

[137] The original court proceedings had been instituted in 1924. The order of the commission was first sustained, but later the decree was modified to permit the company to keep the physical assets of the competitor acquired by means of the stock and also to permit the company to dispose of the shares to its officers, agents, or employees. The Supreme Court, however, refused to allow this modification. The lower court then corrected its decree and allowed the company six months to submit to the commission a report showing how the order had been carried out. After three further extensions of time, the company on September 15, 1928, reported that it had brought action on a debt against the lesser company,—the stock of which it unlawfully held,—had taken judgment by default, and under execution had bid in substantially all of the physical assets of the lesser company in satisfaction of the judgment. The dominant company then disposed of the unlawfully held stock. The commission felt that this acquisition of the physical properties before disposing of the stock was an indirect way of accomplishing what had originally been prohibited. The court, however, approved this method of compliance with the order on the ground that, while the commission might order divestiture of stock, it could not order the company to dispose of the physical properties acquired while holding the stock. The case was then again taken to the Supreme Court, but before the case was argued the company negotiated a sale of the property in dispute and the commission thereupon stipulated to dismiss the proceedings, which was done on May 19, 1930, and the case remanded to the lower court. By the terms of the stipulation the lower court on June 6, 1930, vacated its former ruling. Western Meat Co. *v.* F. T. C., 1 F.(2d) 95 (Sept. 2, 1924), 4F.(2d) 223 (Feb. 17, 1925), 272 U. S. 554 (Nov. 23, 1926), 33 F.(2d) 824 (Jan. 24, 1929), 281 U. S. 771 (May 19, 1930). See: Ann. Rep., 1930, pp. 90–91. Thus, after a judicial history of six years, the commission settled the matter by agreement. In similar cases this measure of administrative suc-

part of 1926, which involved the jurisdiction of the commission to proceed with an investigation on a charge of misrepresentation, was concluded November 4, 1929.[138] And the Supreme Court also settled a five-year litigation which, since it is the first pronouncement of the highest court on the jurisdictional requirement of public interest, merits careful consideration.[139]

cess has not been attained. For example: Aluminum Co. of America *v.* F. T. C., 284 Fed. 401 (June 1, 1922), 261 U. S. 616 (Feb. 23, 1923), and 299 Fed. 361 (June 24, 1924); International Shoe Co. *v.* F. T. C., 29 F.(2d) 518 (Nov. 27, 1928), and 280 U. S. 291 (Jan. 6, 1930).

[138] The jurisdiction of the commission to proceed with an investigation was involved rather than the validity of orders issued, but since it is the sort of litigation history that makes the layman exclaim over "technicalities" and the law's delays, a brief description will not be out of place here. A company was charged with serious misrepresentations, both open and anonymous, as to competitor's products. After the proceedings had been completed before the commission, the complaint was dismissed by the commission on March 23, 1926. But on the same day counsel for the commission was granted the right to reargue the case. After the reargument, the commission recalled its order of dismissal and reopened the case for the taking of further testimony. The company under investigation then sought to have the commission restrained from proceeding further on the ground that, because of the order of dismissal, the commission had lost jurisdiction of the case. The Supreme Court of the District of Columbia, after a number of moves, finally denied this attempt. The company then appealed to the Court of Appeals of the District of Columbia where, on May 6, 1929, the lower court was affirmed. The company then attempted to take the matter to the Supreme Court of the United States, but that court refused to review the case. Then the company sought a rehearing, but this too was denied on November 4, 1929. Royal Baking Powder Co. *v.* F. T. C., 32 F.(2d) 966, and Ann. Rep., 1930, pp. 109–111. In the meantime the company had been engaged in efforts to prevent one of the commissioners from participating in the investigation on the ground of bias and prejudice. Petitions were filed with the commission on May 31 and June 4, 1928; the commission postponed action on these until the final hearing of the case. The company then sought to have the Supreme Court of the District of Columbia force the commission to consider the petitions before proceeding with the investigation, but the court finally determined in favor of the commission. The company then took the matter to the Court of Appeals of the District, but before the case was argued the company had the appeal dismissed, December 31, 1929. Ann. Rep., 1930, pp. 110–111; *Statutes and Decisions*, 1914–1929, p. 704. This ended the several-year attempt to prevent the commission from proceeding with an investigation. It is worth noting that another such attempt was denied January 6, 1930. Macfadden Publications *v.* F. T. C., 37 F.(2d) 822.

[139] The commission had filed in the Court of Appeals for the District of Columbia on May 13, 1924, a petition for enforcement of its order, but the court held that it was without jurisdiction. The Federal Trade Commission Act provided for review and enforcement of orders in the Circuit Courts of Appeals

The case involved the use of the trade name and style of a competitor. The Court of Appeals of the District of Columbia reversed the order of the commission, and the commission took the case to the Supreme Court. The justices of the Supreme Court found it unnecessary to "decide whether the Court of Appeals was justified in all of its assumptions of fact or in its conclusions on the matters of law" because the decision should be affirmed on the "preliminary ground" that the matter was not one of "public interest" as required in the Federal Trade Commission Act but was a private quarrel. That the case involved a private quarrel is clearly shown by the evidence. The name had been used for five years before the commission filed its complaint. As the Supreme Court said, "whatever confusion had originally resulted . . . must have been largely dissipated before the Commission first took action. If the members of the public were in 1920, or later, seriously interested in the matter, it must have been because they had become partisans in the private controversy. . . ."

Notwithstanding the commission's long-standing claim that the question of public interest was entirely within its discretion, this decision on its face has the merit of calling the commission from the investigation of petty and private disputes to more important matters — except that on the basis of other decisions it is difficult to see what authority the commission would be allowed to exercise in matters of consequence. As treated by the lower federal courts, the jurisdictional requirement of public interest had been considerably warped in earlier decisions which justified the commission's protests. Now, for the first time, the Supreme Court specifically dealt with the question: "In determining whether a proposed proceeding will be in the public interest the Commission exercises a broad discretion. But the mere fact that it is to the interest of the

within the territory of which the objectionable practice was used; the territory of the District of Columbia was not specifically mentioned. The Supreme Court, to which the commission appealed, determined that the Court of Appeals of the District of Columbia had jurisdiction. The case was thereupon reinstated in the lower court and on April 2, 1928, the court determined that the trade name in dispute was, in fact, generally descriptive of the business and therefore not within the exclusive use of any person in the absence of further deceptive practices; the order of the commission was, therefore, reversed. The commission then took the case to the Supreme Court, where the reversal of the commission was approved. F. T. C. *v.* Klesner, 6 F.(2d) 701 (June 1, 1925), 274 U. S. 145 (Apr. 18, 1927), 25 F.(2d) 524 (Apr. 2, 1928), 280 U. S. 19 (Oct. 14, 1929).

community that private rights shall be respected is not enough to support a finding of public interest." The commission's "preliminary determination that institution of a proceeding will be in the public interest, while not strictly within the scope of [the provision that findings must be supported by the evidence], will ordinarily be accepted by the courts. But the Commission's action in authorizing the filing of a complaint . . . is subject to judicial review."

Although the commission's claim for discretion is denied in cautious language,[140] the pronouncement of the Supreme Court is in general terms which are not likely to be accepted by the circuit courts of appeals as confining the judicial power to cases as clearly shown to be private and trivial as this instance. Professional criticism continues to condemn the commission for its failure to concern itself with matters of greater magnitude, but it is only fair to point out that the commission's attempts to regulate some of the larger aspects of competition and particularly the enforcement of the Clayton Act have failed through judicial restriction. Furthermore, matters which are not so clearly in the public mind may nevertheless be such that without their elimination other and more serious practices cannot consistently be regulated. Regulation may not necessarily or even advisedly be confined to large scale enterprise.

Two relatively new proceedings reached the Supreme Court in 1930. The first of these involved the acquisition of stock of a competitor in violation of the Clayton Act. The largest manufacturer in an industry had purchased the stock of the largest manufacturer in New England. This the commission found to be unlawful as tending to create a monopoly. The company appealed to the Circuit Court of Appeals for the First Circuit and sought to escape the order of the commission on the ground that the lesser company had become insolvent in the sense that it "was unable to pay its debts as they became due" and that therefore it was no longer a potential or prospective competitor. Both the court and the commission rejected this defense and found that the company was not actually in bankruptcy, and the court pointed out in its opinion that because the company was in financial difficulties did not necessarily mean that it would eventually pass into the hands of competitors. After the filing of the complaint by the commission, the company went through the form of divesting itself of the stock but

[140] The commission's only comment: "The public interest element in the commission's cases is brought out. . . ." Ann. Rep., 1930, p. 9.

acquired the physical properties of the company, which both the commission and the court found to be subterfuge. The court affirmed the order of the commission, and the company sought to have the decision reviewed in the Supreme Court. This was first refused but, on application for rehearing, was granted. On January 6, 1930, the Supreme Court reversed the lower court and thereby allowed the acquisition of the physical properties of the lesser competitor.[141]

The Supreme Court, differing with both the commission and the lower court, determined that "the product of the two companies . . . because of the difference in appearance and workmanship, appealed to the tastes of entirely different classes of consumers" and were "sold to a different class of dealers and found [their] way into distinctly separate markets" and that, therefore, there was no substantial competition between the companies. The Supreme Court also found, unlike the commission and the lower court, that the financial condition of the lesser company was "in gravest doubt," that the sale of its assets "to the only available purchaser in order to avoid what its officers fairly concluded was a more disastrous fate" was lawful, and that the continued separate existence of the lesser company was "wholly within the realm of speculation." Three justices dissented and, relying on the pronouncement in an earlier case that inferences drawn by the commission from proven facts are conclusive upon the courts, asserted that the evidence was sufficient, that the mere fact that the product was not sold to the same distributors was immaterial, that there was abundant evidence that substantial competition existed, that the majority had singled out only part of the evidence upon which to base decision, and that the financial difficulties were not such as to preclude conclusion that the business which was still a going concern would continue its separate existence and thereby maintain competition.

The noteworthy thing about this opinion is the outright rejection of the commission's and lower court's findings and the acceptance of the testimony of the officers of the company:

> . . . The officers . . . testified categorically that there was in fact no substantial competition between the companies . . . but that at most competition was incidental and so imperceptible that it could not be located. The existence of competition is a fact disclosed by observation rather than

[141] International Shoe Co. *v.* F. T. C., 29 F.(2d) 518 (Nov. 27, 1928), 279 U. S. 849 (Apr. 15, 1929), 279 U. S. 832 (May 20, 1929), 280 U. S. 291 (Jan. 6. 1930).

by the processes of logic; and when these officers, skilled in the business which they have carried on, assert that there was no real competition . . . their testimony is to be weighted like that in respect of matters of fact.

And again:

. . . The officers, stockholders and creditors, thoroughly familiar with the factors of a critical situation and more able than commission or court to foresee future contingencies, after much consideration, felt compelled to choose [this course of action]. There is no reason to doubt that in so doing they exercised a judgment which was both honest and well informed; and if aid be needed to fortify their conclusion, it may be found in the familiar presumption of rightfulness which attaches to human conduct. . . .

On other occasions the court has asserted that, where the evidence is capable of different interpretations, the conclusions of the commission are final,[142] or that in such an event the conclusion of the lower federal court is final,[143] but now the Supreme Court rejects all of these rules and substitutes its own interpretation of the evidence.

The second case involved an application by the commission for the enforcement of its order prohibiting the misrepresentation of a product. The Circuit Court of Appeals for the Seventh Circuit, finding the evidence ample and the acts unlawful, affirmed the order of the commission with a modification of one paragraph to make it more specific. The Supreme Court was asked to review the decision, but it refused and thereby sustained the order of the commission as affirmed by the lower court.[144] But this was closely followed by the review of another order respecting false advertising which was treated quite differently by the courts.

Medical advertising had become the chief inquiry in the campaign against false advertising.[145] In one instance, the commission determined that a patent medicine, "obesity cure," was falsely advertised and injurious. The company sought reversal of the commission's order which was granted by a circuit court of appeals. The court first dealt with the question "whether the advertising representations as to the scientific character and the safety of the remedy are statements of fact or are opinions" and held forth at length on the nature of proof: "It is clear that the ad-

[142] Pacific States Paper Trade Ass'n *v.* F. T. C., 273 U. S. 52 (Jan. 3, 1927).

[143] F. T. C. *v.* American Tobacco Co., 274 U. S. 543 (May 31, 1927).

[144] F. T. C. *v.* Kay, 35 F.(2d) 160 (Sept. 18, 1929), *certiorari denied* 281 U. S. 764 (June 2, 1930).

[145] Ann. Rep., 1930, pp. 56–57.

jectives 'scientific' and 'safe' have ordinarily no absolute meaning," said the court. "Nothing is always safe, not even water to drink; nothing is so scientific today that it may not be discarded tomorrow; little is so chimerical today that it may not be scientifically accepted tomorrow. It was long a 'scientific' fact that the world was flat; travel under the sea or in the air was long a scientific impossibility; Darius Green was the archetype of credulous ignorance. These merely illustrate that whether any particular plan or theory is scientific, in a fair sense of the word, is typically and generally a matter of opinion. If sometimes it is a matter of fact, that is exceptional." And then the court — having demonstrated that the matter is not subject to proof — nevertheless concludes: "The fair inference is that the actual harm would be exceptional. There is only the chance that the user may be of the exceptional class. . . ." The commission had decided that the remedy might be advertised as safe only if taken under the supervision of a physician. The company objected that this was an infringement of the right to free speech, which contention the court approved as "forcefully made." The court put its decision upon the further ground that the Federal Trade Commission Act forbids unfair competition — that is, competition which injures competitors and not, as here, practices which mislead or injure only consumers.

The case was then carried to the Supreme Court.[146] Although the Supreme Court did not decide the matter until after the decade under consideration, the opinion is important both as a further discussion on the order and, principally, as a denial of the commission's asserted and formerly approved authority in the only remaining phase of active regulation — false and misleading advertising. The Supreme Court reviewed the case solely upon the question of jurisdiction of the commission — whether the practice was a method of *competition* in commerce. It had long been urged that false and misleading advertising and misbranding was not really an unfair method of *competition*, but the Supreme Court in 1921 determined that this was such a method and was unfair to

[146] Raladam Co. *v.* F. T. C., 42 F.(2d) 430 (July 1, 1930). This court on the same day reversed another order of the commission and determined that furniture need not be labeled as "veneered" though it was not solid hardwood. Berkeley & Gay Furniture Co. *v.* F. T. C., 42 F.(2d) 427. The decision of the Supreme Court in the Raladam case is reported in 283 U. S. 643 (May 25, 1931), *review limited* 282 U. S. 829 (Nov. 30, 1930).

the hypothetical truthful manufacturer or dealer.[147] Now the Supreme Court determined that this previous and leading decision on the point only "inferentially" lent support to what had been the accepted law and found it unnecessary "further to consider the merits of this view." Then, after determining that impairment or unfairness between competitors was a necessary element, the court said, "There is neither finding nor evidence from which the conclusion legitimately can be drawn that these advertisments substantially injured or tended thus to injure the business of any competitor or of competitors generally, whether legitimate or not. . . . It is impossible to say whether, as a result of respondent's advertisements, any business was diverted, or was likely to be diverted, from others engaged in like trade. . . ."

Under this decision, unfairness and injury to the purchaser is insufficient unless at the same time competitors are injured. Although this seems the reasonable conclusion in view of the fact that the act was aimed at the maintenance of competition and prevention of monopoly only, nevertheless the court in effect reverses a decision of eight year's standing and severely limits the practice of the commission in this last phase of active regulation. The remaining authority of the commission in this field is probably illustrated by one of the circuit court of appeals decisions in an instance where confusion with other products resulted from the misrepresentation,[148] but in such a case adequate relief could be secured in the ordinary course of legal redress.

The reports of the commission covering this period emphasize general commercial investigations and the holding of trade practice conferences. The report for the fiscal year ending June 30, 1931, lists as major undertakings investigations conducted under authority of Senate resolutions; comment on legal developments is non-committal.[149] Subsequent decisions on review of Federal

[147] F. T. C. *v.* Winsted Hosiery Co., 258 U. S. 483 (Apr. 24, 1922).

[148] Lighthouse Rug Co. *v.* F. T. C., 35 F.(2d) 163 (Oct. 25, 1929).

[149] "Undertakings of the Federal Trade Commission during the year which have been outstanding because of their comprehensiveness and the wide public interest attaching to them are two general business and industrial investigations conducted under authority of Senate resolutions." Ann. Rep., 1931, p. 5. "Among the major activities . . . were: Examination in public hearings of the financial structure of several large utility holding company groups. . . . Investigation of the amount of electric power transmitted over State boundaries, indicating a much larger total interstate movement of electric energy in 1929 than in 1928. . . . Comprehensive comparison of chain and independent store

Trade Commission orders have not departed from the trends so far described.[150]

IV. The Commission as an Investigative Arm of Congress

The emphasis upon general investigations conducted under Congressional resolutions is significant. For many years, beginning with the period of the war, effort and attention has been increasingly given to these duties until now in the headlines of the commission's reports they have become the major undertakings.[151]

prices in three cities, with greater progress in the chain-store inquiry than shown for the previous year because of having for the first time sufficient field and office force. . . . Holding of 57 trade-practice conferences with that many industries, establishing a record in number of such meetings, and revision of certain rules adopted by industries at trade-practice conferences held with the commission." Ann. Rep., 1931, p. 6, and see p. 7 for recital on legal developments.

[150] Charles T. Morrissey *v.* F. T. C., 47 F.(2d) 101 (misrepresentations; order modified; Feb. 27, 1931); Ohio Leather Co. *v.* F. T. C. (remanded for testimony Nov. 12, 1930, 45 F.(2d) 39; joint motion sustained validating and granting enforcement of order regarding misrepresentations as modified, Apr. 7, 1931); F. T. C. *v.* Non-Plate Engraving Co., 49 F.(2d) 766 (misrepresentation order affirmed, May 4, 1931); Arnold Stone Co. *v.* F. T. C., 49 F.(2d) 1017 (misrepresentation order reversed, May 25, 1931); Shakespeare Co. *v.* F. T. C., 50 F.(2d) 758 (resale price maintenance order modified, June 13, 1931); Marietta Mfg. Co. *v.* F. T. C., 50 F.(2d) 641 (misrepresentation order affirmed, June 16, 1931); Temple Anthracite Coal Co. *v.* F. T. C., 51 F.(2d) 656 (stock acquisition order reversed, July 9, 1931); Flynn Co. *v.* F. T. C., 52 Fed. 836 (order prohibiting threatened suits reversed, Oct. 12, 1931); Vivaudou *v.* F. T. C., 54 F.(2d) 273 (stock acquisition order reversed, Nov. 2, 1931); Consolidated Book Pub. *v.* F. T. C., 53 F.(2d) 942 (sales practice order affirmed, Nov. 25, 1931).

[151] This use of the commission is provided in the Federal Trade Commission Act. The development of the function may have been suggested by the duties of the commission during the war (see: Ann. Rep., 1917, pp. 3, 23–25; 1918, pp. 3–6, 7–8, 9–27, 42–52, 84–86; 1919, pp. 3, 17–37, 97–99), or by the experience with the former Bureau of Corporations. The trade commission carried on the investigative work of the Bureau of Corporations (Ann. Rep., 1915, p. 2), and from the beginning investigations undertaken by the commission itself or at the direction of Congress have been an important item of the duties of the commission. Ann. Rep., 1915, pp. 1–2; 1916, pp. 12, 14–26; 1917, pp. 4–7, 14–21, 23–25.

For the development of the investigative function since the war see: Ann. Rep., 1920, pp. 5–7 (". . . While . . . economic inquiries may be inaugurated by the Commission on its own initiative or made at the direction of the President, they are more frequently undertaken by direction of the United States

During all this time much effort of the legal staff is taken with proceedings in connection with securing information in the course of these investigations.[152] Briefly, the economic division of the commission — which was originally intended to carry on the investigative and publicity efforts of the former Bureau of Corporations [153] — is now the dominant branch of the commission, requiring also the active cooperation of the other divisions of the commission.[154]

Senate or the House of Representatives, or both"); pp. 25–42 ("The most varied and extensive work of the Economic Division was done at the direction of the Senate or House of Representatives. . . ."); 1921, pp. 46–53; 1922, pp. 5–8, 40–55; 1923, pp. 12–15, 61–79; 1924, pp. 74–98; 1925, pp. 1–2, 81–95; 1926, pp. 55–64; 1927, pp. 28–39, 93–97; 1928, pp. vii–ix, 1–4, 17–20, 23–40, 187–191, 194–199; 1929, pp. 8–12, 26–29, 57, 65–69, 71–72, 222–233; 1930, pp. 6–7, 11–14, 32–36, 47–49, 233–245; 1931, pp. 5–6, 17–28, 31–34, 219–234.

At the same time, however, investigations for other branches of the government have fallen off, but these at no time were as numerous or extensive as those required by Congress. See: Ann. Rep., 1921, pp. 42–46; 1923, pp. 2, 78–79; 1924, pp. 3, 74–75, 91–92, 97–98; 1925, pp. 83–86, 90; 1926, pp. 59–60, 63–64; 1927, p. 38.

[152] Ann. Rep., 1922, pp. 2–3, 20, 30–32; 1923, pp. 8–9, 11, 44–45; 1924, pp. 19–20, 61; 1925, pp. 1–2, 58–61; 1926, pp. 1, 3–5, 45–47; 1927, pp. 83–86, 93–95; 1928, p. 17; 1920, pp. 41, 79–84; 1929, pp. 8–11, 57, 73, 109–111; 1930, pp. 9–10, 47–49, 58, 60–61, 105–109; 1931, pp. 75–76, 81–84. The legal department was organized primarily to assist the commission in its regulatory function. Ann. Rep., 1916, p. 4; 1917, pp. 7–8.

Another item of legal work may be noted. "Another branch of the legal work is administration of the act 'to promote export trade,' better known as the Webb-Pomerene law, which offers exemption from anti-trust laws to associations engaged solely in export trade." Ann. Rep., 1930, p. 7; see also: pp. 115–125. These duties of the commission began in 1918.

[153] "The economic division is organized primarily to conduct general inquiries called for by the President, by either house of Congress, or by the commission. . . . This was to be the sole function of the commission according to the bill first prepared for this purpose . . . in 1914, and this bill was passed in that form by the House of Representatives. In other words, the commission as first contemplated was to be a continuation of the Bureau of Corporations. . . . Hence the economic division is practically a continuation of the Bureau of Corporations and has had similar work." Ann. Rep., 1926, p. 55; see also: Ann. Rep., 1915, p. 2.

[154] Contrast this with the situation, for example, in 1924: "Most pressing is the increasing demand upon the energies of the commission in the field of unfair competition." Ann. Rep., 1924, p. 1. "Investigations and reports . . . raise no questions properly within the field of administrative law. . . . The study has, therefore, been limited to the normal and permanent duties of the Commission in administering Section 5 of the Federal Trade Commission Act, and Sections 2, 3, 7, and 8 of the Clayton Act." Henderson, *The Federal Trade Commission* (1924), p. xiii.

V. Summary and Conclusion

In summarizing points of contact and difference between the courts and the commission in the enforcement of regulatory orders to the end of 1930, judicial determinations on the question of interstate and foreign commerce may be excluded since this is a traditional province of the courts in which they can hardly be expected at this time to defer to the opinion of administrative authorities.[155] Likewise, the substantial interpretation of statutes may be excluded for this is regarded as *the* function of the courts.

There are, however, matters wherein the opinion of the commissioners must be considered. This, in fact, was one of the popular reasons for the establishment of the commission — that those who gave their whole time to the problem, and thereby became specialists, should make determinations which should be given effect through the courts.[156] But the history of judicial review of regulatory orders of the Federal Trade Commission clearly discloses that the judges substitute their own opinions for those of the commissioners or, even when sustaining the commission, hold themselves in readiness to reverse or modify orders with which they do not agree. The hopes of those who studied the situation during the first years have not been fulfilled.[157] There are only two instances in which the Supreme Court has expressed or approved a real deference for the judgment of the commission; one of these opinions was handed down by the Supreme Court but later repudiated.[158]

While the courts have not interfered with investigations pending

[155] Ward Baking Co. *v.* F. T. C., 264 Fed. 330 (order reversed, Feb. 26, 1920); Winslow *v.* F. T. C., 277 Fed. 206, *certiorari denied* 258 U. S. 618 (order reversed, Nov. 1, 1921); Utah-Idaho Sugar Co. *v.* F. T. C., 22 F.(2d) 122 (order reversed, Oct. 21, 1927).

[156] For a discussion see: Henderson, *The Federal Trade Commission* (1924), pp. 336–337. ". . . If the Federal Trade Commission is worth maintaining at all, it should have a more important function than merely to record physical facts and occurrences for the benefit of an appellate court." Idem, p. 336.

[157] *Supra*, n. 72.

[158] Arkansas Wholesale Grocers' Ass'n *v.* F. T. C., 18 F.(2d) 866, *certiorari denied* 275 U. S. 533 (commission sustained, 1927).

Pacific States Paper Trade Ass'n. *v.* F. T. C., 4 F.(2d) 457, *affirmed* 273 U. S. 52 (Jan. 3, 1927), but when one of the circuit courts of appeals followed this dicta it was reversed (International Shoe Co. *v.* F. T. C., 29 F.(2d) 518, Nov. 27, 1928, reversed 280 U. S. 291), three justices dissenting on the basis of the former opinion.

before the commission,[159] they examine every phase of the proceedings and every part of the record when a party affected by an order seeks to have its validity tested or when the commission applies to the courts for enforcement.

Accordingly, under the Clayton Act the courts have determined what constitutes price discrimination,[160] tying contracts or leases,[161] and unlawful acquisition of stock of a competitor.[162] As judicially construed, the Clayton Act is — to say the least — of uncertain intendment.[163]

Under the broad prohibition of "unfair methods of competition" [164] it is difficult to determine in the various cases whether the courts are "interpreting" the act or reviewing the sufficiency of the evidence to constitute an accepted offense. The orders of the commission fall into several well-defined groups, although there

[159] F. T. C. *v.* Nulomoline Co., 254 Fed. 988 (Aug. 16, 1918); T. C. Hurst & Son *v.* F. T. C., 268 Fed. 874 (Oct. 20, 1920); Butterick Case (S. C. D. C., not reported, Aug. 12, 1921, appeal dismissed Nov. 1921); Chamber of Commerce of Minneapolis *v.* F. T. C., 280 Fed. 45 (Mar. 27, 1922); Royal Baking Powder Co. *v.* F. T. C., 32 F.(2d) 966, *certiorari denied* Oct. 21, 1929; Macfadden Publications *v.* F. T. C., 37 F.(2d) 822 (Jan. 7, 1930).

[160] Cases involving discrimination between wholesalers or chain store systems and associated retailers: Mennen Co. *v.* F. T. C., 288 Fed. 774 (Mar. 13, 1923); National Biscuit Co. *v.* F. T. C., 299 Fed. 733 (May 5, 1924), *certiorari denied* 266 U. S. 613.

[161] In addition to Fruit Growers' Express *v.* F. T. C., 274 Fed. 205 (June 16, 1921) which was decided upon a question of jurisdiction and in which the appeal was dismissed on stipulation (261 U. S. 629), there were the following: Standard Oil Co. of N. Y. *v.* F. T. C., 273 Fed. 478 (May 11, 1921, commission reversed); Sinclair Refining Co. *v.* F. T. C., 261 U. S. 463 (commission reversed, 1923); B. S. Pearsall Butter Co. *v.* F. T. C., 292 Fed. 720 (July 19, 1923, commission reversed, 1923).

[162] Aluminum Co. of America *v.* F. T. C., 284 Fed. 401 (June 1, 1922), *certiorari denied* 261 U. S. 616 (commission sustained), 299 Fed. 361 (commission reversed to extent of allowing company to acquire physical assets, 1924); F. T. C. *v.* Western Meat Co., 272 U. S. 554 (Nov. 23, 1926, sustaining commission in one instance and reversing it in two; and see: 33 F.(2d) 824 (1929), 281 U. S. 771 (1930); International Shoe Co. *v.* F. T. C., 280 U. S. 291 (Jan. 6, 1930, commission reversed).

[163] Compare: Irvine, *Uncertainties of Section 7 of the Clayton Act*, 14 Cornell L. Q. 28 (1928); *Judicial Interpretation of Section 7 of the Clayton Act*, Comment 39 Yale L. J. 1042; *Clayton Act Section 3 and Patent Protection*, Comment 40 Yale L. J. 954 (1931).

[164] Federal Trade Commission Act, Sec. 5. Compare: Seligson, *Extent of Jurisdiction of the Federal Trade Commission over Unfair Competition*, 9 A. B. A. J. 698, 23 Col. L. Rev. 758 (1923); Montague, *Unfair Methods of Competition*, 25 Yale L. J. 20 (1915).

are some miscellaneous practices which have been the subject of judicial review.

In the field of false or misleading advertising, misbranding of products, or other misleading sales practices — which became by far the larger field of activity of the commission — administrative regulation at first met with substantial success before the courts but later many orders were modified or reversed culminating in a severe restriction at the hands of the Supreme Court.[165] Although commercial bribery is deeply tinged with fraud and unfairness (unless the general prevalence be said to raise it to the level of the lawful), the commission has been unsuccessful in its efforts to regulate the practice.[166] The orders of the commission respecting interference in the channels of trade (usually concerned with the wholesale distribution system or with chain stores) have been sus-

[165] *Commission sustained* (cases listed chronologically): Sears, Roebuck & Co. *v.* F. T. C., 258 Fed. 307 (Apr., 1919); Royal Baking Powder Co. *v.* F. T. C., 281 Fed. 744 (1922); Winstead Hosiery Co. *v.* F. T. C., 258 U. S. 483 (1922); Guaranty Veterinary Co. *v.* F. T. C., 285 Fed. 853 (1922); Fox Film Corp. *v.* F. T. C., 296 Fed. 353 (1924); F. T. C. *v.* Pure Silk Hosiery Mills, 3 F.(2d) 105 (1924); Procter & Gamble Co. *v.* F. T. C., 11 F.(2d) 47 (1926), *certiorari denied* 273 U. S. 718; Louis Leavitt *v.* F. T. C., 16 F.(2d) 1019 (1926); Sea Island Thread Co. *v.* F. T. C., 22 F.(2d) 1019 (1927); Indiana Quartered Oak Co. *v.* F. T. C., 26 F.(2d) 340 (1928), *certiorari denied* 278 U. S. 623; F. T. C. *v.* Balme, 23 F.(2d) 615 (1928), *certiorari denied* 277 U. S. 598 (1928); Bradley *v.* F. T. C., 31 F.(2d) 569 (1929); F. T. C. *v.* Powe, 35 F.(2d) 1017 (1929); Masland Duraleather Co. *v.* F. T. C., 34 F.(2d) 733 (1929); Lighthouse Rug Co. *v.* F. T. C., 35 F.(2d) 163 (1929). *Commission's order modified:* L. B. Silver Co. *v.* F. T. C., 289 Fed. 985 (1923); F. T. C. *v.* Kay, 35 F.(2d) 160 (1929), *certiorari denied* 281 U. S. 764; N. Flugelman & Co. *v.* F. T. C., 37 F.(2d) 59 (1930); F. T. C. *v.* Cassoff, 38 F.(2d) 790 (1930); Bayuk Cigars Inc. *v.* F. T. C., (1930); F. T. C. *v.* Good Grape Co., 45 F.(2d) 70 (1930). *Commission reversed:* Chicago Portrait Co. *v.* F. T. C., 4 F.(2d) 632 (1925), 269 U. S. 555; Ostermoor & Co. *v.* F. T. C., 15 F.(2d) 692 (1927); F. T. C. *v.* American Snuff Co., 38 F.(2d) 547 (1930); Raladam Co. *v.* F. T. C., 42 F.(2d) 430 (1930), 283 U. S. 643 (1930); Berkeley & Gay Furniture Co. *v.* F. T. C., 42 F.(2d) 427 (1930). *Enforcement of order denied:* John C. Winston Co. *v.* F. T. C., 3 F.(2d) 961 (1925); F. T. C. *v.* Standard Education Society, 14 F. (2d) 947 (1926).

Compare: Handler, *Jurisdiction of the Federal Trade Commission over False Advertising,* 31 Col. L. Rev. 527 (1931); *Scope of the Jurisdiction of the Federal Trade Commission over False and Misleading Advertising,* Comment 40 Yale L. J. 617–630.

[166] New Jersey Asbestos Co. *v.* F. T. C., 264 Fed. 509 (1920); Kinney-Rome Co. *v.* F. T. C., 275 Fed. 665 (1921); F. T. C. *v.* Advance Paint Co. (1926); F. T. C. *v.* Grand Rapids Varnish Co., 41 F.(2d) 996 (1929). And see: Winslow *v.* F. T. C., 277 Fed. 206 (1921), *certiorari denied* 258 U. S. 618.

tained only where associated or concerted action has been shown.[167] In the field of resale price maintenance, the commission's authority was sustained in the first case taken to the Supreme Court, but because that leading decision attempted to draw a line between the manufacturer's right to refuse to sell and some of the means of securing information as to price cutters, practical enforcement was always difficult, the circuit courts of appeals freely modified the orders of the commission, and finally attempts to regulate the practice nearly ceased — which is probably due as much to the general belief that there is a proper field for price setting as it is due to lack of success in enforcing the orders.[168] Orders prohibiting instances of imitation of competitor's trade style or name have been tested in only two instances in one of which the commission was successful.[169] Misrepresentation of competitor's products, facilities or financial standing has not been successfully prohibited by the commission.[170] The single order of the commission pro-

[167] National Harness Mfrs.' Ass'n *v.* F. T. C., 268 Fed. 705 (commission sustained, 1920); Western Sugar Refinery Co. *v.* F. T. C., 275 Fed. 725 (commission sustained in part, 1921); Wholesale Grocers' Ass'n *v.* F. T. C., 277 Fed. 657 (commission sustained, 1922); Southern Hardware Jobbers' Ass'n *v.* F. T. C., 290 Fed. 773 (commission sustained, 1923); Raymond Bros.-Clark Co. *v.* F. T. C., 280 Fed. 529 (commission reversed, 1922) *affirmed* 263 U. S. 565 (1924); Arkansas Wholesale Grocers' Ass'n *v.* F. T. C., 18 F.(2d) 866, *certiorari denied* 275 U. S. 533 (commission sustained, 1927).

[168] *Cases listed chronologically:* Beech-Nut Packing Co. *v.* F. T. C., 257 U. S. 441 (commission sustained but order modified, 1922); Mishawaka Woolen Mfg. Co. *v.* F. T. C., 284 Fed. 1022 (order modified, 1922) *certiorari denied* 260 U. S. 748; Butterick Co. *v.* F. T. C., 4 F.(2d) 910 (commission sustained, 1925), *certiorari denied* 267 U. S. 602; Oppenheim, Oberndorf & Co. *v.* F. T. C., 5 F.(2d) 574 (commission sustained, 1925); Hills Bros. *v.* F. T. C., 9 F.(2d) 481 (commission sustained, 1925); Toledo Pipe-Threading Machine Co. *v.* F. T. C., 11 F.(2d) 337 (order modified, 1926); Moir *v.* F. T. C., 12 F.(2d) 22 (order modified, 1926); Q. R. S. Music Co. *v.* F. T. C., 12 F.(2d) 730 (commission sustained, 1926); Ayer *v.* F. T. C., 14 F.(2d) 274 (commission reversed, 1926); *certiorari denied* 273 U. S. 759; American Tobacco Co. *v.* F. T. C., 9 F.(2d) 570 (commission reversed, 1925) *affirmed* 274 U. S. 543 (1927); Cream of Wheat Co. *v.* F. T. C., 14 F.(2d) 40 (order modified, 1926); J. W. Kobi Co. *v* F. T. C., 23 F.(2d) 41 (commission sustained, 1927).

Compare: Stevens, *Resale Price Maintenance as Unfair Competition*, 19 Col. L. Rev. 265 (1919).

[169] Juvenile Shoe Co. *v.* F. T. C., 289 Fed. 57 *certiorari denied* 263 U. S. 705 (commission sustained, 1923); F. T. C. *v.* Klesner, 25 F.(2d) 524 (commission reversed, 1928), *affirmed* on other grounds 280 U. S. 19 (1929).

[170] In addition to the Utah-Idaho Sugar Case (22 F.(2d) 122, 1927), which was decided upon the ground that no interstate commerce was involved, there

hibiting concerted action in fixing prices, though modified in the circuit court of appeals, was affirmed in the Supreme Court.[171] The commission met no more success in its efforts to prevent tying contracts or leases or other analagous practices under the Trade Commission Act than it has under the Clayton Act.[172] Nor has the regulation of price discrimination fared better under the Federal Trade Commission Act than under the Clayton Act.[173] Attempts to regulate other practices such as interference with licensees of a competitor,[174] threats of competition to force dealing,[175] and monopolistic devices,[176] have met with very little success.

In connection with all cases, the courts determine the sufficiency of the pleadings (although this appears to have been the sole ground of decision in only one instance),[177] what shall constitute proof and what conclusions shall be drawn from the evidence, when the matter is of public interest, what amounts to interference with competition, and when monopoly exists or is fostered. If an order of the commission is successful in passing this minute scrutiny, in some courts there is still the troublesome question of enforcement.

Finally, there is difference of opinion between the various courts as well as between the courts and the commission as to the sources of the law of unfair competition. Some courts have pronounced leanings toward the common law; the Supreme Court has said

were the following: John Bene & Sons *v.* F. T. C., 299 Fed. 468 (commission reversed, 1924); Philip Carey Mfg. Co. *v.* F. T. C., 29 F.(2d) 49 (commission reversed, 1928).

[171] Pacific States Paper Trade Ass'n *v.* F. T. C., 273 U. S. 52 (1927) (commission sustained).

[172] In addition to the Gratz Case (253 U. S. 421, June 7, 1920), which was decided by the Supreme Court on the pleadings, and the Fruit Growers' Express Case (274 Fed. 205, June 16, 1921), which was decided upon a question of jurisdiction, there were the following: Standard Oil Co. of N. Y. *v.* F. T. C., 273 Fed. 478 (commission reversed, May 11, 1921); Curtis Publishing Co. *v.* F. T. C., 260 U. S. 568 (commission reversed, Jan. 8, 1923); Sinclair Refining Co. *v.* F. T. C., 261 U. S. 463 (commission reversed, April 9, 1923).

[173] Mennen Co. *v.* F. T. C., 288 Fed. 774, *certiorari denied* 262 U. S. 759 (commission reversed, Mar. 13, 1923); National Biscuit Co. *v.* F. T. C., 299 Fed. 733, *certiorari denied* 266 U. S. 613 (commission reversed, May 5, 1924).

[174] Herman Heuser *v.* F. T. C., 4 F.(2d) 632 (commission reversed, Mar. 2, 1925).

[175] Eastman Kodak Co. *v.* F. T. C., 7 F.(2d) 994 (order modified, 1925), *affirmed* 274 U. S. 619 (1927).

[176] Chamber of Commerce of Minneapolis *v.* F. T. C., 13 F.(2d) 673 (order modified, July 13, 1926).

[177] F. T. C. *v.* Gratz, 253 U. S. 421 (June 7, 1921).

that the decisions under the Sherman Act are pertinent so far as they contain declarations of "public policy"; and all of the courts deny the commission's authority to develop a law of business practice — instead, "it is for the courts, not the commission, ultimately to determine as a matter of law" what shall constitute unfair methods of competition.

As decisions have come from the courts, the field of administrative activity has been narrowed. Toward the end of the decade active regulation was largely confined to misrepresentation of merchandise and resale price maintenance — neither of which could be called an "anti-trust" function of the commission or a serious problem in the maintenance of competition.[178] But resale price maintenance finally became the subject of a general investi-

[178] The commission itself in 1916 recognized that false representations to consumers were not strictly within Section 5. "Thus far the Commission has been of the opinion that at least those cases in which the method of competition restrains trade, substantially lessens competition, or tends to create a monopoly are subject to a proceeding under section 5 of the Federal Trade Commission act. The Commission has gone further than this, however, and in some instances where these elements did not appear, as in certain cases of misbranding and falsely advertising the character of goods where the public was particularly liable to be misled, the Commission has taken jurisdiction." Ann. Rep., 1926, p. 6.

". . . The Federal Trade Commission was organized primarily to deal with the trust problem. . . . In the field of misbranding and of deceptive advertising, valuable though the work has been, the Commission's jurisdiction has been a more or less fortuitous by-product rather than the result of a clear legislative design. Probably if the question of merchandise misbranding had been taken up on its merits, a law similar to the Food and Drugs Act would have been drafted, with its effective combination of administrative and criminal enforcement." Henderson, *The Federal Trade Commission* (1924), p. 339.

"The Commission's great activity in [respect to fraudulent advertising] as well as its activity concerning resale price maintenance, is largely accounted for by the fact that the Beech-Nut case . . . and the Winsted case . . . were the early decisions of the Supreme Court upholding the action of the Commission. The Commission met repeated reversals in the early cases involving other activities. These activities [fraudulent advertising and price maintenance] are scarcely a direct development of the theory of the Federal Trade Commission Act as an Anti-Trust Law. It is questionable whether resale price maintenance is an unfair method of competition. Its illegality is substantially an invention of the Supreme Court and its economic desirability is such a close question that there is no assurance that the activities of the Commission along this line achieve any net gain." J. R. McLaughlin, *Cases on the Federal Anti-Trust Laws* (1930), p. 621, n. 175. And see: Gaskill, *Price Control in the Public Interest* (2 ed., 1931); Seligman and Love, *Price Cutting and Price Maintenance* (1932).

gation, and the orders of the commission dealing with misrepresentation have met with less and less success before the courts. Finally, the commission has taken the view, so far as its regulatory authority is still exercised, that it is a complicated investigator and prosecutor — "merely an administrative and fact-finding body."[179] The development and authoritative enforcement of a law of competition, once the principal function of the commission, has given way to conciliation and cooperation.[180] Of course, in lesser cases the orders of the commission are more effective because of the expense and inconvenience of resort to the courts.[181] Other orders, however, though not enforced or contested are not necessarily effective — they may be disobeyed without risk of penalty, or practices may be modified.[182]

[179] "It is readily conceded . . . that what constitutes an 'unfair method of competition' . . . is a question of law to be finally decided by the court of last resort. . . . But the Commission must necessarily, in the first instance, open the trial by deciding whether or not a given practice is lawful or unlawful so as to give the court an opportunity to adjudicate the question. In doing so, the Commission, though merely an administrative and fact-finding body, acts in a quasi-judicial capacity without appearing to exalt itself into the realm of the judicial branch of the government." Memorandum, May 29, 1929. Commissioner McCullough.

The annual reports for 1929, 1930, and 1931 at pages 14, 18, and 9 in enumerating the functions of the commission simply state: "Jurisdiction is given the commission in determining in the first instance what is or what is not an unfair method of competition. . . ."

It was contemplated that the commission should act as investigator in cooperation with the Department of Justice in the enforcement of the Sherman Act (see: *Federal Trade Commission as Special Master in Anti-Trust*, 30 Harv. L. Rev. 168), but this was not the conception of the commission's function under the substantive provisions of the Clayton Act and Federal Trade Commission Act.

[180] Compare a statement concerning the enforcement of anti-trust laws in general: "Definite agreements in regard to prices and outright monopolies are prohibited, but the executive branches of the government, which are relied upon to enforce these prohibitions, have during the last decade shown less interest in opposing than in promoting cooperation among business men. The place of dissolution suits has been taken by such prophylactic measures as consent decrees, trade practice conference rules and stipulations, so that attempts to apply the criminal penalties of the law have been infrequent and unimportant." Seager and Gulick, *Trust and Corporation Problems* (1929), p. 662.

[181] For an account of the regulatory work including uncontested orders see: Seager and Gulick, *op. cit.*, pp. 499 et seq., 651–653.

[182] But compare: *Public Regulation of Competitive Practices*, pp. 217–218.

There is a growing tendency to criticize and evaluate the administration of the anti-trust legislation of 1914.[183] How far the restraining hand of the judiciary is responsible for the changed activity of the Federal Trade Commission is, of course, a matter of opinion. Had regulatory orders been enforced in greater numbers, certainly the commission would have been more disposed to develop this phase of its duties. On the other hand, to attribute the lack of success entirely to unsympathetic treatment at the hands of the judges would be error — causes are rarely so simple. Personnel and amplifying legislation, among other things, are of first importance.

The courts, having taken the determination of these matters to themselves, have had no easy task. To draw the line of legality between that which hinders competition and that which is desirable to foster and protect business initiative is no simple matter — as inconsistent decisions and difficulties in delimiting those practices which are to be prohibited testify. However, the experiment thus far has been a judicial experiment; the special commission has been ousted so far as the development of the law is concerned. The federal legislature, too, has taken the commission's time and energies, sometimes for needed investigations but too often (at least as judged from the use made of completed inquiries) as a repository for political gestures. Perhaps now, if Congress were persuaded to overhaul the statutes, the courts would be inclined to give the administrative agency a more adequate measure of authority.

[183] Compare: Watkins, *An Appraisal of the Work of the Federal Trade Commission*, 32 Col. L. Rev. 272 (1932); Blaisdell, *The Federal Trade Commission* (1932).

CHAPTER IV

THE INTERSTATE COMMERCE COMMISSION AND THE COURTS

COMPARED with the Federal Trade Commission, the development and present position of the Interstate Commerce Commission affords instruction by way of contrast. Unlike the Trade Commission, the legislative history of the Interstate Commerce Commission develops almost year by year. The judicial relations of the commission so follow statutory developments that it will be necessary to trace this legislative progress as fully as space permits before treating the Transportation Act of 1920 and the 1920–1930 decade.[1] Here Congress has been an active referee and therefore legislative history furnishes materials of first importance. This history is not merely a record of extension of literal authority but in large part is corrective and designed to increase the effectiveness of the commission's efforts. Difficulties in enforcement of orders are removed and limitations imposed by the judiciary in interpreting the statutes are set aside by legislation.

The background of both the Federal Trade Commission and the Interstate Commerce Commission is to be found in the same social and political movements of the last half of the nineteenth century and the first decade of the twentieth. Beginning with the conditions of depression following the Civil War and the consequent movements in industry, there arose a body of decisions, statutes, and constitutional provisions directed at commercial enterprise. Over-expansion was a large factor in the panic of 1873. Anti-trust legislation was marked in the states before the federal government acted.[2] Popular reaction, however, was directed chiefly toward the railroads.

The Interstate Commerce Commission is, of course, a large part of the story of government regulation of "public utilities." Toward

[1] Such a comprehensive study is now appearing under the Commonwealth Fund. Two valuable volumes have already been published. I. L. Sharfman, *The Interstate Commerce Commission* (1931): vol. I, "The Legislative Basis of the Commission's Authority"; vol. II, "Scope of the Commission's Jurisdiction."

[2] Seager and Gulick, *Trust and Corporation Problems* (1929), p. 343 et seq.

the seventies of the last century was a period of railroad building and extension encouraged by every private and public means to tap the wealth of national resources and realize the immediate economic development of a vast domain. History's common denominator finally appeared — great expansion led to scandalous abuse and public assistance turned to public regulation.[3] As in the case of the anti-trust movement, reaction first appeared in state legislation. The authority of regulating agencies ranged from the mere inquisitorial to authoritative regulation. Bitter controversy attended the attempts to attain public supervision, but despite judicial interference which seriously crippled the commissions[4] the policy of public regulation became established in the states.

As state legislation developed, the need for federal regulation became apparent.[5] Railroad extension had opened a continent, and so far as national commerce was concerned state lines were hardly more than features of political geography. Discriminatory practices were common and the subject of chronic complaint. Unlike the present conception of carriers as essentially monopolistic, the public faith was placed in the maintenance of competition. General resort to cooperation between railroads in the form of pooling of traffic or revenues, which followed over-expansion and the ruinous rate wars of the sixties and seventies, coupled with a decision

[3] First Annual Report of the Interstate Commerce Commission, 1887, p. 5.

[4] "In the nineteenth century the United States developed a system of judicial interference with administration. Law paralyzing administration was an everyday spectacle. . . . A reaction from the extreme limitations of administration in our traditional polity, accelerated by the demands of an expanding law of public utilities . . . resulted in a rapid development of administrative bodies of all kinds. . . ." Pound, *Justice According to Law*, 14 Col. L. Rev. 1, 12 (1914), citing Smalley, *Railroad Rate Control*, p. 124: "The gradual growth of the doctrine of judicial review and the gradual development of the methods employed by the courts, have gradually paralyzed the state railroad commissions by destroying their will as well as their power. . . . The commission have become discouraged from the task of rate regulation; most of them pay relatively slight attention to the matter of rates, confining themselves largely to the other and much less important duties imposed upon them."

[5] Bernhardt, *The Interstate Commerce Commission*, 1923, pp. 4–6; and see: Sharfman, *op. cit.*, vol. I.

For federal railroad legislation up to and including the Act of 1887 see: L. H. Haney, *A Congressional History of Railways in the United States*, vol. I, "Congress and the Railway down to 1850" (1908); vol. II, "The Railway in Congress, 1850–1887" (1910). For a list of bills and resolutions see Briggs, *Federal Regulation of Interstate Commerce, 1862–1913* (1913); and see: Miller, *Legislative Evolution of the Interstate Commerce Act* (1930).

of the Supreme Court to the effect that the right to regulate commerce carried over state lines was an exclusively federal function [6] aroused popular demand and made Congressional action imperative if railway regulation was to succeed. The result was the passage of the Act to Regulate Commerce in 1887 and the creation of the Interstate Commerce Commission.[7]

For the purpose of comparison with the Federal Trade Commission it is important to note, at this point, that the policy of public regulation of railroads in its beginnings demanded the maintenance of competition.[8] Monopolistic practices and discrimination were to be stamped out.

I. The Initial Period

The Cullom Act of February 4, 1887, was the first general federal statute providing for regulation of interstate carriers, although not the first act relating to railroads or providing some degree of regulation.[9] The act created the Interstate Commerce Commission. It applied only to carriers of persons or property by railroad or partly by railroad and partly by water between the states and territories or the District of Columbia or to and from foreign countries. The principal substantive provisions were the prohibitions against unreasonable rates, unjust discriminations, undue preference and the charging of a greater amount under substantially similar circumstances and conditions for a shorter than for a longer haul over the same line in the same direction, and pooling of traffic or revenues.

The orders of the commission were not immediately effective unless voluntarily obeyed (as is now the case with the Federal Trade Commission). Upon refusal or neglect to comply, enforcement could be secured only through the federal circuit courts. Upon such application the court could examine the order to determine whether it were valid, and the courts were directed to determine the matter "speedily as a court of equity and without

[6] Wabash Ry. Co. *v.* Illinois, 118 U. S. 557 (1886), and see: Ann. Rep., 1887, pp. 3–4.

[7] Until 1920 the basic statute is customarily referred to as "The Act to Regulate Commerce"; by the Transportation Act of 1920 the designation is changed to "Interstate Commerce Act."

[8] See the account of discriminatory and monopolistic conditions in the first annual report of the commission, 1887, and see also: Ann. Rep., 1892, p. 4.

[9] 24 Stat. 379.

the formal pleadings and proceedings applicable to ordinary suits in equity but in such manner as to do justice." Furthermore, the courts could "direct . . . inquiries . . . needful to enable [them] to form a just judgment" but the report of the commission was to be "*prima facie* evidence of the matters therein stated."

The initial act was wisely regarded as experimental and contained a provision requiring the commission to make recommendations for additional legislation. (The Federal Trade Commission Act 27 years later was similarly regarded and contained a provision for administrative recommendations.[10]) From the very first the Interstate Commerce Commission took this mandate seriously. Although it reported that extensive amendment was unnecessary during the first years,[11] the commission advised legislation in a large number of particulars.[12] These first recommendations of the

[10] See *infra*, p. 184 and n. 44.

[11] "The Commission has not seen occasion for recommending any very considerable changes in the act. . . . Incidentally . . . some need of amendment has been pointed out." Ann. Rep., 1887, and see also the reports for 1888, p. 68; 1890, p. 65.

[12] *The Commission's recommendations for legislation, 1887–1894* (Annual reports indicated by date and page): *Inclusion of other carriers within the act:* Water carriers: 1887, p. 12; 1888, p. 71; 1889, p. 108; 1890, p. 64; 1893, pp. 58–60; 1894, p. 79. Express companies: 1887, pp. 12–15; 1888, pp. 6–9; 1889, p. 107; 1890, p. 64. Sleeping-car companies: 1887, p. 15. Tank cars: 1887, p. 15. In general: 1894, pp. 39–41. *Provision against sudden raising of rates:* 1888, p. 68. *Authority regarding filing and publication of tariffs:* 1887, pp. 15–23; 1888, pp. 16–17, 68; 1889, p. 25 (commenting on amendment passed). *Joint tariffs:* 1894, pp. 31–34. *Penalty for destruction of posted tariff:* 1894, p. 78. *Requirement of notice of intention to reduce rates:* 1888, p. 69; 1889, p. 13 (reduced fares). *Imposition of penal provisions against false billing and rebating:* 1888, pp. 10–11, 69. *More precise definition of "interstate commerce":* 1888, p. 69; 1889, pp. 72–75; 1892, pp. 65–66. *Authority to prescribe rates for carriage of immigrants:* 1889, pp. 41–44. *Interchange of traffic with non-competing roads:* 1888, p. 70. *Amplification of through traffic and through rate provisions:* 1889, p. 107; 1890, pp. 55–58; 1891, pp. 41–53, 68; 1893, pp. 39–50, 78; 1894, pp. 54–60, 78. *Revision of provisions for summoning witnesses and securing reports or records:* 1889, p. 107; 1890, p. 64; 1892, pp. 39, 42–47, 75. *Modification of provisions regarding free passes:* 1889, pp. 9–12, 107; 1890, p. 68. *Provision against ticket sellers' commissions:* 1888, pp. 44–50; 1889, pp. 13–14, 108; 1890, pp. 62–64, 68; 1891, p. 68. *Provision regarding ticket brokerage:* 1889, pp. 19, 108; 1890, pp. 49–55, 68; 1891, p. 68. *Regulation of private car mileage:* 1889, pp. 9–13, 108; 1890, p. 68; 1891, p. 68; 1893, pp. 60–67. *Safety appliance legislation:* 1889, pp. 84–97; 1891, p. 68; 1892, pp. 69–70; 1893, pp. 74–76; 1894, pp. 75–77. *Amendment of penalty provisions:* 1890, p. 68; 1891, p. 68; 1892, pp. 39, 47; 1893, pp. 6–11, 78; 1894, pp. 60, 78. *Modification of provisions for judicial re-*

commission seem to have been genuinely necessary and wise (with the possible exception of the request for authority over labor troubles) and most of them have since become statute, but at this time the recommendations for legislation were accepted only in part.[13]

The first years of the commission's existence were taken up with analysis of the statutory authority and problems and the careful beginnings of active regulation,[14] as were the first years of the later

view: 1890, pp. 9–11, 13–21, 68; 1891, pp. 18–23, 68; 1892, pp. 41, 75; 1893, p. 78; 1894, p. 78. *Amplification of authority to require annual reports from carriers:* 1888, pp. 58–68; 1890, p. 68; 1891, p. 68; 1893, pp. 70–73, 78; 1894, pp. 63–64, 79. *Uniform classification of freight:* Subject discussed: 1888, pp. 34–41; 1889, pp. 48–57; 1890, pp. 31–36. Legislation recommended: 1891, pp. 23–34, 68; 1893, pp. 50–56, 78; 1894, pp. 34–39. *Precise definition of word "line" to prevent avoidance of provisions:* 1892, pp. 47, 75; 1893, pp. 31–36, 78; 1894, p. 79. *Amplification of provisions regarding statistics:* 1892, p. 73. *Authority to prescribe minimum as well as maximum rates:* 1888, pp. 19–24; 1893, pp. 38–39, 78; 1894, pp. 20–24, 78. *Provision for government appeals in penal cases where there is a constitutional question or judgment is given on demurrer or motion:* 1894, p. 79. *Possible amendment of pooling provision:* 1894, pp. 69–73, 79. *Bills of lading:* 1891, pp. 54–65. *Overcharges and undercharges:* 1893, pp. 56–58; 1894, pp. 44–49, 78. *Criminal prosecutions:* 1894, pp. 12–16. *Grant of authority over labor troubles:* 1894, pp. 66–68. *Appointment of special agents to make investigations:* 1890, pp. 6, 26, 68; 1891, p. 11; 1892, p. 74.

13 Previously by Act of August 7, 1888 (25 Stat. 832), duties were imposed on the commission with regard to government-aided railroad and telegraph lines. Ineffectual administration is reported from 1888 through 1895. On March 2, 1889, the initial act was amended to provide, among other things, amplification of penalty provisions, authorization and means for the enforcement of some of the provisions of the act, provision for jury trial in proceedings to enforce the commission's awards of reparation, and the elimination of the Secretary of Interior as an intermediary between the commission and Congress. 25 Stat. 855. The second amendment, February 10, 1891, broadened the commission's power to require the attendance and testimony of witnesses and the production of documentary evidence. 26 Stat. 743. There was also the compulsory testimony act of February 11, 1893, 27 Stat. 443, which while not in terms an amendment of any of the preceding acts, remedied the unconstitutional nature (limited immunity) of Sections 9 and 12(3) of the original act providing for compulsory testimony. The last amendment of this period, February 8, 1895, added a provision for the issuance of joint interchangeable mileage tickets. 28 Stat. 643. At this time the first of the safety and accident prevention laws was enacted conferring additional duties upon the commission. March 2, 1893, 27 Stat. 531. Amended April 1, 1896, 29 Stat. 85.

14 A mind rutted by conceptions of arbitrary administrative action will be disturbed on reading the first reports of the Interstate Commerce Commission by the care with which the powers and purposes are considered, the caution exercised before interfering with the economic structure, and the altogether

Federal Trade Commission. It was not until 1894 that the Interstate Commerce Commission reported that the purposes and requirements of the law were so well understood that the report to Congress would be "mainly devoted to stating what has been done toward securing observance of the law through exercise of the Commission's powers and by proceedings in the courts, and what amendments are necessary to remedy discovered defects in the statute."[15] The transportation companies worked in some harmony with the administrative body; it was not until the second year that carriers refused to comply with the commission's decisions.[16]

Notwithstanding the comparatively substantial body of legislation, defects in the statutes as judicially interpreted soon became apparent. A detailed analysis of the judicial decisions for this period would be unprofitable for comparison. Unlike the Federal Trade Commission cases, until 1906 judicial review of Interstate Commerce Commission orders was not confined to the record before the commission — instead, new evidence was taken in the courts and the proceeding amounted to a new trial before the court. For this earlier period, it should suffice to state the more general defects and the course of administration.

The period after the commission had become settled and till 1897, although some defects in the legislation had already appeared, was one of testing the administration of the act and determining

reasonable and painstaking analysis of the problems and difficulties involved in the regulation of each phase of commercial practice. To choose one of many examples, pooling agreements were popularly considered one of the more vicious practices of the railroads and were prohibited by the Act of 1887; yet the commission in its first report to Congress said, "The pooling system has done much to maintain steadiness in rates, but the managers have not been able by means of it to keep rates up to former standards. It has done something, however, to check a prevailing tendency to consolidation. The motives to consolidation are diminished by any contrivance which removes obstacles to the interchange of business and increases the facilities and conveniences for uninterrupted commercial intercourse." See: Ann. Rep., 1887, pp. 33–36; Ann. Rep., 1901, pp. 47–55. For other examples of cautious administration see: Ann. Rep., 1891, p. 14; 1896, pp. 5–6. Of course, irrespective of administrative attitude, action may be arbitrary in a legal sense. Whether there had been unreasonableness during these years must be determined from the decisions.

[15] Ann. Rep., 1894, p. 1.

[16] Ann. Rep., 1888, p. 11: "The decisions made by the Commission within the year, when against the carriers, have been accepted and conformed to with reasonable promptitude, except in two instances."

before the courts the scope of the commission's authority. In 1893 the commission reported that "resistance to regulation is diminishing and . . . the trend of judicial decision in recent years, with some embarrassing exceptions, has been towards holding interstate rail carriers to more rigid performance of their public functions."[17] But by 1895 the attempts to administer the act were "not entirely satisfactory," [18] and in 1898 the situation was described as "intolerable." [19] The defects in the legislation so far as the provisions for judicial review and enforcement of the commission's orders were concerned appeared almost from the first, but it was not until 1896 and 1897 that the act was so interpreted by the courts that effective regulation of rail transportation was practically impossible. The years 1896 and 1897, therefore, mark a turning point in the work of the Interstate Commerce Commission just as the years 1926 and 1927 mark the turning point in the administration of the anti-trust acts by the Federal Trade Commission.

The defects in the administration of the Interstate Commerce Act as they appeared at this time may be considered as of two classes — the enforcement of the act and the construction of its substantive provisions. In the first place, procedure for enforcement of the orders of the commission through the courts was cumbersome and in practice reduced the commission to little more than a preliminary investigator and prosecutor. As is now true with the Federal Trade Commission, the administrative orders were not binding until passed on by a federal court. Although the commission was required to execute the Act to Regulate Commerce, its decisions were not obligatory and it could not enforce them by process of its own. When enforcement of orders was sought in the courts, new evidence could be introduced which required a new judgment (this time by the judges rather than the administrators). And then there was the probability of appeals through the judicial hierarchy.

This system involved two major defects. In allowing new evidence to be produced in court the same case was not presented that had been before the commission. Carriers found it unnecessary to disclose the whole evidence to the commission but could present entirely new matter to contest attempted enforcement. And secondly, the fact that orders were of no effect until passed upon

[17] Ann. Rep., 1893, p. 11.
[18] Ann. Rep., 1895, pp. 5–6.
[19] Ann. Rep., 1898, pp. 5–6.

by the courts and the further loss of time because of appeals delayed enforcement, whereas the nature of the subject demanded speedy and authoritative action — which Congress had recognized in the original act when the courts were adminished to act "speedily . . . and without formal pleadings and proceedings."

The commission complained that its determinations were not even accorded the weight of findings made by a master in chancery or a referee and that the only effect of the investigation and determination of the commission was to shift the burden of proof in the proceedings before the courts.[20] The commission reported to Congress that it received complaints, gave notice, held hearings, received evidence, made investigation, considered and gave decision:

> Now, after all this has been gone through with, what is the effect of the order thus made? Really nothing whatever. If the carrier declines or neglects to obey, it suffers no penalty and incurs no loss. The act provides that any person interested in an order of the Commission, or that the Commission itself, may file a petition in the United States circuit court in the proper district, asking to have the order enforced, and the court is instructed to determine whether the order is a proper one and, if so, to enforce it. . . .
>
> Upon the trial before the Commission the testimony is all reduced to writing, but no part of this can be used, except by stipulation, upon the trial in the circuit court. The testimony upon both sides must be entirely retaken. Nor is either party in any way confined to the testimony previously given nor the issues previously made. The result, of course, is that the case made before the circuit court may be entirely different from the case made before the Commission, so that the proceeding is not, in any proper sense, a review of the correctness of the decision of the Commission. If the circuit court, after a full hearing, is of opinion that the order ought to be complied with, it so decrees; if not, it refuses to enforce the order. From the decree of the circuit court, either enforcing or refusing to enforce the order, an appeal lies to the circuit court of appeals, and from that court, in most cases, to the United States Supreme Court.[21]

---

[20] "With this exception . . . the hearing may proceed, so far as the original defendant is concerned, as though there had never been any investigation before the Commission, or any report and decision made by it; or at least the facts found by the Commission may be controverted by other testimony, and new facts may be established by entirely new evidence. This certainly seems rather an impotent conclusion of so much labor and expense as is usually involved in a proceeding before the Commission; and it is hardly credible that either Congress or the commercial interests of the country, or the general public, supposed that the law would bear this construction." Ann. Rep., 1891, pp. 20–21 at p. 21.

[21] Ann. Rep., 1897, pp. 27–37, 31.

This difficulty appeared as soon as enforcement of orders was attempted. The commission began recommending amendments in 1890, and these legislative proposals became the chief features of the reports to Congress.

The second major defect in the regulation of carriers was the restricted character of the substantive provisions of the statutes. In some respects the original legislation was incomplete, in others judicial interpretation "disclosed" vital omissions of authority. To illustrate, two of the more important features of the original act — fixation of rates [22] and long-and-short-haul rate uniformity [23]

[22] The commission interpreted the original act as conferring power to investigate rates and also power to prescribe the remedy. Rates were fixed only in correcting abuses and not in the first instance. However, in 1896 the Supreme Court stated that it was unable to find any provision of the act "that expressly or by necessary implication" conferred such power. Cin., N. O. & Tex. Pac. Ry. *v.* I. C. C., 162 U. S. 184 (1896). After this pronouncement the power of the commission over rates was made more doubtful by various decisions in the lower courts. Finally the Supreme Court determined that the commission had no power to "prescribe a rate for the future, although its right to pass upon the reasonableness or unreasonableness of a rate already paid" and of which complaint had been made could not be questioned. I. C. C. *v.* Railway Co., 167 U. S. 479 (1897). Thereafter the commission's orders had no prospective operation; all it could do was declare illegal one rate after another in the hope that the carrier would finally comply. For a further discussion see: Sharfman, *The Interstate Commerce Commission* (1931), I, 27.

[23] One of the abuses which led to the establishment of the commission was the practice of local discrimination by competing railroads whereby higher rates were paid at small non-competitive points than in localities where there was competition. This form of discrimination was made unlawful when circumstances and conditions were "substantially similar." For some years the railroads made attempts to adjust their rates in accordance with this legislation, but in 1892 judicial interpretation began which complicated matters and made regulation difficult — including the "line" decisions by which a carrier could become an entity for the transportation of through freight legally separate from that under which it engaged in local freight carriage over the same system and which the commission reported "invaded the very jurisdiction of the law itself." Ann. Rep., 1893, p. 35. The commission recommended legislative definition. Although the Supreme Court did not concur in all of the interpretations of the lower federal courts, in 1896 it decided that "competition, whether of trade centers or of railroads, must be recognized as a factor in the determination of the similarity of circumstances and conditions under which the [act] should apply." I. C. C. *v.* Alabama Midland Ry. Co., 168 U. S. 144 (1897). And see also: East Tennessee Ry. Co. *v.* I. C. C., 181 U. S. 1 (1901); I. C. C. *v.* Clyde Steamship Co., 181 U. S. 29 (1901). Competitive conditions had given rise to the practice which the act sought to correct, and yet the

— ultimately became ineffective. Substantive provisions became seriously restricted or uncertain in other respects such as the application of the provisions against discrimination, undue preference, and prejudice. There was a lack of specific provision in such matters as through routes and rates and joint rates, filing and posting of tariffs, penal provisions, and in the requirements for statistical data.[24]

By 1897 the decisions defining the powers of the Interstate Commerce Commission, as the dissenting justice in an important commerce commission case said, had gone "far to make that Commission a useless body for all practical purposes, and to defeat many of the important objects designed to be accomplished by the various enactments of Congress relating to interstate commerce. The Commission was established to protect the public against the improper practices of transportation companies. . . It has been shorn, by judicial interpretation, of authority to do anything of an effective character. It is denied many of the powers which . . . were intended to be conferred upon it. Besides, the acts of Congress are now so construed as to place communities on the lines of interstate commerce at the mercy of competing railroad companies. . . ."[25] And the commission, after fully reporting on the

courts determined that this very factor justified differences in rates. Exceptions to the prohibition, addressed by the act to the commission, were now so recognized by the courts that application to the administrative body was unnecessary. The long-and-short-haul provision collapsed.

[24] Although the courts found the statutes too vague in some respects for effective regulation of carriers by the commission, they found another use for the Interstate Commerce Act. The commission reported that in addition to cases arising from the orders of the commission "attention should be called to orders, injunctions, and opinions arising out of railway labor troubles, which have been partially based upon sections of the act to regulate commerce. That provisions intended to bring about general interchange of traffic with connecting lines on equal terms . . . have been found so weak as to be incapable of forcing a railroad company to haul the loaded car of a connecting carrier at established local rates, and yet can be successfully invoked by a railroad company to restrain its employees from obstructing or in any way interfering with the prompt forwarding of interstate traffic over its own and connecting lines, is a condition of affairs which not plain people alone, but those supposed to be versed in the law, find it extremely difficult to understand." Ann. Rep., 1894, p. 13. Somewhat the same history is to be noted in connection with the Sherman Act. See: Jones, *Historical Development of the Law of Business Competition*, 36 Yale L. J. 207, 228 (1926).

[25] I. C. C. *v.* Alabama Midland Ry. Co., 168 U. S. 144, 176 (1897).

administration of the law as interpreted and enforced by the courts,[26] stated its position:

> The Interstate Commerce Commission can conduct investigations and make reports. It can, perhaps, correct in a halting fashion some forms of discrimination. It collects and publishes statistical information which would be of value if, under the law, it could be obtained and published within a reasonable time. It performs a valuable service in adjusting differences between the carrier and the shipper which never reach the stage of a formal complaint. But, by virtue of judicial decision, it has ceased to be a body for the regulation of interstate carriers. It is proper that Congress should understand this. The people should no longer look to this Commission for a protection which it is powerless to extend.[27]

Although there was some attempt at conciliatory or cooperative action,[28] the commission (unlike the later Federal Trade Commission) did not cease attempts to exercise authority and continued to point out the necessity for legislation. Aside from the statements of the commissioners or judges, it is commonly asserted that the courts in cavalier fashion substituted their own views for those of the commission in specific instances and, by interpretation, devitalized regulation.[29] Certainly there is much in the situation upon which to base such views. At the same time, however, the more vital defects are not entirely attributable to the attitude of the courts but are in some measure the result of the experimental

[26] Ann. Rep., 1897, pp. 6–51. See also: Hening, *The Interstate Commerce Commission before the Federal Courts*, 31 Am. L. Reg. (N. S.) 156 (1892).

[27] Ann. Rep., 1897, p. 51.

[28] Conferences with railroad presidents: Ann. Rep., 1899, pp. 8–12. Settled and discontinued cases: Ann. Rep., 1899, pp. 43–44; 1900, pp. 48–52; 1901, pp. 21–22; 1902, pp. 21–22; 1903, pp. 44–46; 1904, pp. 41–42; 1905, pp. 55–57.

Of the 208 informal complaints filed with the commission during the three years 1898, 1899, and 1900 "175, or 69.71 per cent., had been settled in one way or another by informal action on the part of the Commission." Newcomb, *Work of the Interstate Commerce Commission* (1905), p. 18.

[29] ". . . At almost every step, the Commission was hindered by the open hostility of the railroads and the unsympathetic attitude of the courts. . . . The Commission's orders were reversed with startling frequency, not only on technical grounds and as a result of major changes in the record, but also because of differences of judgment between the Commission and the courts in large matters of economic policy." Sharfman, *op. cit.*, I, 23–24. "By the close of the nineteenth century, the commission's functions, through the causes ascribed, were attenuated practically to those of a mere publicity body. Its field of activity was limited to enforcement of the safety laws, statistical work, and various independent investigations." Bernhardt, *op. cit.*, p. 16.

nature of the law. At least the commission in reporting to Congress so regarded conditions and took the position that, irrespective of the merits of the interpretations, particular points were matters for legislation.

Accordingly, still maintaining that no fundamental changes were necessary or even desirable, the commission emphasized the necessity of legislation to effectuate the original purposes and policy of the Act to Regulate Commerce.[30] The Interstate Commerce Commission frankly admitted that regulation was unsatisfactory and that it was powerless to administer effectively the policy of the statutes. The reports to Congress from 1895 to 1906 are a continuous record of defects and recommendations for legislation.[31] At the close of the years 1895, 1896, and 1897 the legislative recommendations were made in detail. Thereafter, the needs having been fully formulated, the commission continued to emphasize the

[30] Ann. Rep., 1895, p. 11; 1896, p. 114; 1898, pp. 5–6; 1899, pp. 5–8; 1900, p. 5; 1901, p. 5.

[31] *Recommendations for legislation, 1895–1905:* (References to annual reports to Congress by year and page). *Witnesses and records:* 1895, pp. 6–10, 19–20, 111 (*prima facie* effect of certain records); 1896, pp. 23–28, 116 (*prima facie* effect of records). *Judicial review: and enforcement of orders:* 1895, pp. 11–20, 110; 1896, pp. 114–115; 1897, pp. 27–37, 140–143; 1898, p. 90; 1905, p. 12. *Power to fix rates:* 1895, pp. 20–21, 110–111; 1896, p. 115; 1897, pp. 6–9, 149–150 (import and export rates), 2–23, 26–27, 140–143 (joint rates); 1903, pp. 13–17; 1904, pp. 5–10; 1905, pp. 9–10. *Tariffs, filing and enforcement:* 1895, pp. 21–24, 74–77 (bills of lading), 111–112 (joint tariffs); 1896, pp. 54–55, 102–103, 116 (joint tariffs); 1897, pp. 46–48; 1898, pp. 83–90, 140–142; 1905, pp. 7–8, 8–9 (import and export rates). *Statistics, reports, accounts:* 1895, pp. 60–64, 111; 1896, p. 116; 1897, pp. 80–83, 146–147; 1898, pp. 78–79; 1899, pp. 63–64; 1900, p. 74; 1901, p. 59; 1903, pp. 17–22; 1905, pp. 11–12. *Safety appliances:* 1895, pp. 91–95, 112; 1901, pp. 78–81 (accident reports); 1902, pp. 62–69 (accident reports); 1903, pp. 96–107; 1904, pp. 97–105 (accident reports); 1905, pp. 13–14 (accident reports). *Pooling and traffic agreements:* 1895, pp. 96–102; 1897, pp. 49–51. *Private cars:* 1902, pp. 80–82; 1903, pp. 22–26; 1904, pp. 10–19; 1905, pp. 10–11. *Ticket brokerage:* 1895, pp. 103–107; 1896, pp. 104–105; 1897, p. 61. *Passes:* 1896, pp. 105–107. *Special agents:* 1895, pp. 108-109, 111; 1896, p. 116. *Uniform classification of freight:* 1895, pp. 109–110, 111; 1896, pp. 115–116; 1897, pp. 62–71; 1899, pp. 12–20; 1900, pp. 14–21. *Interchange of traffic:* 1895, pp. 110, 111. *Application of penalties to corporations:* 1895, pp. 111; 1896, p. 115. *Long-and-short-haul:* 1897, pp. 37–46, 146. *Enforcement of penal provisions:* 1897, pp. 60–61, 140–143, 148–149. *Through routes and rates:* 1897, pp. 71–75, 147–148. *Valuation:* 1903, pp. 26–32; 1905, pp. 88–92 (discussion of method). *Terminal railroads:* 1904, pp. 19–23; 1905, pp. 10–11. *Carriers and practices subject to the act:* 1905, pp. 6–7. *Elevator charges:* 1905, pp. 10–11.

situation by reference to previous reports and by constant illustration.[32]

Notwithstanding the ineffectiveness of the statutes and the appeals of the commission, the period is characterized by a lull in legislative activity. Political interest was absorbed in currency legislation, the Spanish American War, the Philippines, and trust problems. There was also, of course, the opposition of great transportation systems and financial combinations. At the same time, however, the tendency toward monopoly (consolidation and financial combination) and the rise in rates were not unnoticed. Many bills were introduced, but only four acts were passed. These were not expressly amendatory of the Interstate Commerce Act and only one was of substantive importance.[33]

In spite of differences of subject matter and the newness of the

[32] Ann. Rep., 1898, pp. 5–6: "In previous communications to the Congress . . . attention has been called to the vital respects in which the act . . . has proved defective and inadequate. . . . We are unable to add anything to the presentation then made. . . . Meanwhile the situation has become intolerable. . . ." And see pp. 6–22.

"The requests of the Commission for needful amendments have been supported by petitions and memorials from agricultural, manufacturing, and commercial interests throughout the country; yet not a line of the statute has been changed and none of the burdensome conditions which call for relief have been removed or modified." Ann. Rep., 1899, pp. 5–8.

And see to the same effect the reports for 1900, pp. 5–8; 1901, pp. 5–16; 1902, pp. 5–18; 1903, pp. 7 and 13–32; 1904, pp. 5–29; 1905, pp. 5–14.

[33] *Accident Reports Act.* March 3, 1901, 31 Stat. 1446. See: Ann. Rep., 1901, p. 62 et seq. Subsequently repealed by the Act of May 6, 1910, 36 Stat. 350, which latter has become the present accident reports act.

Expediting Act. February 11, 1903, 32 Stat. 823. To alleviate delays in proceedings before the courts, precedence was given the cases and the period for appeals was shortened. But this, while important, was not the real difficulty.

Elkins Act. February 19, 1903, 32 Stat. 847. The act dealt forcefully by penalties with discriminations and deviations from published tariffs and thereby supplemented the weaker provisions of the Act to Regulate Commerce. It was passed at the demand of the carriers themselves — and has been characterized as "a truce of principals to abolish piracy." As a matter of fact, these provisions, by making personal discriminations more difficult, actually assisted the general rise of rates, and though beneficial in the administration of the letter of the law the act was not without defects — in the estimation of the commission it fell far short of the necessary legislation. Ann. Rep., 1903, pp. 7–12; 1905, p. 13.

Provision was made in the legislative, executive, and judicial appropriation act of February 25, 1903, 32 Stat. 904, for immunity of witnesses in proceedings in the courts under the Act to Regulate Commerce.

administrative device, the history of the judicial relations of the Interstate Commerce Commission and its position at the beginning of the century bear remarkable resemblance to the Federal Trade Commission today.

As noted in connection with the Federal Trade Commission a quarter of a century later, it was with concerted action that the courts permitted governmental interference.[34] Section 5 of the original Act to Regulate Commerce prohibited pooling arrangements, but traffic associations were reorganized and continued to regulate competitive rate-making. Although pooling agreements were illegal, other protective measures were adopted by the carriers to prevent rate wars which had previously been so disastrous. The Supreme Court determined that carriers' contracts or combination in restraint of trade were prohibited by the Sherman Act,[35] but concerted rate making continued.

The commission was not unmoved by obvious discrepancies in the state of affairs — the essentially monopolistic nature of railroads, the ruinous effects of certain forms of competition and competitive practices, the ineffectiveness of the Act to Regulate Commerce, the application of the Sherman Act to carriers, and the inevitable tendency toward railroad consolidation.[36] It was this state of the law, however, that led to railroad consolidation which in turn — because of the popular attitude toward monopoly — stimulated effective regulation. Increasing prosperity in the closing years of the nineteenth century and the desire to avoid legislative and judicial prohibitions against pooling and traffic agreements led to consolidation of carriers. But this was also the "trust busting" era. Ineffective public regulation and the organization of vast private transportation systems under unified control did not withstand the temper of the times. Rising rates and the public horror of monopoly, together with the assistance of the progressive elements of the Roosevelt administration, finally broke through

[34] Fear of combination has, of course, strong roots in the common law. For some interesting materials see: Dicey, *Law and Public Opinion*, reprinted 1920, Appendix, Note 1 and pages cited.

[35] United States *v.* Trans-Missouri Freight Association, 166 U. S. 290 (1897).

[36] *Cooperative action among railroads:* Ann. Rep., 1896, pp. 86–91; 1899, pp. 8–12; 1900, pp. 8–14; 1901, p. 16. *Essential unity of railroad interests:* 1888, pp. 25–30. *Tendency to consolidation:* 1889, pp. 76–80; 1890, p. 64; 1902, pp. 5–6. *Prosecutions under the Sherman Act:* 1895, pp. 86–87; 1898, pp. 10–22. The recommendations on the pooling clause are parts of this problem; see notes 12 and 31.

laissez-faire propaganda and the agitation against bureaucratic regulation. The original legislation had been placed on the statute books twenty years before and an administrative agency provided; legislation to effectuate the policy of 1887 was now forthcoming. (It may be noted that the "spectre of monopoly" which first led to a vitalizing of railroad regulation was part of the movement which resulted in the establishment of the Federal Trade Commission a decade later.)

II. The Revival of Legislation and Beginnings of Effective Administration

A rising political and popular sentiment was first reflected in minor legislation and in the enforcement of the anti-trust act.[37] Then a period of more effective railroad regulation began with the Hepburn Act of June 29, 1906.[38] On the legislative side there was both a vitalizing and extension of authority. By the Hepburn Act authority was granted the commission to prescribe just and reasonable maximum rates or charges, regulations, or practices, but only after hearing and upon complaint (the Senate eliminated provisions that the commission pass upon reasonableness of proposed schedules of rates prior to their taking effect). Definitions were amplified. Express companies, pipe lines carrying oil, and sleeping-car companies (but not carriers entirely by water) were brought under the act. Duties of the carriers were specifically stated. There was definite provision for statistical and accounting reports, access to records, penalties for non-compliance or false entries, and it was made unlawful for carriers to keep other accounts, records, or memoranda than those prescribed or approved by the commission. The commission was enlarged from five to seven members.

The importance of the Hepburn Act, however, lies in the provisions for enforcement of the commission's orders. The procedure of judicial review and enforcement and the delays incurred thereby had been the principal defect in prior legislation. Now all orders of the commission (except those for money payments) were to take effect within such reasonable time as the commission might pre-

[37] For a convenient reference see: Jones, *Historical Development of the Law of Business Competition*, 36 Yale L. J. 207, 229 et seq. (1926).

[38] 34 Stat. 584. The effective date of the act was changed by joint resolution (34 Stat. 838) which provided that the act should take effect 60 days after its approval by the President.

scribe, and were to remain effective for two years unless suspended, modified, or set aside by a court or by the commission itself. The circuit courts might restrain the enforcement of an order, although this injunctive process could only be exercised after a hearing and upon not less than five days' notice to the commission. In the case of disobedience of an order which had become final, the courts were directed to compel enforcement provided the order had been "regularly made and duly served." Thus the burden or initiative in all cases appealed to the courts was shifted from the commission to the carrier. Instead of rulings becoming effective only upon affirmation by the highest courts, they were now to be effective from the date prescribed by the commission unless judicial action intervened. The act also provided for appeals directly to the Supreme Court with privilege of precedence upon its docket. There shortly followed three acts dealing with witnesses and immunities, permissible passes, and carrier's records.[39]

Although the Hepburn Act was promising from the standpoint of effective regulation, there were still weaknesses in the state of the statutory law. Rate fixing, under the new legislation, was still unsatisfactory. Although the commission might prescribe future rates on complaint, it could not suspend rate advances prior to their taking effect. The shipper had the burden of showing that rates already in effect were unreasonable, and furthermore such reparation as might be awarded him was no compensation for loss of business in the intervening period. Often no one was sufficiently interested to undertake complaint; others were fearful. Accordingly, the rise of the general rate level begun years before continued. The commission recommended legislation.[40] Also, the new legislation had not vitalized the long-and-short-haul provision. The manufacturing centers and interests had resisted any amplification of these provisions, but the South and West were not content.

The movement which began with the Hepburn Act, spurred by

[39] 38 Stat. 798, June 30, 1906. Provided that the immunity under the Acts of February 11, 1893, February 19, 1903, and February 25, 1903, should extend only to a natural person testifying in obedience to a subpoena.

35 Stat. 60, April 13, 1908. Defining "employees" and "families" in the permissible pass provision.

35 Stat. 648, February 25, 1909. Authorizing the commission to designate carriers' records which might be destroyed after a reasonable time and to prescribe the length of time they should be preserved.

[40] Ann. Rep. 1907, pp. 7, 9–10; 1908, pp. 10–12, 95; 1909, pp. 6–7.

the further though brief experience since 1906, led to the Mann-Elkins Act of 1910.[41] By the more important provisions the commission was given authority to suspend changes in rates pending examination as to reasonableness, the long-and-short-haul clause was renewed by eliminating the qualifying phrase ("under substantially similar circumstances and conditions") which as interpreted by the courts had made the original policy in this respect inoperative (there were also some additions to the long-and-short-haul provisions), and any doubt of the commission's authority to undertake investigations on its own motion was removed. The authority of the commission was also extended to telegraph, telephone, and cable companies. To meet one judicial decision [42] the commission was authorized after due hearing to order such through routes as it might deem desirable and to prescribe joint rates therefor; and to care for another interpretation [43] it was provided that the shipper, with some exceptions to be prescribed by the commission, could designate the route by which shipment was preferred. To relieve congestion and prevent delay as well as to provide a specialized tribunal for the review of Interstate Commerce Commission cases, a Commerce Court was established as had been recommended by President Taft. The five judges of this court were to have exclusive jurisdiction over cases for the enforcement of any order of the commission (other than those for payment of money), suits to set aside the orders of the commission, suits to enjoin illegal discriminations or departures from published rates, and proceedings to compel the filing of reports or keeping of prescribed accounts or to compel the movement of traffic or furnishing of facilities.

This legislation is sometimes regarded as a definite milepost in interstate commerce regulation.[44] It affirms the revived legislative

[41] 36 Stat. 539. The Judicial Code of March 3, 1911, repealed the provisions relating to the Commerce Court. It also transferred to the federal district courts the jurisdiction of the circuit courts. 36 Stat. 1167.

[42] I. C. C. *v.* Northern Pacific Ry. Co., 216 U. S. 538 (1910).

[43] Southern Pac. Co. *v.* I. C. C., 200 U. S. 536 (1906).

[44] "The Interstate Commerce Act of 1887 . . . was enacted by Congress to prevent interstate railroad carriers from charging unreasonable rates and from unjustly discriminating between persons and localities. The railroads availed themselves of the weakness and cumbrous machinery of the original law to defeat its purpose, and this led to various amendments culminating in the amending Act of 1910 . . . in which the authority of the Commission in dealing with the carriers was made summary and effectively complete." Chief Justice

policy, but it is by no means the culmination of either administrative or legislative development of the subject.

Although the Mann-Elkins Act might be regarded as a full measure of authority to be given an administrative tribunal, the stream of legislation extending the authority of the commission continued. Valuation of railroad property, further restriction on competitive practices and monopoly, and the amplification of laws regarding safety of passengers, employees, and property were among the more important subjects of Congressional action.[45] By the Panama Canal Act of August 24, 1912, the Act to Regulate Commerce was amended to forbid railroads to continue ownership or operation of water lines when competition with an existing water route would thereby be lessened, and gave the commission jurisdiction to determine the fact of competition and authorize continuance of existing water-line operation by railroads under some circumstances; the basic act was further amended to confer additional authority upon the commission respecting connections between carriers, through routes, maximum joint rates, or proportional rail rates, and to require equal treatment of water lines by a rail line.[46] As the development of regulation progressed the importance of valuation became increasingly apparent, and finally Congress enacted the Valuation Act of March 1, 1913.[47] In 1914

Taft in Railroad Comm. of Wis. *v.* Chicago etc. R. Co., 257 U. S. 563, 582 (1922).

[45] In addition to the statutes mentioned presently in the text, there were: Act of August 24, 1912, 37 Stat. 558 (commission given some authority over parcel post). Act of August 1, 1914, 38 Stat. 627 (providing for transportation of field parties of the commission).

[46] 37 Stat. 566. Authority over water carriers subsidiary to railroads, but not over all water carriers as the commission had recommended.

[47] 37 Stat. 701. For some years the commission had been pointing out the need of a more adequate system for determination of value of railroad interests as a prerequisite to anything like scientific regulation. Ann. Rep., 1903, pp. 26–32; 1905, pp. 88–92 (discussion of method); 1907, pp. 149–150; 1908, pp. 83–85, 96; 1909, p. 6; 1910, p. 37; 1912, p. 70. While particular rates might be adjusted with reference to related charges, whenever an entire rate schedule was questioned no measure was available. Although the original Act to Regulate Commerce required the commission to report annually "the cost and value of the carriers' property, franchise, and equipment," no method or basis for determining value was prescribed, nor was the commission given authority to make such determination. In some respects this is the most far-reaching legislation of the period. The work of valuation (the commission was authorized to investigate, determine, and report the value of all property owned or used by every common carrier subject to the provisions of the Act to Regulate

the commission was given jurisdiction to administer some of the provisions of the Clayton (Anti-Trust) Act respecting carriers.[48] The development of safety regulation and requirements was regarded by the commission as one of its important duties;[49] legislation was recommended, and a number of statutes were enacted.[50]

Although subsequent events have shown the effectiveness of the legislation of 1906 and 1910, at the time of passage there is no confident note in the reports of the commission, and as had been the case after the passage of the original Act to Regulate Commerce in 1887, the first years are given to careful analysis and interpretation of the new statutes.[51] The volume of work immediately increased,[52] but the commission was particularly apprehensive of the treatment to be accorded its orders in the courts under the Hepburn Act.[53] Enforcement difficulties had been one of the principal reasons for the ineffectiveness of the original legislation; it was to remedy this situation that amendments had been rec-

Commerce) begun in 1913 was not complete in 1930. Ann. Rep., 1922, pp. 70–71; 1923, p. 13; 1928, p. 56; 1929, pp. 64–65. See particularly Ann. Rep., 1923, p. 15, on the magnitude and difficulties.

48 38 Stat. 730. See: Ann. Rep., 1915, pp. 26–27; 1916, p. 30.

49 See the introduction to the Annual Report for 1911, p. 1.

50 *Infra*, p. 130, n. 97.

51 Ann. Rep., 1906, p. 5 (Hepburn Act); Ann. Rep., 1910, p. 5 (Mann-Elkins Act).

52 ". . . 5,156 complaints have been filed with the Commission for consideration and action. . . . The number of formal cases and investigations instituted during the year was 415, relating directly to the rates and practices of 2,236 carriers. This shows a very great increase over previous years, as the number of such complaints filed in 1905 was 65 and 82 in the year 1906, while the total number filed during the six years previous to 1907 was 350, or 65 less than in the present year. . . . The work of the Commission in all its branches has increased to such an extent that it seems almost impossible to prepare a statement that will show the relative yearly increase with any degree of accuracy." Ann. Rep., 1907, pp. 118–119 et seq. See also: Ann. Rep., 1908, pp. 6–7 (reporting an annual increase in formal complaints of 33½ per cent and the holding of 573 hearings and investigations). "Immediately following the passage of the Mann-Elkins law the Commission was called upon to exercise what is perhaps the most far-reaching and fundamentally important power conferred upon it by that act, namely, the authority to suspend proposed advances in rates pending investigation. . . ." Ann. Rep., 1910, pp. 5–6. It is not until 1915 that the number of complaints begins to decrease, although the activities of the commission continue to grow in number and extent. Ann. Rep., 1915, p. 1.

53 Awaiting judicial test of the new legislation, the commission announced some practical jurisprudence of distinctly Austinian flavor. Ann. Rep., 1907, p. 6.

ommended for fifteen years and finally placed upon the statute books.

It was not until 1909 that a test of the new legislation in the courts was possible. At the close of 1908 the commission noted with concern the pendency of suits which, in determining the scope of judicial control, would determine the success of the Hepburn Act.[54] Not until 1911 did the commission report that the new legislation had invigorated the system of regulation.[55]

Before discussion of judicial pronouncements under the new legislation, mention must be made of the Commerce Court established by the Mann-Elkins Act of 1910. The idea of a special court to pass upon determinations of the commission had been vigorously opposed, and the Commerce Court was the subject of controversy from the time of its establishment. It lasted three years. How much instruction the "experiment" affords is a matter of opinion.[56] At all events, its significance for the purposes of this study lies in the fact that administration relations with the courts had become so important that a special court was established; that such a tribunal existed is eloquent testimony that the experience of twenty-five years had made the problem of judicial relations a matter of first importance in the legislative development of administrative regulation.

The Commerce Court was not wholly specialized, for the judges (after the terms of the first bench had expired) were to be selected from the circuit judges for five-year terms and no judge was to be eligible for reassignment until the lapse of a year after his first assignment. If the proponents of the new court expected it to lend sympathetic ear to the pleas of the administrative commission, they were disappointed. The Commerce Court reversed the commission only to be itself reversed by the Supreme Court.[57] The career of the Commerce Court, which had been created upon the approval of the Mann-Elkins Act in 1910, was terminated at the close of 1913.[58]

[54] Ann. Rep., 1908, p. 20.

[55] "The Hepburn Act . . . marked the beginning of a new era in the strength and administration of the law. . . ." Ann. Rep., 1911, p. 1.

[56] See: Frankfurter and Landis, *The Business of the Supreme Court* (1927), pp. 153–174; Sharfman, *The Interstate Commerce Commission* (1931), I, 60–70.

[57] See the discussion and statistics in Frankfurter and Landis, *op. cit.*, p. 165 n. 95: "94 cases were docketed in the Commerce Court. 43 decisions were rendered, including one rehearing. Appeals were taken in 22 cases, of which 13 were reversed, 2 modified, and 7 affirmed."

[58] 38 Stat. 208.

Aside from the experience with the Commerce Court, the record of the relations between the commission and the courts after 1906 is altogether different from that of the previous period. Specific legislation and procedural reforms had not been without effect. Although the principal period of decisions for the purposes of this study is the decade 1920–1930, the new character of judicial control may be noted.[59] It is not that there was an abrupt change of relations or that the courts found immediately a new technique for the treatment of administrative questions, but that new principles were developed which indicate a substantial trend toward permitting an administrative rather than a judicial regulation of railroads. There was no longer a new trial or a judicial reconsideration of the whole case.[60]

First to be noted are the judicial statements on the scope of review. In 1910 Chief Justice White announced, in an opinion sustaining an order of the commission, that in determining whether an order should be suspended or set aside the courts must consider:

> (*a*) all relevant questions of constitutional power or right;
> (*b*) all pertinent questions as to whether the administrative order is within the scope of the delegated authority under which it purports to have been made; and, . . .
> (*c*) whether even although the order be in form within the delegated power, nevertheless it must be treated as not embraced therein, because the exertion of authority which is questioned has been manifested in such an unreasonable manner as to cause it, in truth, to be within the elementary rule that the substance, and not the shadow, determines the validity of the exercise of the power. . . .
> Plain as it is that the powers just stated are of the essence of judicial authority, and which, therefore, may not be curtailed, and whose discharge

[59] See: Tollefson, *Judicial Review of Decisions of the Interstate Commerce Commission*, 11 Minn. L. Rev. 389, 504 (1927); and for an early discussion see: Newcomb, *Force and Effect of the Orders of the Interstate Commerce Commission*, 23 Harv. L. Rev. 12 (1909).

[60] "Originally the duty of the courts to determine whether an order of the Commission should or should not be enforced carried with it the obligation to consider both the facts and the law. But it had come to pass . . . that in considering the subject of orders of the Commission, for the purpose of enforcing or restraining their enforcement, the courts were confined by statutory operation to determining whether there had been violations of the Constitution, a want of conformity to statutory authority, or of ascertaining whether power had been so arbitrarily exercised as virtually to transcend the authority conferred although it may be not technically doing so." Chief Justice White in Procter & Gamble *v.* United States, 225 U. S. 282, 297–298 (1912).

may not be by us in a proper case avoided, it is equally plain that such perennial powers lend no support whatever to the proposition that we may, under the guise of exerting judicial power, usurp merely administrative functions by setting aside a lawful administrative order upon our conception as to whether the administrative power has been wisely exercised.

Power to make the order and not the mere expediency or wisdom of having made it, is the question.[61]

These views were repeated in a number of decisions which followed, and in 1912 the judicial statement was revised to include the doctrine of divisibility of law and fact. "... The orders of the commission are final unless ... based upon a mistake of law. But questions of fact may be involved in the determination of questions of law, so that an order, regular on its face, may be set aside if it appears that [the] rate is so low as to be confiscatory and in violation of the constitutional prohibition against taking property without due process of law; or if the commission acted so arbitrarily and unjustly as to fix rates contrary to evidence, or without evidence to support it; or if the authority therein involved has been exercised in such an unreasonable manner" as to amount to an excess of authority.[62] And the labelling of functions as legislative or judicial was continued and persists into the 1920 decade. However insufficient these statements may be as working formulas, they display a disposition on the part of the judiciary to set aside certain matters as the peculiar province of the commission. The same tendency may be seen in another form in the recognition that there is a sphere of activity committed to "a tribunal appointed by law and informed by experience" with which the courts should not interfere.[63] As time goes on it becomes apparent that the principal inquiry is the sufficiency of evidence upon which administrative findings may be based. Toward this requirement all doctrines of review and constitutionality tend. "A finding without evidence is arbitrary and baseless," for any other construction "would nullify the right to a hearing." [64]

In addition to these statements of deference toward the administrative agency, two doctrines under which the courts exclude themselves from interference with administration indicate the judicial policy to confine railway regulation to the commission,

[61] I. C. C. *v.* Ill. Cent. R. Co., 215 U. S. 452, 470 (1910).

[62] I. C. C. *v.* Union Pac. R. Co., 222 U. S. 541, 547 (1912).

[63] Ill. Cent. R. Co. *v.* I. C. C., 206 U. S. 441, 454 (1907).

[64] I. C. C. *v.* Louisville etc. R. Co., 227 U. S. 88, 91, 93 (1913).

"informed by experience." The first of these — the doctrine of primary jurisdiction of the commission — secures to the administrative agency exclusive authority over the greater part of railroad regulation; the courts may not, in the first instance, entertain proceedings. In pronouncing decision in a reparation case in 1907 the doctrine was confirmed by the Supreme Court. ". . . The existence of . . . power in the courts, independent of prior action by the commission, would lead to favoritism, to the enforcement of one rate in one jurisdiction and a different one in another, would destroy the prohibitions against preferences and discrimination," and "if the power existed in both courts and the Commission to originally hear complaints on this subject, there might be a divergence between the action of the Commission and the decision of a court. . . . A conflict would arise which would render the enforcement of the act impossible." [65] In addition to the demand for uniformity, there is quite as much basis for the doctrine in the desire or necessity for an exclusively administrative regulation.

As a corollary to the doctrine of primary jurisdiction, in 1912 Chief Justice White, in an opinion reversing a Commerce Court decision, disclaimed for the judiciary jurisdiction to interfere where the commission had refused to act.[66] Under this doctrine of so-called negative orders the courts may not force a particular determination by refusing to accept an administrative refusal to act — neither by review of negative orders nor by mandamus may the courts compel the commission to come to a decision.

These doctrines — particularly those limiting the scope of review — leave a wide margin for judicial control. Doctrines of judicial review, of course, do not preclude abstract consideration of a record, but consideration of interstate commerce cases does not take place *in vacuo*. There is a record of the evidence and facts before the courts in each case, and the legislation of 1906 and 1910, together with legislative and administrative history since 1887, comprise a body of legal materials which the courts use increasingly to test the commission's exercise of authority. Judicial appreciation of the legislative policy and of necessities have to great extent filled the gaps in doctrine. This will become apparent from the study of decisions under the legislation of 1920.

A word is necessary regarding the judicial treatment accorded a

[65] Texas etc. R. Co. *v.* Abilene Cotton Oil Co., 204 U. S. 426, 440–441 (1907).

[66] Procter & Gamble Co. *v.* United States, 225, U. S. 282 (1912).

different type of administrative determination. Reparation orders — awarding damages to shippers for overcharges and discriminations — unlike other orders of the commission must be enforced through the courts and there may be a jury trial. They do not become binding until some party in interest institutes proceedings in a federal court, and it is provided by statute that the orders of the commission in this field have the effect of *prima facie* evidence. Unless the defendant produces further evidence in the judicial proceeding, the findings and order of the commission may not be rejected where appropriate findings have been made by the commission.[67] The Supreme Court has said that "the statutory provision merely established a rule of evidence" and "it leaves every opportunity to the defendant to contest the claim." [68]

The great war in Europe brought on a critical condition in the United States transportation system. Necessity for reform in railroad regulation was increasing. In conformity with the original policy of the commission, legislation was regularly recommended as needs became apparent.[69] From 1915 to 1917 several statutes

[67] Meeker *v.* Lehigh Valley R. Co., 236 U. S. 412 and 434 (1915).

[68] Mills *v.* Lehigh Valley R. Co., 238 U. S. 473, 482 (1915).

[69] The formal recommendations of the commission from 1906 to 1920 are noted in connection with significant legislation. Other suggested or recommended legislation not noted elsewhere includes: (Annual reports by year and page): *Damages for misquotation of rates:* 1908, pp. 16–17, 95. *Witnesses:* 1908, pp. 17–20, 95; 1916, pp. 66, 91 (intimidation of witnesses); 1917, p. 68. *Preservation of records:* 1908, p. 95. *Authority to route traffic:* 1909, p. 7. *Clarification of authority to investigate without complaint:* 1909, p. 8. *Amplification of authority over through rates:* 1909, p. 7. *Authority to prescribe general regulations as to movement of traffic:* 1909, pp. 9–10. *Authority to require statistics on water transportation:* 1909, p. 53. *Amplification of authority over tariffs* (extensions, etc.): 1911, pp. 4–5. *Clarification of authority over telephone, telegraph and cable tariffs:* 1911, pp. 5–6, 96–97; 1912, p. 70; 1913, p. 3. *Authority to require uniform freight classification:* 1911, pp. 7, 97; 1912, p. 70; 1913, p. 82; 1914, pp. 24–25; 1915, pp. 12–15. *Request to be relieved of authority over street railroads in the District of Columbia:* 1911, pp. 94–95, 97. *Request to be relieved of duties regarding parcel post rates:* 1913, pp. 79–80, 83. *Modification of provisions for limitation of actions:* 1913, pp. 80–81; 1914, p. 65; 1915, p. 68; 1916, pp. 78–79; 1917, p. 68. *Definition of rebating* (failure of carriers to collect charges): 1913, p. 81. *Authority to defend suits in courts* (rather than Department of Justice): 1913, pp. 81–82. *Authority over the construction and maintenance of physical properties:* 1913, p. 82. *Authorization to examine records of carriers:* 1913, pp. 14, 82; 1914, p. 65; 1915, p. 69; 1917, pp. 68–69. *Authority to suspend certain schedules:* 1916, pp. 65, 91. *Modification of reparation provisions:* 1916, pp. 75–78; 1919, pp. 17–21, 53. *Modification of Panama Canal Act:* 1917, p. 69. *Authority to establish standard operating rules:* 1917, p. 99; 1919, p. 53. *Prohibition of trespassing on*

were enacted changing or affecting the regulation of transportation.[70]

As the war in Europe continued abnormal conditions demanded

carriers: 1916, pp. 66–67; 1917, p. 99. *Subjection of holding companies to the act:* 1919, pp. 21–22, 53.

Formal suggestions were not made hurriedly or with respect to details of relatively little importance. See: Ann. Rep., 1912, p. 71.

[70] The Mann-Elkins Act of 1910 had required carriers to make reasonable rules for the exchange, interchange, and return of cars, but neither that act nor subsequent acts gave specific authority to the commission to prescribe rules relating to car service. The commission had recommended legislation in 1906 and 1907. Ann. Rep., 1906, pp. 16–18; 1907, pp. 7–8. The confusion of the World War made the situation acute. Report on Car Supply Investigation, 42 I. C. C. 657 (1917). Ann. Rep., 1916, pp. 67–74, 91; 1917, pp. 62–63. The Esch Car Service Act was approved May 29, 1917, 40 Stat. 101, whereby the commission was given broad power to issue directions on the movement, distribution, exchange, interchange, and return of cars (in emergencies the commission was given summary powers).

The accumulated duties of the commission — the variety, complexity, and extent of its functions — made reorganization necessary. The commissioners requested relief. Ann. Rep., 1915, p. 68; 1916, p. 92. The commission reported some internal reorganization as early as 1913 (Ann. Rep., 1913, p. 1) and in 1917 the Act to Regulate Commerce was amended to enlarge the commission from seven to nine members with authority to separate into divisions, each with authority to act on matters assigned by the full commission but subject to rehearing. 40 Stat. 270. On October 17, 1917, the commission adopted the divisional form of organization and steps were taken to insure harmonious policies and uniform results. Ann. Rep., 1917, pp. 59–61. Because of abnormal conditions, the existing rate structure was legalized to prevent controversies between shippers and carriers as to past practices and rates; this, too, was done at the recommendation of the commission. Ann. Rep., 1916, p. 92.

Cummins Amendments: The Hepburn Act included the so-called Carmack Amendment regarding the liability of carriers for damages to goods in transit. In 1915 and 1916 the Cummins Amendments changed this portion of the Interstate Commerce Act. 38 Stat. 1196, and 39 Stat. 441.

The Naval Service Appropriations Act, approved in 1916, amended the Act to Regulate Commerce to require prompt delivery in time of peace of shipments for the United States. 39 Stat. 556. Army Appropriations Act, 39 Stat. 646 (1916), provided for reduced rates to members of the National Guard. An Act of February 17, 1917, provided that the Interstate Commerce Act should not be construed to prevent free transportation for the trustees of the Cincinnati Southern Railway (39 Stat. 992). The Porto Rico Civil Government Act, 39 Stat. 964 (1917), provided that the Safety Appliance Acts should not apply to Porto Rico (recommended by the commission, Ann. Rep., 1915, pp. 67–68; 1916, p. 93). And by the Act of July 28, 1916 (39 Stat. 412), the commission was directed to fix and determine the basis and amount of compensation for carriage of mail and service.

increased capital when capital was scarce and the transportation system as a factor in national defense took on an altogether new aspect. The continuous rise of the general price level reduced the net income of the railroads. Until the entry of the United States into the European conflict, the problem had been one of railroad relief. As early as 1915 measures had been adopted to investigate the general problem of regulation.[71] But events moved too swiftly for formal recommendations on the general problem.

III. The War and Federal Control

The development of regulation of commerce had been adapted to times of peace. The transportation system from the standpoint of a nation involved in war was another matter. In August, 1917, the President was authorized to give priority to such traffic as he might deem important to the national defense in time of war.[72] When the nation entered the war the need of the moment was unity of operation. Voluntary efforts toward concerted action were limited by existing law.[73] The commission recommended unified control.[74] The President by proclamation of December 26, 1917, assumed control of transportation systems in the country effective January 1, 1918.[75] Congress promptly provided legislation to effectuate the President's proclamation.[76] The Act to Regulate Commerce was not amended, but of course its provisions were affected. Rates were initiated by the President and filed with the commission, but the latter could not suspend their operation.

[71] President Wilson's message of December 7, 1915, recommended the appointment of "a commission of inquiry to ascertain by a thorough canvass . . . whether our laws as at present framed and administered are as serviceable as they might be in the solution of the problem." Congress by joint resolution complied on July 20, 1916 (39 Stat. 387) by providing for a joint subcommittee to investigate the system of government regulation and "also the subject of government ownership of all public utilities."

[72] 40 Stat. 272. The Hepburn Act had provided for precedence to carriage of troops and materials of war in time of war or threatened war, and the Naval Appropriations Act, 39 Stat. 604 (1916), required speedy carriage of government shipments in times of peace.

[73] See: Annotated Act (1929), v. 1, note p. 84.

[74] Special Report, December 5, 1917. Reprinted in Ann. Rep., 1918, pp. 4–9.

[75] Under authority of the Army Appropriations Act, 39 Stat. 645 (August 29, 1916), and other enabling powers. Assumption of control of railway express and telephone and telegraph systems followed, November 16 and July 22, 1918.

[76] 40 Stat. 451. March 21, 1918.

Rates were to some extent still subject to the requirements of the Act to Regulate Commerce, except that the commission was required to give consideration to the fact of unified national control and, when passing upon the question of reasonableness, to the President's certification of necessity and his recommendations.

The period of federal possession and control lasted twenty-six months — from December 28, 1917, to March 1, 1920. Management and regulation were for the most part merged. The summary powers of management vested in the Executive left little authority to the commission — instead, the commission in a special advisory capacity aided by statistical information on hand rendered assistance in the management of the carriers and administration of the federal control statutes.[77]

For the purposes of this study the activities of the commission during the period of federal control are hardly pertinent. Even where the commission continued to make determinations and administer the act, abnormal conditions were such that comparison would be unprofitable.

So far as basic change in the regulation of carriers is concerned — the abandonment of the orthodox competitive policy — the movement began before the entrance of the nation into war. The war period and the federal control period did, of course, bring into relief the nature of the transportation system and problem. The government had taken over the railroads when they were seriously threatened with breakdown and had made them serve during the trying conditions of war. Investigation of the entire scheme of railroad regulation, begun in 1916,[78] had been interrupted. A period of centralized control and management had intervened before conditions had become sufficiently settled for further consideration of the problem. Widely divergent opinions — proposals for federal ownership, continued federal control, or return to private ownership under regulation of varying degrees — made the railroad problem again a matter of paramount interest. Comprehensive revision of the law was in the air.[79]

The carriers emerged from the war subject to a somewhat changed policy of regulation. The former "restrictive" basis of regulation was abandoned for a policy which recognized to a greater

[77] See: Ann. Rep., 1918, particularly at pages 10–20.

[78] *Supra*, n. 71. And see: *Hearings on Extension of Tenure of Government*, 65th Cong., 3 Sess., v. 2, 3.

[79] See: Ann. Rep., 1918, pp. 2–9; 1919, pp. 1–9.

extent the essentially monopolistic nature of the transportation system.[80] These changes of policy involve the problem from the standpoint of sound economic adjustments, whereas this study is concerned with administration — particularly the relations between the administrative agency and the courts. However, the administration of the new legislative policy during the post-war decade furnishes excellent material for the study and comparison of inter-governmental relations of a matured commission.

IV. The Transportation Act of 1920

The railroads were returned to private control and the regulatory legislation thoroughly overhauled by the Transportation Act of 1920.[81] Although the departures in policy — which were quickly recognized on all sides [82] — do not so much concern us here, this extensive and intensive treatment in the form of legislation indicates the public importance of the subject and the determination to continue effective governmental control.

Aside from the provisions for the return and reestablishment of private management [83] and those which concern labor relationships,[84] there were amendments of the first importance as well as

[80] Annotated Act (1929), v. 1, note p. 85. Ann. Rep., 1919, p. 1. Clark on *Interstate Commerce* (1919) (Testimony of Commissioner Clark before the Senate Committee on Interstate Commerce).

[81] February 28, 1920, 41 Stat. 456.

[82] For materials on judicial recognition see *infra*, n. 134. "In all of the preceding acts the prohibitory or punitive element was largely dominant. Because of the railroad abuses in the past, Congress, as well as the State legislatures, followed a policy of restraint and compulsion rather than one which permitted freedom of action. The burdens carried by the railroads during the Great War and while under Federal control demonstrated as never before the vital part they played in our economic life, and that if they were to continue as going concerns, legislation under which they were to be turned back to their owners must be of a constructive and not deterrent character." Commissioner Esch, *The Breadth of the Commerce Clause*, National Ass'n of Railroad and Utilities Commissioners, 38th Annual Convention, November 10, 1926. "The adoption of the Transportation Act marks the beginning of a new approach in railroad regulation. . . . The basic contribution, evidenced by the character of many of its provisions, lay in the statutory recognition of a positive public responsibility, in the exercise of the Commission's regulating functions, toward the establishment and maintenance of an adequate transportation service." Sharfman, *The Interstate Commerce Commission*, I, 177.

[83] Secs. 200–210.

[84] Secs. 300–316. See: Ann. Rep., 1920, pp. 1–3.

new matter.[85] There was a modification of the emphasis upon enforced competition but subject, in specific instances, to the approval of the commission; pooling might be authorized, though enforcement of orders was dependent upon the assent of the carriers involved (the removal of restrictions upon consolidation relegated these provisions to a subordinate place), with the approval of the commission one carrier might acquire control of another under lease or in any other manner "not involving the consolidation of such carriers into a single system for ownership and operation," [86] and subject to some restrictions the commission was to formulate a plan for the consolidation of railways into a limited number of systems. Control over securities was a field of activity recommended since 1907 [87] and now authorized by the Act of 1920; the commission was given "exclusive and plenary" jurisdiction, directed to review the financial transactions and approve or order changes as condition of approval, and given supervisory power to be exercised by issuing supplemental or modified orders. The provisions respecting rates were substantially expanded; minimum as well as maximum rates might be prescribed,[88] the long-and-short-haul clause was amplified,[89] a rule for the determination of rates was stated, there was provision for recapture of excess earnings the proceeds of which were to be used as loan funds and reserve funds,[90]

[85] Secs. 400–441.

[86] See: Ann. Rep., 1907, pp. 22–24.

[87] Ann. Rep., 1907, pp. 23–24; 1908, pp. 85–86; 1909, pp. 8–9; 1910, pp. 35–37; 1911, pp. 90–92, 97; 1912, pp. 70–71; 1913, p. 82; 1914, p. 65; 1915, p. 69; 1916, p. 92; 1917, p. 69. See also: Special Address to Congress, President Wilson, *Messages and Papers of the Presidents*, XVII, 7913 at 7916; Cong. Rec., Vol. 51, 1963; Jacobs, *Interstate Commerce Commission and Interstate Railroad Reorganizations*, 45 Harv. L. Rev. 855–866 (1932).

[88] This was advocated as early as 1893. Ann. Rep., 1893, pp. 38–39. And see also: the Annual Reports for 1897, pp. 140–150 and 143; 1898, p. 23 and 26–27.

[89] For discussion see: Vanderblue, *The Long and Short Haul Clause since 1910*, 36 Harv. L. Rev. 426 (1923). The provisions regarding the long-and-short-haul clause were first regarded as declaratory of the practice of the commission (Ann. Rep., 1920, pp. 47–78), but later the commission thought the new legislation adopted a "less liberal policy in dealing with departures from the long-and-short-haul rule" (Transcontinental Cases of 1922, 74 I. C. C. 48, 70).

[90] These provisions are prefaced by the statement that "it is impossible (without regulation and control in the interest of the commerce of the United States considered as a whole) to establish uniform rates upon competitive traffic which will adequately sustain all the carriers which are engaged in such

the authority of the commission to apportion joint rates was extended, and finally express legislative basis for cooperation between state and federal authorities was provided[91] and the commission authorized to prescribe intrastate rates where necessary to remove discrimination resulting from state action. The significant change in the rate-making provisions is the attempt to provide for regulation of the general rate level as well as for adjustment of particular rates. Other important provisions gave the commission power of supervision and control over the supply and use of the facilities of carriers to eliminate discrimination and insure adequate attention to the public needs.[92] The number of commissioners was increased from nine to eleven.[93]

This description of the lengthy Transportation Act is neces-

traffic and which are indispensable to the communities to which they render the service of transportation, without enabling some of such carriers to receive a net railway operating income substantially and unreasonably in excess of a fair return upon the value of their railway property. . . ." Sec. 15a (5). Carriers receiving such excess income are declared to hold part of it "as trustee" for the United States. Half of the excess was to be placed in a reserve fund for the carrier; the other half is to be paid to the commission for a "general railroad contingent fund." There were limitations upon the use of the "reserve fund," and the general fund was to be used for loans to carriers.

[91] Recommended by the commission: Ann. Rep., 1916, pp. 80–91, 92; 1917, pp. 58–59, 68. State and federal authorities cooperate in other than rate-making. See for example: Colorado *v.* United States, 271 U. S. 153, 166–167 (cooperation in abandonment proceedings). For the establishment of cooperation under the new legislation see: Ann. Rep., 1922, pp. 8–9, 233–234; 1925, pp. 1–2, 273–277; Proceedings, National Ass'n of Railroad and Utilities Commissioners: 1922, pp. 63–73, 426–431; 1925, pp. 41–74, 244–259.

[92] In case of "emergency" — shortage, congestion, etc. — the commission is given summary powers.

[93] The commission made a "reexamination of . . . administrative machinery and internal organization," and continued to function by divisions. See: Ann. Rep., 1920, pp. 3–6, and at p. 5: "The diversity and importance of the various duties now cast upon us, and the need for their expeditious performance, seem to have been recognized by the Congress in making possible this division of work and responsibility among our members. Necessarily, more than ever before individual commissioners must assume the initial responsibility for certain lines of work. As all petitions for rehearing are brought before the whole commission, and as our internal regulations provide for the free and full interchange of information and views as to all work in progress, including frequent conferences of the entire body as the occasion arises, it is possible to coordinate and harmonize the actions of the various divisions into a consistent general policy." See also: Ann. Rep., 1921, p. 1. In 1928 the commission requested authority to delegate authority to individual commissioners and members of the staff. Ann. Rep., 1928, p. 83.

sarily much restricted. However, enough has been said to disclose the nature of legislative development of railroad regulation. The commission continued to recommend legislation as the need arose,[94] although Congress has complied in few particulars. Other [95] and subsequent statutes extending or amending the powers of the commission [96] and safety legislation [97] are in general important and

[94] *Infra*, n. 206.

[95] The Merchant Marine Act of 1920 imposed certain duties on the commission in cooperation with the Shipping Board. Ann. Rep., 1921, pp. 11–14. The Inland Waterways Act as amended by the Denison Act of May 29, 1928, imposed other duties on the commission. Ann. Rep., 1929, p. 78; 1930, pp. 72–73.

[96] June 10, 1921, 42 Stat. 27. The Act of 1920 had provided for consolidation or acquisition of control of carriers. This statute added a paragraph covering telephone companies. Ann. Rep., 1921, pp. 19–20.

June 7, 1922, 42 Stat. 624. Amendment of Sec. 192 (the Valuation Act) by modifying details required in respect to land valuation.

August 18, 1922, 42 Stat. 827. Directing commission to require carriers to issue interchangeable mileage or script coupon tickets at just and reasonable rates.

June 7, 1924, 43 Stat. 633. Prescribed a period of limitations for institution of shippers' proceedings to recover overcharges and modified provisions extending this period.

January 30, 1925, 43 Stat. 801. (Hoch-Smith Resolution; statement of principle and policy in rate-making with particular reference to agriculture). Ann. Rep., 1925, pp. 37–41; 1926, pp. 36–39; 1927, pp. 67–72; 1928, pp. 63–68; 1929, pp. 69–73; 1930, pp. 61–68. See: Sharfman, *op. cit.*, vol. I; and Robinson, *The Hoch-Smith Resolution and the Future of the Interstate Commerce Commission*, 42 Harv. L. Rev. 610 (1929).

July 2, 1926, 44 Stat. 835. Amendment of Sec. 20 (11) — the Cummins Amendment — by extending the liability imposed regarding reconsigned or diverted shipments.

February 26, 1927, 44 Stat. 1247. Amendment of Sec. 20 (1) by providing for carrying a blind person with a guide for one fare.

March 4, 1927, 44 Stat. 1446. Permitted the commission to approve reduced rates in case of calamitous disaster, relieved consignees who are agents only from liability for undercharges discovered subsequent to delivery, extended the period during which the commission might suspend the operation of proposed schedules, amplified provisions regarding liability of carriers for loss of goods, and provided limitations on claims arising out of federal control.

April 23, 1930, 46 Stat. 251. Modification of requirements as to liability for carriage, notice, and filing of claims.

[97] Safety acts are ordinarily treated separately in the study of interstate commerce legislation — as a parallel body of legislation rather than an "organic aspect of the basic statute." Sharfman, *op. cit.*, I, 247. Ann. Rep., 1911, p. 1. The work of the Bureau of Safety and Bureau of Locomotive Inspection is now reported separately.

interesting but do not warrant an extension of this phase of the discussion.

At the close of 1920 [98] the commission reported the passage of the act [99] and, as after the enactment of previous important legislation, the careful beginnings of administration [100] including necessary reorganization of the commission.[101] The test of the new legislation before the courts was impending. It is not until 1922 that cases involving the orders of the commission begin to reach the Supreme Court in numbers.

V. Judicial Control of Administration, 1920–1930

How far the administration of the statutes has been left to the Interstate Commerce Commission remains to be examined — whether the courts allow the administrative agency to work out principles and make determinations in the light of specialized

The development of safety legislation dates from 1893. *Supra*, p. 104 n. 13. In this field, as well as with respect to general regulation, the federal government had been preceded by the states. Ann. Rep., 1889, pp. 44–45, 84–101, 293–340; 1891, p. 337; 1892, p. 70.

The commission in its annual reports has steadily recommended legislation. Prior to 1906 see n. 31, *supra*. Ann. Rep., 1906, pp. 70–76; 1907, pp. 7, 122–139; 1908, pp. 48–57, 95; 1909, pp. 40–51; 1910, pp. 37–46; 1911, pp. 80–92, 97; 1912, pp. 59–60, 62–66, 71; 1913, pp. 62–64, 67–72, 82, 83; 1914, pp. 49–56, 65; 1915, pp. 51–57, 69; 1916, pp. 53–56, 79–80, 92; 1917, pp. 47–48, 69; 1918, pp. 51–53.

And Congress has accepted the recommendations with comparative regularity. Safety Appliance Acts: 27 Stat. 531 (1893), 29 Stat. 85 (1896), 32 Stat. 943 (1903), 36 Stat. 289 (1910); Medals of Honor Act: 33 Stat. 743 (1905). Hours of Service Acts: 34 Stat. 1415 (1907), 39 Stat. 61 (1915). Accident Reports Acts: 31 Stat. 1446 (1901), 36 Stat. 350 (1910). Locomotive Inspection Acts: 35 Stat. 476 (1908), 36 Stat. 913 (1911), 38 Stat. 1192 (1915), 43 Stat. 659 (1924). Investigation of train control devices authorized: 34 Stat. 838 (1906), 35 Stat. 317, 325 (1908), 38 Stat. 212 (1913). Transportation of explosives: 35 Stat. 554 (1908), 35 Stat. 1134 (1909), 41 Stat. 1444 (1921) recommended Ann. Rep., 1920, pp. 74–77 and 78, and see also: Ann. Rep., 1921, pp. 47–78. The Act of 1920 (Sec. 441) grants blanket authority to the commission without prescription of specific devices for train control.

[98] The period covered by the annual reports during the decade 1920–1930 is November 1 to October 31.

[99] Ann. Rep., 1920, p. 1.

[100] See, for example: Ann. Rep., 1920, pp. 9–11 (rates), 11–25 (emergency powers, car service and facilities), 26–33 (financial provisions), 47–49 (long-and-short-haul), 26–27 (consolidation of carriers).

[101] Ann. Rep., 1920, pp. 3–6 (divisions of the commission), 26 (organization of Bureau of Finance), 42–43 (Bureau of Traffic), 56–57 (Bureau of Service). The Bureau of Service was reorganized in 1925. Ann. Rep., 1925, pp. 54–58.

judgment or whether (as with the Federal Trade Commission) they determine not only the validity of rules and principles but also application to specific situations.

The present statutes under which the commission operates confer powers so broad that they may be considered delegations of legislative authority limited only as to subject matter; the legislative intent to give wide discretion to the administrative agency is clear. "The language of the Act fairly teems with expressions which explicitly evince the intent of Congress that the commission should be guided by its own informed judgment in the exercise of the authority conferred upon it. Not only does the requirement, in numerous connections, that the arrangements sanctioned or prescribed shall be 'just and reasonable' set up standards which are inherently discretionary in character, but grants of power are frequently vested in the Commission with more precise recognition of its freedom of action." [102]

Statutory Provisions. It will be recalled that under the original Act to Regulate Commerce the report of the commission on proceedings in the courts was to be "*prima facie* evidence of the matters therein stated"; but procedure which amounted to a new trial in the courts made the commission's determinations of little consequence. The Hepburn Act of 1906 provided that on proceedings for the enforcement of reparation orders the "findings and order of the Commission shall be *prima facie* evidence of the facts therein stated"; restraint of other orders was recognized only incidentally and without specification of the effect to be accorded the determinations of the commission. When the Valuation Act was passed in 1913, it was provided that final values fixed by the commission should be "*prima facie* evidence of the value of the property in all proceedings." The relief afforded by the Hepburn Act is not to be found in any delimitation of the scope of judicial review, but in the provision that the orders of the commission (except those for money damages) become operative without the intervention of a court, the burden or initiative in contesting orders thereby being shifted to the private parties affected. The Commerce Court Act of 1910 specifically recognized suits to set aside, enjoin, annul, or suspend in whole or part any order of the commission. When the Commerce Court was abolished in 1913, jurisdiction was transferred to the district courts. Under the Transportation Act of 1920 the prevail-

[102] Sharfman, *The Interstate Commerce Commission* (1931), II, 357–358, and discussion following.

ing situation was unaffected. Enforcement of orders for the payment of money still takes place through the courts and the "findings and order of the commission" are "*prima facie* evidence of the facts stated therein." Final valuations, likewise, are to be "*prima facie* evidence" of value in all proceedings. The jurisdiction of the courts to annul other orders is simply recognized by the judicial code without limitation as to scope of review,[103] and after an order has become binding a disobedient carrier may be forced to comply by resort to the courts but the court is limited in such a proceeding to a determination of whether "the order was regularly made and duly served and . . . the carrier is in disobedience." So far as review of the commission's orders (except valuations and reparation awards) is concerned, as distinguished from enforcement after violation, the courts are left to work out the respective spheres of judicial and administrative authorities — to determine the nature and scope of judicial review. Even the *prima facie* effect to be given reparation orders and valuations might do no more than shift the duty of first going forward with evidence.

In examining the decisions on review of Interstate Commerce Commission orders, it hardly seems necessary to take up the progress year by year, as was done in connection with the Federal Trade Commission, since the decisions of the courts have not changed the entire course of administration within the decade. For convenience the subject matter will, therefore, be treated as a whole without insistence upon any tight classification according to legal doctrine or subject matter.[104]

The decisions of the courts are, of course, the chief source of information on administrative-judicial relations together with the reports and records of the Interstate Commerce Commission. As noted above in connection with the Federal Trade Commission, it is the decisions of the Supreme Court which settle the course of judicial relations. Accordingly, those contests of administrative action which reach the highest court will comprise the substance of the following exposition of judicial review in action. However,

[103] 38 Stat. 219. There are also provisions which affect the procedure and course of appeal through the various courts.

[104] A study of judicial review of Interstate Commerce Commission orders from the standpoint of doctrine and functions may be found in Sharfman, *The Interstate Commerce Commission* (1931), II, 384–452, and in Tollefson, *Judicial Review of Decisions of the Interstate Commerce Commission*, 11 Minn. L. Rev. 389 (1927).

some of the decisions of the Supreme Court which do not involve the validity of the commission's regulatory orders are immaterial here — legal proceedings involving access to records of carriers,[105] access to valuation records of the commission,[106] the construction of orders,[107] claims of shippers against carriers,[108] contests of state authority in the field of regulation,[109] and attempted tests of constitutionality.[110] Also, cases which became moot as a result of the legislation of 1920 [111] and those involving adjustments arising out of the federal control period [112] may be excluded.

[105] Clyde Steamship Co. *v.* United States, 281 U. S. 744 (1930) (*denying certiorari to* 36 F.(2d) 691).

[106] United States ex rel. St. Louis etc. Ry. Co. *v.* I. C. C., 264 U. S. 64 (1924).

[107] Central New England Ry. Co. *v.* Boston etc. Co., 279 U. S. 415 (1929).

[108] Am. Ry. Exp. Co. *v.* Lindenburg, 260 U. S. 584 (1923) (damages to goods in transit; order of the commission incidentally involved); Davis *v.* Portland Seed Co., 264 U. S. 403 (damages alleged to result from rates imposed in violation of the long-and-short-haul provisions) (1924); Atlantic Coast Line R. Co. *v.* Standard Oil Co. of Kentucky, 275 U. S. 257 (1927) (shipper's claim to benefit of intrastate rates).

[109] Lehigh Valley R. Co. *v.* Bd. of Pub. Utility Commrs., 278 U. S. 24 (1928) (state authority in elimination of grade crossing); Napier *v.* Atlantic etc. R. Co., 272 U. S. 605 (1926) (authority of the states in regulation of locomotive equipment).

[110] State of Texas *v.* I. C. C., 258 U. S. 158 (1922) (attempted test of constitutionality of labor provisions and provisions for regulation of intrastate rates).

[111] United States *v.* Alaska S. S. Co., 253 U. S. 113 (1920) (involving order of the commission prescribing forms of bills of lading).

[112] Administration of deficit, claims, and income guaranty provisions of the Act of 1920 and the 1921 amendment in connection with the termination of federal control came before the courts in a number of cases. Applications for mandamus in connection with orders of the commission denying claims of carriers were refused by the courts in three instances: United States ex rel. Chicago etc. Co. *v.* I. C. C., 265 U. S. 292 (1924) (*affirming* 288 Fed. 648; the order of the commission excluded a refrigerator car company from the guaranty provisions); United States ex rel. Abilene etc. Ry. Co. *v.* I. C. C., 270 U. S. 650 (1926) (*denying certiorari to* 8 Fed.(2) 901; the commission had determined that a carrier was not under federal control and therefore not entitled to benefit of deficit provisions); United States ex rel. Cripple Creek etc. R. Co. *v.* I. C. C., 273 U. S. 706 (1926) (*denying certiorari to* 11 F.(2d) 650; the commission had refused to settle a claim on the basis that the carrier operated a railway system). The commission's power to correct advances to carriers under the guaranty provisions was sustained by the Court of Appeals of the District of Columbia, which decision the Supreme Court refused to review. Northern Pac. Ry. Co. *v.* I. C. C., 275 U. S. 572 (1928) (*denying certiorari to* 23 F.(2d) 221). In 1928 the Supreme Court determined that the "orders" of the commission certifying to the Secretary of the Treasury amounts due under the

Before entering upon the course of judicial review of the various types of orders of the Interstate Commerce Commission during the decade 1920–1930, judicially expressed limitations upon the power of the courts should be noted.[113] In the first place, the doctrines limiting the scope of judicial review which were announced after the passage of the Hepburn Act have been repeated, although the Supreme Court in recent years has not laid particular stress upon them. The distinction between "questions of law" and "matters of fact" is preserved (which, of course, means no more than that it is the policy of the courts to leave some matters to the sound discretion of the administrative agency),[114] and the Supreme Court disclaims for the judiciary any authority over the weight of the evidence, soundness of reasoning, the application of administrative precedents, or the wisdom of the commission's action.[115]

guaranty provisions were not regulations of commerce but were a purely legislative incident of the war and therefore not subject to review. Great Northern Ry. Co. *v.* United States, 277 U. S. 172 (*affirming* 22 F.(2d) 865). Decisions on the federal control provisions of the Act of 1920, in which the validity of orders of the commission are not involved, are: Marion etc. Ry. Co. *v.* United States, 270 U. S. 280 (1926) (validity of compensation fixed by board of referees); New York Central R. Co. *v.* N. Y. etc. R. Co., 271 U. S. 124 (1926) (reparations allowed by state authority affecting the rate level and jurisdiction of the commission following the termination of federal control); United States *v.* Guaranty Trust Co. of New York, 280 U. S. 478 (1930) (involving priority of government claims found due by the commission). A reparation order of the commission based upon the Federal Control Act was sustained by a circuit court of appeals and the Supreme Court refused to review the decision. Mellon *v.* World Publishing Co., 275 U. S. 561 (1927) (*denying certiorari to* 20 F.(2d) 613).

[113] See: *Judicial Power to Set Aside Orders of the Interstate Commerce Commission*, Note 41 Harv. L. Rev. 381 (1928).

[114] Compare the discussion in Seaboard Air Line Ry. Co. *v.* United States, 254 U. S. 57, 62 (1920). There are also some statements indicating the survival of distinctions between legislative and judicial functions: Baltimore etc. Co. *v.* United States, 264 U. S. 258, 263, 264–265 (1924). United States *v.* Los Angeles etc. R. Co., 273 U. S. 299, 309 (1927).

[115] "To consider the weight of the evidence before the Commission, the soundness of the reasoning by which its conclusions were reached, or whether the findings are consistent with those made by it in other cases is beyond our province." "The finding of reasonableness, like that of undue prejudice, is a determination of fact by a tribunal 'informed by experience.' . . . This court has no concern with the correctness of the Commission's reasoning, with the soundness of its conclusions, or with the alleged inconsistency with findings made in other proceedings before it." Virginian Ry. Co. *v.* United States, 272 U. S. 658, 663, 666 (1926). See also: Western Paper etc. Co. *v.* United States, 271 U. S. 268, 271 (1926); Chicago etc. Ry. Co. *v.* United States, 274

"The courts will not review determinations of the Commission made within the scope of its powers, or substitute their judgment for its findings and conclusions," for "these matters are left by Congress to the administration tribunal appointed by law and informed by experience." [116] The one constantly expressed limitation upon the commission is that the findings be "supported by substantial evidence," in which case they are "conclusive unless there was some irregularity in the proceeding or some error in the application of rules of law." [117] There is a positive deference toward the administrative judgment in these doctrines or principles of judicial review.[118]

In other important respects the courts have continued to refuse to interfere in the regulation of transportation. First, the courts will not themselves originate regulation in those matters which Congress has placed within the jurisdiction of the commission; and secondly, in some instances where the administrative agency has refused to act the courts will not interfere.

The first of these limitations — the doctrine of primary jurisdiction — was announced by the Supreme Court in 1907. There are several reasons for this limitation upon the jurisdiction of the courts — the desire for a uniform administration of the law rather

U. S. 29, 33–34 (1927); New England Divisions Case, 261 U. S. 184, 204; Assigned Car Cases, 274 U. S. 564, 580 (1927).

[116] United States *v.* New River Co., 265 U. S. 533, 542 (1924); Chicago etc. Ry. Co. *v.* United States, 270 U. S. 287, 294 (1926); Assigned Car Cases, 274 U. S. 564, 581 (1927); Virginian Ry. Co. *v.* United States, 272 U. S. 658, 666.

[117] "The determination whether a rate is unreasonable or discriminatory is a question on which the finding of the Commission is conclusive if supported by substantial evidence, unless there was some irregularity in the proceeding or some error in the application of the rules of law." "In making its determinations the Commission is not hampered by mechanical rules governing the weight or effect of evidence. The mere admission of matter which under the rules of evidence applicable to judicial proceedings would be deemed incompetent does not invalidate its order." Western Paper etc. Co. *v.* United States, 271 U. S. 268, 271 (1926). And see also: Virginian Ry. Co. *v.* United States, 272 U. S. 658, 663 (1926).

[118] Compare: "While under these principles of decision, as will appear in due course, there is ample room for judicial interference, without precise definition as to its scope, it is significant that the basic question thus open to the determination of the courts is the possession of power by the Commission rather than the wisdom or expediency of its exercise. This mode of approach has been repeatedly stressed by the Supreme Court and constitutes the controlling doctrine in all matters of review." Sharfman, *The Interstate Commerce Commission* (1921), II, 392.

than a regulation differing between courts and the commission and between the different courts (any lack of agreement between a judicially developed body of law and administrative practice would eventually result in the supremacy of judicial precedents), the necessity for administrative autonomy, and the general purpose to secure a specialized regulation of carriers.[119] But of course not all litigation affecting railroads is withdrawn from the courts; it is only those matters which have been committed to the *discretion* of the commission which must first be passed upon by the administrative body.[120] Where the question is whether or not a matter falls within the scope of the commission's authority, it may be raised before a determination is made by the commission; while the commission in the exercise of its administrative discretion or judgment must often determine whether the subject matter is within its jurisdiction, yet if such question is presented to a court before the commission has acted the court will determine the matter. Accordingly, the doctrine of primary jurisdiction has not been applied to such questions as whether a matter is for federal regulation by the Interstate Commerce Commission or the proper subject of state regulation,[121] but when the exercise of federal authority is placed in the commission the federal courts may not interfere before the commission has determined the matter.[122] Akin to the doctrine of primary jurisdiction is the contention, sometimes raised, that carri-

[119] *Supra*, pp. 121–122.

[120] For a discussion and list of cases see: Great Northern Ry. Co. *v.* Merchants' Elevator Co., 259 U. S. 285 (1922) (construction of tariff held the proper subject of judicial action without first resort to the commission).

[121] Texas & P. Ry. Co. *v.* Gulf etc. Ry. Co., 270 U. S. 266 (1926) (determination of whether proposed construction was an "extension" and therefore a matter of federal administration or an "industrial track" and for state regulation); Texas etc. R. Co. *v.* North Side Belt Ry. Co., 276 U. S. 475 (1928) (whether proposed terminal railroad would be an interstate carrier); Missouri-K.-T. R. Co. *v.* Northern Oklahoma Rys., 25 Fed.(2d) 689 (1928), *certiorari denied* 278 U. S. 610 (whether proposed state railroad would engage in interstate commerce; the commission had already denied application for permission to construct).

The federal courts also determine whether state authority is ousted by Congressional action: Railroad Commission of California *v.* Southern Pac. Co., 264 U. S. 331 (1924); Alabama etc. Ry. Co. *v.* Jackson etc. Ry. Co., 271 U. S. 244 (1926); Midland etc. R. Co. *v.* Barkley, 276 U. S. 482 (1928).

[122] Board of Railroad Commissioners of North Dakota *v.* Great Northern Ry. Co., 281 U. S. 412 (1930) (a district court may not enjoin enforcement of intrastate rates as discriminatory against interstate commerce pending investigation by the commission); Jeanneret *v.* Chicago etc. R. Co., 17 F.(2d) 978

ers must first exhaust the administrative remedy — by appearing in the administrative hearings and by seeking rehearings or modification of orders.[123]

A second limitation upon resort to the courts is the principle that the courts may not coerce administrative action — the so-called doctrine of affirmative-and-negative orders. The basis of this denial of judicial authority, first announced in 1912,[124] lies in the difficulty of forcing the exercise of administrative discretion and the further consideration that such interference would amount to judicial exercise of the administrative function. Yet denials of relief by the commission, when not subject to judicial control or review, leave the applicant without further recourse. On the one side there is the impracticability of coercing administrative action toward any particular decision involving the exercise of discretion, and on the other side there is inconsistency in allowing a review of affirmative orders but denying appeal when the commission refuses to act. Doubtless the doctrine was less objectionable in the earlier days of regulation when the function of the commission was the correction of abuses rather than the control of a national transportation system under complete regulation; in the former situation a denial of relief by the commission amounted to no more than an unsuccessful equity action, but under the present system of complete regulation a denial to one party may amount to a grant to another.

However, further abstract discussion is perhaps unprofitable, for the Supreme Court carefully considers the effect of the particular orders and the application of the doctrine is not merely a matter of form.[125] An order of the commission which is in form negative —

(1927), *certiorari denied* 275 U. S. 531 (reparation may not be secured in the courts on general rate orders of the commission — where no particular claim has been presented and passed on by the commission).

[123] United States *v.* Abilene etc. Ry. Co., 265 U. S. 274 (1924). (In the adjustment of divisions of joint rates contesting carriers had not taken part in the hearings before the commission nor had they sought to have the commission modify the order, but the Supreme Court determined that a district court had acted within its discretion in refusing to dismiss the order for failure to exhaust the administrative remedy.) See also: Beaumont etc. R. Co. *v.* United States, 282 U. S. 74, 87 (1930). The Supreme Court has held that the administrative remedy must first be exhausted before valuations are reviewable unless there be "willful" disregard of law. Delaware etc. Co. *v.* United States, 266 U. S. 438 (1925).

[124] *Supra,* p. 122 n. 66.

[125] See: United States *v.* Los Angeles etc. R. Co., 273 U. S. 299, 309–310 (1927).

a denial of relief — but which in effect continues an emergency rule beyond the time of emergency amounts to a change of status and is subject to judicial consideration.[126] Where the commission finds as a preliminary matter that it has not jurisdiction, on judicial proceedings to compel the commission to consider the case the Supreme Court has determined the law and sustained the commission without reference to the doctrine of negative orders.[127] The fact that an order is permissive does not preclude judicial review,[128] but when the commission has denied reparation it cannot be compelled to reconsider and award reparation.[129] Irrespective of the merits of this much-disputed doctrine of negative orders, it is further evidence of the judicial policy of non-interference with administrative discretion.

In addition to "negative" orders, there are other determinations of the commission which the courts will not examine. An order reopening tentative valuations is not subject to court review;[130] and although the commission may be compelled to consider certain

[126] United States *v.* New River Co., 265 U. S. 533 (1924). The order of the commission denied a petition to revert to the rule for distribution of facilities existing before the period of federal control and continued the wartime rule. "The effect of the order is to grant relief sought" by those who preferred the new rule.

[127] I. C. C. *v.* United States ex rel. City of Los Angeles, 280 U. S. 52 (1929). The commission had approved establishment of a union station but determined that it was without authority to compel carriers to establish such station. Thereupon, proceedings were instituted to compel the commission to consider evidence for the entry of an order requiring the construction, but when the case reached the Supreme Court the commission's interpretation of its authority was sustained without consideration of the propriety of mandamus.

[128] Baltimore etc. Co. *v.* United States, 264 U. S. 258 (1924). (Order approving plans for acquisition of control of carriers by another carrier is reviewable.)

[129] I. C. C. *v.* United States ex rel. Waste Merchants' Ass'n, 260 U. S. 32 (1922) (reparation asked for improper denial of services refused by the commission on the ground that the tariffs had not been violated and the rates were reasonable); United States ex rel. Donner Steel Co. *v.* I. C. C., 8 F.(2d) 905 (1925) *certiorari denied* 270 U. S. 651 (reparation for excluding party from customary allowances and services was denied by the commission on the ground that no damages had been shown although the practice was discriminatory); Bartlesville Zinc Co. *v.* I. C. C., 30 F.(2d) 479 (1929), *certiorari denied* 279 U. S. 856 (reparation for unlawfully imposed demurrage charges was denied by the commission on the ground that the charges had been assessed substantially in compliance with the applicable tariff).

[130] Delaware etc. Co. *v.* United States, 266 U. S. 438 (1925).

evidence in determining final valuations,[131] an order fixing a final valuation is not reviewable since the subject may be canvassed when the valuation is used in regulation.[132] And the courts will not determine jurisdiction in advance to avoid possible future complications, since the pronouncement of the court would amount to a declaratory judgment.[133]

A more important preliminary consideration is the ready and constant judicial recognition of legislative policy and appreciation of the necessities of administration. The policy of Congress is broadly interpreted and translated into action in judicial decisions sustaining the commission's exercise of authority. The policy of the legislation of 1920 was immediately recognized and became the basis of decision in a series of important cases.[134] Attacks upon the commission's authority are tested in the courts by consideration

[131] Kansas City Southern R. Co. *v.* I. C. C., 252 U. S. 178, 187 (1920).

[132] United States *v.* Los Angeles etc. R. Co., 273 U. S. 299 (1927).

[133] Piedmont & N. R. Co. *v.* United States, 280 U. S. 469, 476–477 (1930).

[134] See, for example, the following excerpts from extended discussions in the decisions of the courts: "The act made a new departure. [The former] control which Congress through the Interstate Commerce Commission exercised was primarily for the purpose of preventing injustice by unreasonable or discriminatory rates against persons and localities, and the only provisions of the law that inured to the benefit of the carriers were the requirement that the rates should be reasonable in the sense of furnishing an adequate compensation for the particular service rendered and the abolition of rebates. The new measure imposed an affirmative duty on the Interstate Commerce Commission to fix rates and to take other important steps to maintain an adequate railway service for the people of the United States." Chief Justice Taft in Wisconsin Railroad Commission *v.* Chicago etc. R. Co., 257 U. S. 563, 585 (1922). "The Transportation Act of 1920 introduced into the federal legislation a new railroad policy. . . . Theretofore, the effort of Congress had been directed mainly to the prevention of abuses; particularly, those arising from excessive or discriminatory rates. The 1920 act sought to ensure, also, adequate transportation service. That such was its purpose, Congress did not leave to inference. The new purpose was expressed in unequivocal language." Mr. Justice Brandeis, in the New England Divisions Case, 261 U. S. 184, 189 (1923). And see also: Dayton-Goose Creek Ry. Co. *v.* United States, 263 U. S. 456 (1924), in which the constitutionality of the provisions for recapture of excess earnings and use of part of such fund for relief of carriers in straightened financial circumstances is sustained upon the basis of the new legislative policy to provide for an adequate national transportation system. The effect of cumulated legislation on particular subjects is illustrated by the decisions in Chicago etc. Ry. Co. *v.* United States, 274 U. S. 29, 36–37 (1927); Assigned Car Cases, 274 U. S. 564 (1927); Atchison etc. Ry. Co. *v.* United States, 279 U. S. 768, 776–777 (1929); Wisconsin R. Comm. *v.* Chicago etc. R. Co., 257 U. S. 563, 582–584.

of administrative practice, the purposes of the statutes, and the consequent practical demands of administrative power.[135]

The Decisions of the Courts

A survey of decisions of the Supreme Court and of decisions which that court refused to review during the years 1920 to 1930 will disclose more accurately the nature of the judicial control of the Interstate Commerce Commission. For convenience, the regulatory orders of the commission as they come before the courts may be treated according to the subject matter — rates, practices, valuation, reparations, and so on, and the various types of orders may also be classified according to the statutory provisions for judicial review or enforcement. Judicial review over the larger class of orders (involving all but valuation and reparation orders) has not been provided in the legislation except that jurisdiction has been placed in certain federal courts. Accordingly, judicial control over these orders, in which the courts have had to work out their own principles of review, will be treated first.

Reasonable Rates. **Excluding those decisions in which the controversy has become moot,[136] or in which the appellants were without standing to contest the order,[137] or which involve special statutes (railway mail pay),[138] the commission's orders fixing reasonable rates were tested in the Supreme Court in five instances during the decade. All of the orders of the commission under its general rate-fixing powers were sustained. The first, involving the commission's decision on an inter-sectional rate controversy, was**

[135] This mode of judicial consideration is strikingly illustrated in the following cases: R. Comm. of Wisconsin *v.* Chicago etc. R. Co., 257 U. S. 563 (1922) and State of New York *v.* United States, 257 U. S. 591 (1922), both involving federal authority over state rates; United States *v.* Illinois Central R. Co., 263 U. S. 515 (1924); Baltimore etc. R. Co. *v.* United States, 264 U. S. 258, 270 (1924) (joinder of parties); United States *v.* American Ry. Exp. Co., 265 U. S. 425 (1924) (through routes in express); State of Colorado *v.* United States, 271 U. S. 153, 163 (1926) (abandonment of intrastate spurs); Alabama etc. Ry. Co. *v.* Jackson etc. Ry. Co., 271 U. S. 244, 250 (1926) (exclusive jurisdiction of commission over connections); Beaumont etc. Ry. Co. *v.* United States, 282 U. S. 74 (1930) (fixing divisions of joint rates by groups without determining dissimilarities between carriers within the groups).

[136] Anchor Coal Co. *v.* United States, 279 U. S. 812 *denying certiorari to* 25 Fed.(2) 462.

[137] Alexander Sprunt & Son *v.* United States, 281 U. S. 249.

[138] Missouri Pac. R. Co. *v.* United States, 271 U. S. 603; United States *v.* New York Central R. Co., 279 U. S. 73.

sustained as "clearly within the broad discretion vested in the commission."[139] In the second, despite recitals which lent support to the complaint that the commission had attempted to equalize rail rates with rail-and-water rates, the court determined that it would be "quite unfair to conclude that the commission undertook to exercise an authority entirely different and distinct from that which the complaint specifically invoked."[140] And in the third case, the Supreme Court again refused to consider the motives of the commission but insisted that the commission had exercised "only its function of determining the reasonableness of rates."[141]

[139] This test of the commission's order involved rates on naval stores from southern points. New rates, as fixed by the commission in a series of orders, were contested as discriminatory between localities and in violation of the long-and-short-haul provisions. The commission was sustained in a three-judge district court, and the Supreme Court, confining itself to the single question whether the administrative determination was supported by substantial evidence, likewise sustained the commission. Certain established routes, if retained, would have been violative of the long-and-short-haul provisions. The commission refused to change the rates and instead directed that these routes be abandoned. Western Paper Makers' Chemical Co. *v.* United States, 271 U. S. 268 (1926), *affirming* 7 F.(2d) 164 (1925).

[140] The commisson had determined that existing rates on combined rail-and-water transportation were unreasonable and prescribed proper rates. There had been no previous joint rates, but the commission determined that joint rates were desirable and in the public interest. In effect the court refused to consider the grounds upon which the commission had acted and instead accepted the form of the complaint and words of the order as indicating the authority exercised. (In other decisions — notably valuation — the court has not been so sparing in the scope of review.) As to the sufficiency of the evidence, the court determined that the order rested upon established facts and circumstances in addition to the comparison to which the carrier objected. Sufficient statutory authority for the commission to establish through routes by rail and water was found; the Act to Regulate Commerce, the Panama Canal Act, and the Transportation Act of 1920 were construed in the light of broad and expanding legislative policy. That the commission had not specified the particular statutes under which it would investigate was held immaterial since the "allegations in matters of fact were sufficient to authorize the commission to consider the case" under the disputed statutory provision. "To plead the law relied on, is no more necessary in a proceeding before the commission than it is in a judicial proceeding." Chicago etc. Ry. Co. *v.* United States, 274 U. S. 29 (1927), *affirming* 6 F.(2d) 888.

[141] The case involved an order of the commission cancelling increased proportional rates on grain and grain products. In the competition of carriers of grain to gulf ports, a railroad sought to raise rates to the junction with another road so that it would have for itself an advantage in carrying grain destined for export after transfer to other carriers. The commission found the increased rates unjustified and ordered them cancelled. In seeking to have the commis-

However, in two administrative orders issued under legislation enacted for the benefit of special interests, the commission was reversed; in each case the difficulties were due to the ambiguous nature of the legislation — the Supreme Court determined that the commission had taken political gestures too seriously.[142]

sion's order set aside, the carrier offering the increased rates contended that the commission lacked authority to cancel the rates because by so doing it compelled the carrier to participate in a through route and rate and thereby short haul itself. The routing was said to be only an "incident." In short, the commission's power to pass upon the reasonableness of rates is sustained regardless of incidental effect or possible motive. The contention that the commission had interfered with through routes and rates was labelled a fiction since when grain was delivered at the junction it was impossible to say whether it would be carried to any particular further destination. The "faint contention" that there was insufficient evidence was dismissed as "clearly unfounded." United States *v.* Atchison etc. Ry. Co., 279 U. S. 768 (1929), *affirming* 33 F.(2d) 345 (1928).

[142] In 1922 Congress, upon pressure from commercial travellers' associations, provided for the issuance of nontransferable interchangeable scrip coupon tickets "at just and reasonable rates." Act of August 18, 1922, 42 Stat. 827. The commission, with some reluctance and difficulty, ordered carriers to issue the scrip at prescribed rates. The district court and the Supreme Court, however, annulled the order of the commission on the ground that, in granting reduced fares rather than just rates under the circumstances, the commission had "erred in reading the wishes that originated the statute as an effective term of the Act passed." New York Central R. Co. *v.* United States, 263 U. S. 603 (1924), *affirming* 288 Fed. 951 (1923).

The second instance occurred in connection with similar special legislation. Congress in 1925, with agricultural conditions in mind, directed the commission in adjusting rates to consider the "conditions which at any given time prevail" in the different industries "so far as it is legally possible to do so, to the end that commodities may freely move." Hoch-Smith Resolution (*supra*, n. 96). For a discussion see: Sharfman, *The Interstate Commerce Commission* (1931), I, 227–235. In the attempt to secure the benefits of this legislative expression, fruit growers protested the rates on fruits from California points. The commission found them unreasonable and prescribed proper rates. A district court sustained the commission but the Supreme Court determined that the Congressional action made no change in the basic law, that agricultural products were not placed in a "most favored" class as the commission thought had been intended, and that existing rates had not been condemned by the joint resolution of Congress. Ann Arbor R. Co. *v.* United States, 281 U. S. 658 (1930), *reversing* 30 F.(2d) 940 (1928). Instead, the Supreme Court construed the words of Congress to mean no more than that the existing law was to be enforced, which interpretation can hardly be criticized since the words of the resolution are loose, ambiguous and obviously motivated by the desire to do something (if no more than make a political gesture) in behalf of hard-put agricultural industries.

Divisions of Joint Rates. In correcting or prescribing the divisions of joint rates between carriers the commission was three times sustained in the Supreme Court and as many times reversed. The reversals, however, were all put upon the ground of error in procedure. The commission was sustained in its determination of the mileage basis for division of rates,[143] there was a broad judicial interpretation of the commission's authority over joint rates under the legislation of 1920 so that weaker roads could be assisted through a larger share of the rates and the national transportation system thereby strengthened so long as no confiscatory rates were imposed upon the stronger roads,[144] and on the ground of necessity

[143] The first case involved an order of the commission fixing switching allowances and divisions. A sawmill company was owner of a short railroad connecting with a trunk line. The two carriers joined in establishing through routes and joint rates on products from the company's mills to points on the trunk line and beyond. The division or allowance given the short line out of the joint rates was large. The commission determined that this allowance was so large as to amount to a rebate to the sawmill company and to discriminate against another lumber company served also by the same short line; proper division of the joint rates was fixed by order of the commission. This was sustained in a district court, and the Supreme Court — reviewing the reasonableness of the order — also sustained the commission. The matter in dispute was the distance travelled over the short line — upon which the division of the rate was based. The short line contended that part of the carriage on the trunk line involved in weighing cars should be included in the total short or "tap line" carriage. The commission found that weighing on the trunk line was unnecessary and that to allow this additional distance would give an undue advantage to this particular tap line over similarly situated lines. The Supreme Court determined that the administrative order was not arbitrary or unreasonable and sustained the commission. Louisiana & P. B. Ry. Co. *v.* United States, 257 U. S. 114 (1921), *affirming* 274 Fed. 372 (1921).

[144] The Act of 1920 conferred upon the commission power to apportion joint rates among the carriers who were parties to the rate and directed the commission to give consideration, among other things, to the importance to the public of the transportation service rendered by the several carriers, to the financial condition of the carriers, and to the character of the services rendered. Under these provisions the railroads of New England sought a larger division of the rates on freight moving between their territory and other sections of the country. After extensive proceedings the commission fixed the divisions of rates, increasing the portions allotted to the New England carriers by 15 per cent. A suit to set aside the order of the commission was unsuccessful in the district court. On appeal to the Supreme Court it was contended that the order was void because the purpose was not to establish just divisions of rates but to relieve the financial needs of the New England lines. In answer, the court in its opinion pointed out the new policy and new conditions in the post-war transportation system. The new legislative policy contemplated a national

the commission was permitted to fix divisions of rates between groups of carriers upon average or group conditions rather than upon specific investigation of each carrier.[145] For procedural error,

transportation system, but the situation was complicated by the weak financial condition of the carriers — particularly those in certain sections of the country. "It was necessary to avoid unduly burdensome rate increases and yet secure revenues adequate to satisfy the needs of the weak carriers. To accomplish this two new devices were adopted: the group system of rate making and the division of joint rates in the public interest. Through the former, weak roads were to be helped by recapture from prosperous competitors of surplus revenues. Through the latter, the weak were to be helped by preventing needed revenue from passing to prosperous connections." The court found sufficient authority and sufficient evidence upon which the commission could act. Since confiscatory rates had not been shown, the court found no unconstitutionality in the exercise of such authority. No discrimination was found in the order against individual lines or lack of due consideration of their needs; the group order was found unobjectionable. The hearing, specific provisions of the order, and the evidence were found sufficient. New England Divisions Case, 261 U. S. 184 (1923).

[145] The order of the commission prescribed the basic formula for determination of future divisions of joint rates at western points. A district court, in a suit to set aside the commission's order, denied the injunction but granted a stay of the order pending appeal. The Supreme Court then sustained the order of the commission. The carriers contended that the statutory provisions required the commission to determine the divisions of each carrier upon a consideration of its own rights and needs and did not authorize the commission to base its order upon group conditions or upon average conditions in the group, but the Supreme Court determined that the commission "need not under all circumstances take specific evidence as to each rate of every carrier. When considering divisions of numerous joint rates applicable to traffic passing through gateways between different territories the commission may make the required determinations and establish bases for divisions between groups of carriers in the respective territories upon evidence which it reasonably may deem typical and to have sufficient probative weight to justify the necessary findings and the order in respect of each rate." Under this rule the evidence was held sufficient. As to the argument that within the groups of carriers there were widely divergent individual situations, the court said that so wide a range of rates of return had been shown that "if approximate similarity in that respect is essential to the order, its basis cannot be sustained." "The reports satisfactorily show that the findings as to average group conditions taken as a whole are sustained by substantial and persuasive evidence." And the court held that a study of the record "leads to the opinion that, notwithstanding the wide differences in rates of return between carriers the basis adopted will not, at least on that account, result in unjust and unreasonable divisions." This method of fixing group divisions was held constitutional and no want of parties was found. Beaumont, etc. Ry. Co. *v.* United States, 282 U. S. 74 (1930), *reviewing* 36 F.(2d) 789 (1929). The decision is notable as a recognition of the difficulties of regional rate-making — the commission is not held

however, the commission was reversed for failure to undertake full and specific investigation [146] and for use of evidence not submitted at hearing.[147]

to a meticulous consideration of individual carriers which, the court realized, would be a practical impossibility.

[146] The first of the cases in which the Supreme Court felt the commission had exceeded its authority involved the share of joint rates received by a short railroad in the Southwest owned by a sulphur company. After extensive investigation into the division of rates of many railroads, and further investigation into the operation of this particular short line, the commission found the allowances to the short line unreasonable and, in effect, a rebate to the industrial concern which owned the line; proper divisions were prescribed. This action was sustained in a district court, but the Supreme Court reversed the order. Although the commission had engaged in extensive proceedings, involving many railroads and rates, the Supreme Court felt that, because the final investigation involved only the short line, "the commission evidently undertook to deprive the Brimstone Company of receipts supposed to exceed a fair return on its property and award the same to connecting carriers without evidence tending to show they were in need or had or would receive more or less than a fair return from agreed divisions, or that the joint rates themselves were unfair and unjust, or that the agreed divisions were 'unjust, unreasonable, inequitable, or unduly preferential or prejudicial as between the carriers.'" And the court further determined that the commission was without authority to make its adjustments operative until after the final order — although in this case there had been earlier orders directing the carriers to adjust the divisions of joint rates. "The power to require readjustments for the past is drastic. It may reasonably exist in cases where the particular rate has been approved by the Commission after full hearing; it ought not be extended so as to permit unreasonably harsh action without very plain words." Two justices dissented. In view of all the proceedings and the numerous orders, it does not appear that the commission acted arbitrarily or in reckless disregard of the rights of parties. Brimstone R. etc. Co. *v.* United States, 276 U. S. 104 (1928), *reversing* 17 F.(2d) 165.

In the second instance of reversal, the commission had found the practice of carriers at St. Louis which required railroads on the west side of the Mississippi to bear the expense of transfer of westbound freight across the river unreasonable; the commission shifted the burden to the lines on the eastern side of the river and commended the carriers to a study of the divisions of rates with view to readjustment. The commission had issued its order as a regulation of "practices" but the court determined that this was in effect a division of rates which could only be ordered upon substantial evidence whereas in this particular investigation by the commission "the propriety of divisions was not the subject of inquiry and investigation." On the other hand, the court held that in view of the extensive adjustments in former years there was a "strong presumption" that the general level of rates had been adjusted to include reasonable compensation for the services. The administrative practice in other instances was

Notd 147 will be found on following page.

Discriminations in Rates in Interstate Commerce. Discriminatory rate cases may be treated in two groups — discriminations in interstate rates and discriminations between interstate and state rates. In the field of interstate rate discriminations, the commission was reversed in an attempt to equalize lumber rates between different sections of the country through equalization of shippers' privileges, [148]

deemed insufficient to supply the necessary support for the order of the commission. Accordingly, the district court which had sustained the commission was reversed and the case sent back for further proceedings. Baltimore etc. R. Co. *v.* United States, 277 U. S. 291 (1928). The case reached the Supreme Court a second time, 279 U. S. 781 (1929).

[147] In the third instance of reversal for procedural error, an order of the commission was involved which readjusted the divisions of joint rates in favor of a southwestern railway system. A district court and the Supreme Court reversed the commission. The court found that the necessary parties had been included in the proceedings before the commission, the authority of the commission to establish divisions was sustained on much the same grounds as the New England Divisions Case, and the restriction of adjustments to those carriers making physical connection with the relieved carrier was approved. The Supreme Court, however, approved the reversal of the commission on two grounds: evidence in the form of annual reports had been considered in making the determination although not submitted at the hearing and, secondly, there was no evidence in the record of the proceedings showing the individual joint rates or how these were divided. The commission sought to justify the use of outside evidence on the basis of a reference made by the examiner during the hearing and maintained, so far as objection to lack of evidence of particular divisions was concerned, that the evidence on divisions as a whole could be taken as showing the typical and proper division of particular rates; these arguments the court rejected as insufficient to give notice to the carriers of the evidence they must meet. United States *v.* Abilene etc. Ry. Co., 265 U. S. 274 (1924), *sustaining* 288 Fed. 102 (1923).

[148] An eastern creosoting company petitioned the commission for removal of discriminations alleged to result from the refusal of eastern carriers to allow creosoting in transit. Carriers in the South and West granted certain privileges in treating forest products at intermediate points of shipment. The eastern carriers refused to grant such privileges to anyone. They did not, therefore, in their own territory favor one shipper and deny another, but they were parties to joint rates and through routing from southern and western carriers which allowed such privileges. An eastern lumber company asserted discrimination as between it and companies allowed the privileges at the other end of the through routes. The commission ordered the eastern carriers to "remove the discrimination" and was sustained in a district court, but the Supreme Court determined that, while the commission might have ordered the eastern lines to establish such privilege or might have ordered the other lines to discontinue the practice, it could not by simply ordering the eastern lines to remove the discrimination force them to allow the privilege or cancel their joint rates (which was the effect of the order since the eastern lines had no control over

and was sustained in two cases involving local discriminations.[149]

Discriminations between State and Interstate Rates. The commission is authorized by the Interstate Commerce Act, as amended by the Transportation Act of 1920, to remove discriminations between "persons and localities in intrastate commerce on the one hand and

the other groups of carriers). The discrimination arose from local conditions on carriers in another section of the country, and the court held that "participation in joint rates does not make connecting carriers partners." "What Congress sought to prevent . . . was not differences between localities in transportation rates, facilities and privileges, but unjust discrimination between them by the same carrier or carriers." The court came to this conclusion because otherwise "only uniformity in local privileges and practices or the cancellation of all joint rates would afford to carriers the assurance that they were not in some way violating the provisions" of the statute. This decision is a reflection of the difficulties involved in the regulation of a transportation system which serves a continent and yet is subject to regional private control. Central R. Co. of N. J. *v.* United States, 257 U. S. 247 (1921).

[149] Carriers from southern territory had established through lumber rates to northern markets regardless of varying distances within the "blanket" southern territory, but mills on one of the connecting carriers were charged a slightly higher rate. The commission found that rates to the junctions were not unreasonable but that they subjected some of the lumber companies to undue prejudice in view of lower rates allowed at other competing points. The carriers were ordered to desist from charging higher through rates than were contemporaneously charged for like services from other points within the territory. Two of the connecting carriers sought to restrain the enforcement of the order. One district court sustained the commission and another sustained the protesting carriers. In the Supreme Court the contention that the connecting carriers were not subject to the orders of the commission because they did not participate in the other rates, in comparison with which the discrimination arose, was dismissed as "unsound" because the proceedings were aimed at the relation of rates and otherwise "relief on the ground of discrimination could never be had against preferential rates given by a great railway system to points on its own lines which result in undue prejudice to shippers on short lines connecting with it." As to supporting evidence, the court held that, although mere discrimination was not enough unless injustice is shown, though the lower rates on main lines were the result of other and legitimate motives, and notwithstanding the fact that the law did not attempt to equalize opportunities between localities, there was sufficient support in the evidence considering all the factors — as the commission had — in spite of the fact that the rates separately considered might be reasonable. On this point, the opinion of the Supreme Court does not set forth evidence or facts but defers to the judgment of the commission. As to taking property without due process of law — the confiscatory nature of lower rates — the court pointed out that the rates might be equalized by raising some of them or the divisions of through rates might be readjusted. Any distinction on the basis of the type of combined

interstate or foreign commerce on the other hand," and is also authorized to remove "discrimination against interstate or foreign commerce." Rigid judicial censorship over administrative interference with state authority, in view of the historic state rights insistence and the established authority of the courts to delineate the federal system, is to be expected. In removing discriminations arising from state rates fixed by state authority, the courts in previous years had put the burden on the commission to show clearly that the rates established by federal authority should have precedence over state rates. "An order of a subordinate agency, such as the Commission, should not be given precedence over a state rate statute otherwise valid, unless, and except so far as, it conforms to a high standard of certainty." [150] This doctrine was

rate was denied by the court. United States *v.* Illinois Central R. Co., 263 U. S. 515 (1924).

In the second case, the commission had fixed rates on coal shipped in interstate commerce. Certain mines on the Virginian railway were excluded from western markets because joint rates with connecting carriers had not been established and the combination rates over the two carriers were prohibitive. Other mines on the line, because of reciprocal agreements by the Virginian with another carrier entered for other purposes than to provide for westward moving freight, enjoyed connections and practicable rates to the West. The commission found the rates both unreasonable and prejudicial; through rates were prescribed and the carrier was ordered to fix reasonable district rates. A district court sustained the commission and the Supreme Court found that "there clearly was substantial evidence to support every fact specifically found." The fact that the discrimination was unintentional was deemed immaterial. The carrier contended that the rates to the West enjoyed by some of the mines could not be used as standards of reasonableness because they were "the outcome of competitive strain and stress through long periods of development" and were made "in practical, if not absolute, disregard of distance, and all transportation conditions that ordinarily are taken into consideration in the making of rates" and were "below the level at which maximum reasonable rates might be sustained." But the Supreme Court said "the finding of reasonableness, like that of undue prejudice, is a determination of fact by a tribunal 'informed by experience,'" that the court had "no concern with the correctness of the commission's reasoning, with the soundness of its conclusions, or with the alleged inconsistency with findings made in other proceedings before it," and determined that the voluminous record disclosed substantial evidence to support the administrative finding. An argument based on possible consolidation of operation with another carrier was dismissed as "appropriate for consideration by the Commission." Virginian Ry. Co. *v.* United States, 272 U. S. 658 (1926).

[150] Illinois Central R. Co. *v.* State Public Utilities Commission, 245 U. S. 493, 509 (1918). See also: American Express Co. *v.* Caldwell, 244 U. S. 617, 627 (1917).

reannounced by the Supreme Court under the new legislation so far as discriminations in favor of state localities or persons were concerned, but the amended act included a provision for regulation of differences affecting interstate commerce as a whole.

Those decisions which involve only the primary jurisdiction of the commission,[151] the original jurisdiction of the Supreme Court,[152] the discretion of district courts in granting preliminary injunctions,[153] or the determination whether carriers are subject to the jurisdiction of the commission [154] may be excluded from this discussion. In three notable decisions the amplified authority and the discretion of the commission over state rates was sustained;[155]

[151] "The grounds for invoking [the] principle of preliminary resort to the commission are even stronger when the effort is made to invalidate intrastate rates upon the ground of unjust discrimination against interstate commerce." Board of R. Commrs. *v.* Great Northern Ry. Co., 281 U. S. 412 (1930). May 19, 1930.

[152] State of North Dakota etc. *v.* Chicago etc. Ry. Co., 257 U. S. 485 (1922).

[153] State of Alabama *v.* United States, 279 U. S. 229 (1929).

[154] Village of Hubbard *v.* United States, 266 U. S. 474 (1925).

[155] The first judicial test of the exercise of administrative authority under the new legislation involved orders of the commission attempting to remove discriminations between persons and localities and also the adjustment of state rates to the general scheme of national regulation. The commission directed carriers to remove discriminations arising from lower state rates and the carriers secured an injunction to prevent the state railroad commission and other state officials from interfering with the maintenance of the fares ordered by the Interstate Commerce Commission. When the case reached the Supreme Court, the order of the commission was considered as of two parts — one part concerning discriminations between persons and localities and the other discriminations against interstate commerce in general. As to discriminations between state travellers or localities and interstate commerce, the Supreme Court found sufficient evidence (consisting of numerous typical instances) but found that the order affected all rates within the state — without a saving clause to prevent injustice in particular cases such as had previously been held necessary — and that therefore the broad order could not be justified on the basis of discriminations against persons or places alone. To justify the order as a correction of discrimination against interstate commerce as a whole, the court undertook a broad interpretation of the entire legislative history with particular reference to the problems and policy of the legislation of 1920. The low state rates, which the commission ordered changed, made a serious drain on the revenues of interstate carriers, whereas the new legislation "imposed an affirmative duty on the Interstate Commerce Commission to fix rates and take other important steps to maintain an adequate railway service for the people of the United States" in which duty "intrastate rates and the income from them must play a most important part." The words of the amended statute were found to "aptly include a kind of discrimination against interstate commerce which the operation of the new act for the first time makes important and which would seriously

in fact the extension of central authority by way of legislative and administrative action into the field once conceived to be the prerogative of the states is one of the marked developments in the federal system.[156]

obstruct its chief purpose." The necessities of national regulation of railroad rates were preferred to claims for complete state control of intrastate rates; "effective control of the one must embrace some control over the other in view of the blending of both in actual operation." The Supreme Court affirmed the lower court and the order of the commission. R. Comm. of Wisconsin *v.* Chicago etc. R. Co., 257 U. S. 563 (1922).

This decision, so far as it sustained the commission's order against discrimination against interstate commerce as a whole, involved only the authority of the commission — the construction of the statute. A second proceeding pertaining to rates in New York was decided the same day on a consideration of the evidence. In this second case, the railroad commission of New York had increased the state rates on some freight but denied increases on other freight and passenger rates. There was also a state statute fixing passenger fares. The commission directed carriers to remove discriminations against interstate commerce by increasing the state rates. Here again those attacking the order were sustained on the point of discrimination in favor of state localities and persons. As to discrimination against interstate commerce as a whole, the Supreme Court found sufficient evidence to justify the order of the commission since otherwise, by depletion of revenues, interstate carriers would be seriously handicapped and thereby the adequacy of the national transportation system impaired. State of New York *v.* United States, 257 U. S. 591 (1922).

A third case involved reduced rates on materials consigned to governmental authorities. The Interstate Commerce Act, since 1889 (25 Stat. 855), has contained a clause allowing free carriage or reduced rates on federal and state property. After the Interstate Commerce Commission had increased rates in southern territory, the railroad commission of Tennessee increased state rates proportionally, excepting materials for the construction of public highways. The Interstate Commerce Commission then found that this exception involved a discrimination and ordered the rates fixed at the level of the interstate rates. Carriers and the State of Tennessee were involved in a contest of the commission's order, and the commission was reversed in a three-judge district court on the ground that reduced rates on such commodities were expressly authorized. But the Supreme Court, construing the commerce act in its entirety, determined that preferential rates might be allowed only where they did not subject to prejudice or disadvantage any person, locality, or class of traffic; if the lower rate results in giving such undue preference to a single company or local industry over others in the state or in other states, the rates are unlawful. The court found that the proceeding of the commission fell within this rule and that the administrative determination was conclusive since the evidence on which the commission acted had not been introduced in the suit. The lower court was reversed and the commission sustained. State of Tennessee *v.* United States, 262 U. S. 318 (1923).

[156] For a full discussion see: Sharfman, *The Interstate Commerce Commission* (1931), II, 191–247.

Discriminatory Charges. Three orders of the commission correcting discriminations in charges were sustained by the Supreme Court. Discriminations arising from competitive conditions were removed,[157] and penalty charges remaining from wartime were ordered discontinued.[158]

[157] In the first case, carriers had been absorbing switching charges at Richmond only where there were competing lines serving the same point in the city at which freight was received for carriage. The commission found this practice discriminatory and directed the carriers to cease. The carriers contested the order on the ground that the carriage was not a "like and contemporaneous service" within the terms of the statute, but the district court and the Supreme Court sustained the commission. ". . . The statute aims to establish equality of rights among shippers for carriage under substantially similar circumstances and conditions and . . . the exigencies of competition do not justify discrimination against shippers for substantially like services." Seaboard Air Line Ry. Co. *v.* United States, 254 U. S. 57 (1920).

In another case, a few industrial plants at a manufacturing center were exempt from charges for switching over connecting carriers. This discrimination, resulting from comity between carriers and based on competitive conditions in a section of the city, the commission determined was improper and ordered the carriers to desist. A district court enjoined enforcement of the order but the Supreme Court sustained the commission. As a "matter of law," the Supreme Court held that competing carriers might not interchange traffic at one point in the industrial center and thereby accord manufacturing plants an advantage over other plants in the same district not situated to benefit by the comity between competing carriers. United States *v.* Pennsylvania R. Co., 266 U. S. 191 (1924).

[158] The Director-General of railroads in 1919 had established a penalty charge to prevent undue detention of equipment during emergency. The charge in modified form remained in force throughout the period of federal control and was thereafter continued by the carriers. On complaint, in 1920, the commission found that conditions had changed and that, while the charges in the past had not been unreasonable, for the future they should be canceled. The order of the commission was protested by lumber dealers who customarily shipped direct from mills to their own lumber yards and had little occasion to use the reconsignment privilege; they claimed that they were injured because jobbers were relieved from the penalty charge and because without the penalty provisions there was danger of car shortage which would affect their shipments and also affect a short line railway they were building. The Supreme Court affirmed the commission on the ground that discriminations against the appellants had not been shown, could be removed if they arose in the future, and that any future car shortage could be handled by the commission when it arose. The authority of the commission was not considered since the carriers were not complaining and the lumber companies who had complained were not entitled to contest the order. Edward Hines Yellow Pine Trustees *v.* United States, 263 U. S. 143 (1923). See also: Turner etc. Co. *v.* Chicago etc. Ry. Co., 271 U. S. 259 (1926).

— *Connections.* Connections between carriers, not including decisions respecting the primary jurisdiction of the commission,[159] have been the subject of Supreme Court decision in three instances. The commission was sustained in each case. In the first of these, carriers were compelled to traffic and enter reciprocal arrangements with an electric line as they were accustomed to do between themselves,[160] in the second a railroad was directed to furnish transportation service from a state barge canal,[161] and in the third a carrier was directed to make a switching connection with an industrial plant.[162]

Services between Carriers. The single case involving services between carriers which reached the Supreme Court concerned the exercise of the emergency powers of the commission. The Act of

[159] Alabama etc. Ry. Co. *v.* Jackson etc. Ry. Co., 271 U. S. 244 (1926).

[160] A district court and the Supreme Court denied application for injunction to restrain enforcement of the order. The contention of the carriers that this was in effect a requirement for through routes and joint rates which could only be made upon a finding of public necessity the Supreme Court held without merit, since the order left the steam carriers free to remove the discrimination by abandoning the cooperation among themselves. The carriers also contended that the circumstances were different as between the steam and electric carriers (the differences being mainly of size), but the court held that it would not "substitute its judgment for that of the commission" and that the differentiating circumstances were not such as to negative the discrimination. The assertion that to allow connection would give the electric carrier part of their business and thereby deprive them of their property without due process of law was dismissed as "without merit." Finally, the court refused to consider the contention that the electric line was not engaged in the general transportation of freight as required under the terms of the statute, since the commission had found this fact and the evidence had not been introduced in the judicial proceedings. Chicago etc. Ry. Co. *v.* United States, 270 U. S. 287 (1926).

[161] The carrier secured an injunction against enforcement of the order on the ground that the commission was without authority where the only substantial party to the proceeding was not a carrier but a state. The Supreme Court, however, sustaining the commission, determined that it could make the order at the application of a state or of its own motion, that the order was within the scope of authority of the commission and not impaired by the fact that part of the commerce affected was intrastate. United States *v.* N. Y. Cent. R. Co., 272 U. S. 457 (1926).

[162] The commission found the connection practicable, safe, and commercially justifiable. In contesting the action of the commission, the carrier presented novel interpretations of the Interstate Commerce Act — chiefly the failure of Congress to prescribe specifically for the instant case. The order was sustained in a district court and the Supreme Court found the evidence sufficient and the authority under the amended statutes ample. Dering Coal Co. *v.* Cleveland etc. Ry. Co., 275 U. S. 404 (1928).

1920 confers upon the commission certain summary powers — authority to issue in some cases orders "with or without notice, hearing, or the making or filing of a report," if it finds that an emergency exists. The commission was reversed in an attempt to use the emergency power to handle a threatened situation in the normal course of transportation.[163]

Car Service. Excluding decisions involving the primary jurisdiction of the commission,[164] a series of cases involving the supply of cars for coal mines reached the Supreme Court. In the distribution of cars to mines, the commission had for years prescribed rules as it was authorized to do. During the war period a new rule was put in force and was continued after the termination of federal control. The original rule favored mines so located that they enjoyed the facilities of two or more carriers. The substituted rule made the situation of "local" and "joint" mines more nearly equal in that the demands of either type of mine were limited to the same proportion of cars (based upon the tonnage shipped by each mine). The order of the commission was sustained in the Supreme Court.[165]

[163] A carrier had been accustomed, in the interchange of traffic, to switch with its own equipment over its own property the freight received from another line. It threatened to discontinue this service because payment demanded therefor had been refused. The commission ordered the service continued. The carrier contested the order on the ground that it was not a proper exercise of the emergency power. The commission was sustained in the lower court, but the Supreme Court determined that the emergency power of the commission did not justify the order since no general emergency power was granted and the particular instance was not included within the enumeration in the statutes. Peoria etc. Ry. Co. *v.* United States, 263 U. S. 528 (1924).

[164] Midland Valley R. Co. *v.* Barkley, 276 U. S. 482 (1928). An action in a state court for alleged discrimination in furnishing cars to coal mines during a shortage was held to involve a determination of reasonableness and require "the exercise of the regulating function of the Commission."

[165] Mines located on two or more lines sought to have the prior rule reinstated and the "local" mines resisted the change. The commission concluded to continue the new rule. A district court reversed the commission, but the Supreme Court determined that on the facts the order of the commission was "not so arbitrary or unreasonable as to transcend the power conferred upon it." One judge dissented on the ground that the removal of differences or advantages of location constituted a deprivation of property without due process of law. United States *v.* New River Co., 265 U. S. 533 (1924).

The second case to reach the Supreme Court on this subject was a criminal proceeding for fraudulently inducing carriers to transport coal in violation of an order of the commission (issued under emergency powers) requiring coal cars furnished mines in certain order according to the purposes for which the coal was to be used. The Supreme Court transferred the case to a circuit court

Then, after long investigation and experiment, the commission revised the assignment of cars to coal mines and ordered the abandonment of the previous system of assignment on the ground that it was discriminatory. The change was made to improve the service and prevent particular mines (including those operated by railroads) from securing, at a particular time, more than their rateable share of the aggregate coal transportation facilities. Under the former system, mines which owned cars or for whom cars for their individual use had been set aside by the carriers had an advantage over mines depending upon a proportional share of the unassigned cars of the carriers. Under the new rule ordered by the commission, all mines were to receive a proportional share of the total cars irrespective of assignment or ownership. Again the commission was sustained.[166] Thus, after long administrative experimentation, the efforts of the commission to regulate the troublesome matter of coal car supply were completely successful before the Supreme Court.

Through Routes. In contests over orders involving through routes, the commission was successful in the Supreme Court in establishing through routes for express [167] but was reversed in the

of appeals on the ground that the constitutional issues — deprivation of property, interference with state powers, and grant of preference to the ports of one state over those of another — were frivolous, and the circuit court of appeals sustained the order as within the emergency powers conferred by the Act of 1920. Avent *v.* United States, 266 U. S. 127 (1924); Id., 15 F.(2d) 616 (1926).

[166] A district court restrained enforcement of the order of the commission, but on appeal the commission was sustained. The Supreme Court found no objection to the order on constitutional grounds since Congress could exclude private cars from interstate railroads or prescribe conditions under which they could be used and could prescribe how carrier-owned cars be used, and further since the order of the commission had not diverted the private cars of one shipper to use by another because the owner could use the surplus elsewhere or lease the surplus. The statutory authority of the order was found ample. The order — particularly attacked because of its general application — was found not unreasonable or arbitrary on the evidence and in light of the problem and history of attempts to discover a proper rule to remove discriminations and provide adequate service. The court found that the order was not invalid as an attempt to equalize industrial fortune and opportunity. One judge dissented, taking "a temperate and dependable statement concerning the scope and effect of the order" from the brief of counsel attacking the order and referring to "the carefully-prepared opinion of the court below," on the ground that the action of the commission was an unwarranted interference with the private management of railroads. Assigned Car Cases, 274 U. S. 564 (1927).

[167] The larger of the two railway express companies serving the United States refused to establish through routes and joint rates at all points served

attempt, as the Supreme Court thought, to assist a weaker railroad by establishing through routes over its lines.[168]

by either or both of the companies. Instead, it limited its concurrence to routes between the exclusive points of one company and the points exclusively served by the other, thus attempting (since it was the larger company) to secure for itself the entire haul or the longest possible haul on most express. The commission ordered the establishment of some of the through routes originally asked by the smaller company and shippers. A district court held the order void on the ground that the authority of the commission to establish through routes applied, in the words of the statute, only to "carriers by railroad," in which class, the court determined, express companies were not included. But the Supreme Court pointed out that this limitation was contained in a proviso in the statute and that the granting clause conferred authority broadly to include all carriers — hence, the limiting proviso was applicable to railroads only but the general authority applied to all carriers. To exempt express companies, said the court, would be to preserve the existing monopoly of the American Express Company and deprive the commission of power to foster the competition found necessary to secure such service. The court also determined that the through routes might be established although existing transportation was adequate. Here again, legislation following an earlier adverse decision of the Supreme Court aided in interpretation. The evidence before the commission indicating the desirability of the order — chiefly the stimulus of competition — was found sufficient. The complaint of the express company against allowing the shipper to choose his route was found insufficient because, among other things, to give the shipper "the privilege of directing the routing is a corollary of the establishment of competitive routes." United States *v.* Am. Ry. Exp. Co., 265 U. S. 425 (1924).

[168] The carrier had not been able to earn dividends and had long sought to increase earnings by having its line made a part of through routes for interstate traffic not beginning or ending thereon. The commission held numerous hearings, made different determinations, and finally a majority of the commissioners approved the establishment of the through route with a saving proviso to prevent violation of the long-and-short-haul section of the Interstate Commerce Act. A district court restrained enforcement of the commission's order and the Supreme Court affirmed the decision thus reversing the commission. The opinion of the Supreme Court pointed out that the commission had not found that traffic could be handled more advantageously over the proposed new through routes, that the statutes do not give the commission authority to establish all the through routes it might believe necessary or desirable in the public interest since there is a proviso against short-hauling a carrier. This limitation on the power of the commission was inserted to preserve to each carrier the long hauls on its own line; through routes were not to be established which would thereby provide a shorter way over connecting carriers and thereby deprive a railroad of its customary traffic. The commission sought to avoid conflict with this limitation on its authority by providing in the order that the through routes should not apply to traffic originating on or received by the larger carrier who had resisted the order; but this, the court said, was insufficient to protect the carrier's long haul. Materials from the legislative

Abandonment. Aside from those decisions involving the primary jurisdiction of the commission [169] or the proper interest of parties to contest orders,[170] orders involving abandonment of railroad lines reached the Supreme Court in two instances. In the first case the commission authorized abandonment of a line wholly within the State of Texas, but the Supreme Court limited the order to permit abandonment of interstate carriage only; [171] and in the second case the commission's authorization for abandonment of a spur in the State of Colorado was sustained on the ground that its continued maintenance was a burden upon interstate commerce.[172]

history offered by the commission in construction of the statute were rejected on the familiar ground that "where the language of an enactment is clear and construction according to its terms does not lead to absurd or impracticable consequences, the words employed are to be taken as the final expression of the meaning intended." (But then the court proceeded to say that legislative history, in fact, supported their interpretation.) Similarly, legislative acceptance of administrative construction was rejected by the court, and the court refused to be bound by asserted administrative practice and precedents and denied the existence of such settled course of administrative procedure. United States *v.* Missouri Pac. R. Co., 278 U. S. 269 (1929). The commission's error in this case was the attempt to relieve a financially distressed carrier and thereby provide for the much-mentioned "adequate railway service for the people of the United States."

169 *Supra*, n. 121.

170 Pittsburgh etc. Ry. Co. *v.* United States, 281 U. S. 479 (1930).

171 The carrier had originally served an extensive lumber industry but the timber had been removed and mills dismantled. Of the remaining business of the road, three-fourths was interstate. The State of Texas sought to have the certificate of the commission set aside. The proceeding was dismissed in a district court, but on appeal the Supreme Court restricted the scope of the order. The Supreme Court, limiting itself to interpretation of the authority of the commission, determined that while the abandonment of interstate carriage might be authorized the commission had no power to allow abandonment of purely state carriage. The practical effect of this decision is to subject the carrier to the duty of continuing operation merely because of incidental state business unless released by state authority. State of Texas *v.* United States, 258 U. S. 204 (1922). See: State of Texas *v.* Eastern etc., 264 U. S. 49 (1924).

172 An interstate railroad was granted permission to abandon a spur which was located entirely within the State of Colorado. The state contested the order, but both in the district court and on appeal the commission was sustained. The Supreme Court determined that federal authorities could authorize the abandonment of the state spur if it were found to be a burden upon the interstate service of the carrier and consequently upon interstate commerce as a whole. "Congress has power to authorize abandonment because the State's power to regulate and promote intrastate commerce may not be exercised in such a way as to prejudice interstate commerce." The evidence and findings were held sufficient. State of Colorado *v.* United States, 271 U. S. 153 (1926).

Finance. In the regulation of financial transactions of carriers, "exclusive and plenary" authority over which was given the commission by the legislation of 1920, only one case reached the Supreme Court during the decade and the proceeding was dismissed for failure to institute the suit properly.[173]

Consolidation of Carriers and Acquisition of Control. The single decision on consolidation of carriers under the new legislation furnishes no satisfactory statement of the law.[174] Judicial exposition of the law regarding acquisition of control of carriers by other carriers is hardly more satisfactory. In one case the commission was reversed on the pleadings,[175] and a second was dismissed for failure to institute proceedings in the proper judicial district.[176]

[173] Venner *v.* N. Y. Cent. R. Co., 271 U. S. 127 (1926). For the commission's functions in connection with reorganizations see: Jacobs, *The Interstate Commerce Commission and Interstate Railroad Reorganization*, 45 Harv. L. Rev. 855 (1932).

[174] A state supreme court held that a consolidation of carriers without permission of the Interstate Commerce Commission was permissible. The court felt that while the statute gives the commission authority to approve and authorize acquisitions of control, yet "when taken in connection with other paragraphs of that section, it must be construed as only prohibiting the commission from giving its approval to any consolidation prior to the adoption of a complete plan (as provided in the act), but not as prohibiting the voluntary consolidation of carriers under state laws." The United States Supreme Court, in a one-sentence memorandum opinion, affirmed the decision on the ground that the amended Interstate Commerce Act "has not as yet been made applicable to cases like this." Snyder *v.* N. Y. etc. R. Co., 118 Ohio St. 72, 160 N. E. 615, 619 (1928); Id., 278 U. S. 578 (1929). On the general subject see: Simpson, *The Interstate Commerce Commission and Railroad Consolidation*, 43 Harv. L. Rev. 192, 244–249.

[175] The commission had authorized the lease of a junction railroad by another and purchase of control of the latter by a third railway system. A suit to set aside the order was dismissed in a district court but the Supreme Court reversed the lower court on the pleadings — lack of evidence to support the finding of public interest had been one of the grounds on which the order was attacked and this was not denied in the commission's motion to dismiss the suit. The court also held the order reviewable as an affirmative order or one not wholly within the discretion of the commission, and further determined that protesting carriers, who were competitors using the terminal road in dispute, were entitled to challenge the order. Three justices dissented on the ground that the contesting carriers were without legal standing to protest the order. The commission thereupon, after hearing, modified one of the conditions in the original report, and the judicial proceeding was dismissed on motion of the contesting carriers. Baltimore etc. R. Co. *v.* United States, 264 U. S. 258 (1924); Id., Dist. Ct. N. D. Ill., January 15, 1929.

[176] Home Furniture Co. *v.* United States, 271 U. S. 456 (1926).

Valuation and Reparation Orders. In the review of those orders of the commission thus far considered, the statute is silent on the weight to be given the determinations of the commission. But in two classes of orders — valuation and reparation — the statute provides that the orders of the commission shall be *prima facie* evidence in the courts.

Valuation. Valuation of carriers may, for the purposes of this study, be considered in three stages — tentative valuations, final valuations, and the use of final valuations for the purposes of regulation. The statute provides that before a valuation shall become final the carrier shall be given notice and opportunity for protest and hearing.[177] The final values as fixed by the commission are to be "*prima facie* evidence of the value of the property in all proceedings" under the Interstate Commerce Act "and in all judicial proceedings for the enforcement" of the act "and in all judicial proceedings brought to enjoin, set aside, annul, or suspend, in whole or in part, any order of the Interstate Commerce Commission." [178] (If, upon the trial of any action involving a final value fixed by the commission, evidence is introduced which is found by the court to be different from that offered at the hearing before the commission "or additional thereto and substantially affecting" the final valuation fixed by the commission, before the court may render judgment the commission must be given an opportunity to consider the new evidence, and if it desires, to modify its original order.[179]) These provisions have been judicially compared to reparation orders — as only establishing "a rebuttable presumption," cutting off "no defense," interposing "no obstacle to a full contestation of all the issues," taking "no question of fact from either court or jury," and being "at most . . . merely a rule of evidence." [180]

The Supreme Court refused to review a tentative, unreported valuation on the ground that it was "no more than an *ex parte* appraisement without probative effect," and held that a suit to set

[177] Interstate Commerce Act, Sec. 19a (h) and (i).

[178] Idem, Sec. 19a (i).

[179] Idem, Sec. 19a (j).

[180] United States *v.* Los Angeles etc. R. Co., 273 U. S. 299, 311 (1927). In determining that these provisions are no violation of the due process clause, the Supreme Court compared valuation orders with reparation orders and quoted from a prior decision involving reparation orders. See also: U. S. ex. rel. St. Louis etc. R. Co. *v.* I. C. C., 264 U. S. 64, 77 (1924).

it aside would not lie in absence of willful disregard of the law.[181] The courts also refused to interfere when the commission reopened a tentative valuation for reconsideration of items not protested by the carrier.[182] In another litigation the Supreme Court compelled the commission to consider certain evidence which the commission, on the ground of impracticability, had refused to examine.[183] After the commission had corrected the tentative figures, the carriers sought to compel the commission to consider still further evidence, but this the courts refused.[184] The carriers then appealed from the

[181] A carrier sought to have set aside the tentative figures, against which it had filed a protest on the ground that there was not full compliance with the provisions of the statute. The petition was dismissed in a district court and the Supreme Court also sustained the commission. The statute authorizes protest and hearing on tentative valuations; this administrative remedy, the court held, must be exhausted and final action taken by the commission before the valuation is reviewable. Delaware etc. Co. *v.* United States, 266 U. S. 438 (1925).

[182] The carrier brought suit to annul the commission's order reopening the valuation. The carrier's objection to other items of the tentative valuation had been filed and the protest was still pending. A district court dismissed the proceeding on the ground that jurisdiction to enjoin an order of the commission includes only those which compel "the doing or abstaining from doing acts embraced by a previous affirmative command of the commission" and does not include "orders relating to practice or procedure." That is, the district court confined jurisdiction to a review of orders making changes in tentative valuations and excluding orders, such as here involved, which merely reopen the matter. The Supreme Court, in a memorandum opinion, affirmed the decision. New York etc. Ry. Co. *v.* United States, 273 U. S. 652 (1927).

[183] The carrier sought to compel the commission to consider evidence on the present cost of condemnation and damages, or of purchase. This had been the ground of a protest by the carrier against the tentative valuation, but the commission had declaimed to modify the tentative figures. The courts of the District of Columbia denied the petition, but the United States Supreme Court reversed the lower courts and granted the request of the carrier. The statute provided for consideration of the evidence. For refusal to follow the words of the statute the commission was reversed and the lower courts were directed to compel the commission to consider the evidence. United States ex rel. Kansas City S. R. Co. *v.* I. C. C., 252 U. S. 178 (1920).

[184] The commission corrected the valuation in conformity with the first decision of the Supreme Court, and then the carriers sought to compel the commission to fix and report exchange values, to supplement analyses of methods, to report — aside from valuation — other values or elements of value, to estimate original cost to date, and to include in the value of properties certain values represented by ownership of capital stock and a trackage right. The courts of the District of Columbia again denied the petition of the carrier, and this time the Supreme Court sustained the lower courts and the commission

final valuation order, but in the meantime the Supreme Court had determined that final valuation orders were not subject to review until actually used in ordering some affirmative action such as fixing rates, and accordingly the commission's order was not disturbed.[185] The first and only case during the decade in which the validity of a final valuation order was determined by the Supreme Court also involved the administrative exercise of authority to recover excess earnings from a carrier under new provisions of the Act of 1920. In the investigations which led to an order for the recapture of excess earnings, the final valuation of the carrier as previously fixed by the commission was used to determine fair return. In reviewing the order the Supreme Court determined that the commission acted in excess of its authority since it had not given (in the words of the statute) "the consideration to all the elements of value recognized by the law of the land for rate-making

by refusing to review the case. United States ex rel. Kansas City S. R. Co. *v.* I. C. C., 269 U. S. 570 (1925).

[185] Pending appeal from a decision of a district court annulling the final valuation, the Supreme Court handed down its decision in the *San Pedro Valuation Case* and upon the basis of this intervening decision the Supreme Court, in a memorandum opinion, reversed the district court and sustained the commission. United States *v.* Kansas City R. Co., 275 U. S. 500 (1927).

In the *San Pedro Case* the objections urged in the suit to set aside the final valuation order were practically the same as those in the *Kansas City Case.* The Supreme Court found it unnecessary to examine these objections to final valuation orders because, it determined, orders of the commission fixing final valuation were not subject to review since they are not affirmative orders. Final valuation orders were characterized as "the exercise solely of the function of investigation." As a practical matter, the court pointed out that "errors may be made in the final valuation of the property of each of the nearly 1800 carriers" thus making for an enormous volume of litigation while it was "at least possible that no proceeding . . . ever be instituted, either before the Commission or a court, in which the matters . . . complained of [would] be involved or in which the errors alleged [would] be of legal significance." The fact that final valuations were to be *prima facie* evidence of the value of the property in all proceedings under the statutes was held no violation of the due process clause, additional evidence might be introduced if and when the valuation were used, and the arguments that false or improper valuations might mislead the public or the commission were held unpersuasive. "The investigation was undertaken in aid of the legislative purpose of regulation. In conducting the investigation, and in making the report, the Commission performed a service specifically delegated and prescribed by Congress. Its conclusions, if erroneous in law, may be disregarded. But neither its utterances, nor its processes of reasoning, as distinguished from its acts, are subject for injunction." United States *v.* Los Angeles etc. R. Co., 273 U. S. 299 (1927).

purposes." Briefly, the legislative reference to "the law of the land" was held to incorporate into the statute the prior decisions of the Supreme Court on the ascertainment of value; the commission refused to accept one element of value included in the much criticized judicial "rule" (reproduction cost), and therefore — although the court held that the weight to be accorded this element was not involved — in refusing to consider it at all the commission exceeded its authority.[186]

Reparation Orders. The statutory provisions for enforcement of orders of the commission finding damages due shippers because of

[186] The three-judge district court, to whom a petition to enjoin the order of the commission was first addressed, held that it was unnecessary to examine the correctness of the commission's valuation or method of ascertaining value because, taking the value asserted by the carrier, the return allowed was not confiscatory under a prior opinion of the Supreme Court. On appeal the Supreme Court sustained the lower court in its ruling on the matter of interest on the recaptured fund and in the ruling that earnings were recapturable even though the commission had not yet fixed a general level of rates but reversed the commission on the valuation. "The report of the Commission is long and argumentative. Much of it is devoted to general observations relative to the method and purpose of making valuations; many objections are urged to doctrine approved by us; and the superiority of another view is stoutly asserted. It carefully refrains from stating that any consideration whatever was given to present or reproduction costs in estimating the value of the carrier's property. Four dissenting Commissioners declare that reproduction costs were not considered; and the report itself confirms their view. Two of the majority avow a like understanding of the course pursued." ". . . This Court has declared the law of the land concerning valuations for rate-making purposes. The Commission disregarded the approved rule and has thereby failed to discharge the definite duty imposed by Congress." The lower court had determined that the recapture order of the commission did not deny a fair return on the investment and was therefore valid. With this limited view of the scope of judicial control the Supreme Court did not agree: "Whether the Commission acted as directed by Congress was the fundamental question presented. If it did not, the action taken, being beyond the authority granted, was invalid." The decision of the court, from which three justices dissented, is a demand for formal administration — for an ostensible examination of the judicially-established "elements of value" reckoned on different bases. Instead of reviewing the actual order (its effect, arbitrariness, or failure to allow a fair return) the majority of the court seize upon the reasoning of the commission (which was brought into relief by the opinions of the dissenting commissioners) and find therein evidence not of arbitrary or confiscatory action but of failure to follow, formally, the judicial "rule" for determining value. The commission was not guilty of willful action; the difficulties encountered by the commissioners in the conscientious administration of the law are made the basis for annulling the order of the commission. St. Louis etc. Ry. Co. *v.* United States, 279 U. S. 461 (1929).

illegal charges by carriers differ in two important respects from the enforcement of orders so far considered. In the first place, the orders do not become binding when made by the commission but must be enforced through the courts (like the orders of the Federal Trade Commission), and secondly, it is provided in the act that in judicial proceedings for the enforcement of reparation orders the "findings and order of the Commission shall be *prima facie* evidence of the facts therein stated." (As with the Federal Trade Commission, the emphasis is on the "facts" but the findings of the Interstate Commerce Commission are given only *prima facie* effect while those of the trade commission are to be "conclusive" in the courts.) The provision that reparation orders be given *prima facie* effect on proceedings for judicial award of damages has been described by the courts as only establishing "a rebuttable presumption. It cuts off no defense, interposes no obstacle to a full contestation of all the issues, and takes no question of fact from either court or jury. At most therefore it is merely a rule of evidence." [187] And the trial in the district courts has been characterized as *de novo*. [188] However, in a case where the trial court has before it only the record upon which the commission acted, the Supreme Court has held that the findings of the commission, from which the existence of interstate commerce was apparent, ought to be accepted by the trial courts "as conclusive" where there is "ample evidence" to sustain them.[189]

Aside from the refusal of the courts to compel the commission to exercise its discretion and make awards of reparation [190] and excluding those decisions which involve only procedure or jurisdiction in the narrower sense,[191] six reparation orders came before the

[187] Meeker *v.* Lehigh Valley R. Co., 236 U. S. 412, 430, 431 (1915), quoted in United States *v.* Los Angeles etc. R. Co., 273 U. S. 299, 311 (1927).

[188] Montrose Oil Refining Co. *v.* St. Louis-San Francisco Ry. Co., 25 F.(2d) 750, 754 (1927) ("The case is here de novo . . ."), *affirmed* 25 F.(2d) 755 (1928), *certiorari denied*, 277 U. S. 598.

[189] United States *v.* Erie R. Co., 280 U. S. 98, 102 (1929). But compare the doctrine of Crowell *v.* Benson, 52 S. Ct. 285 (1932) in which in other fields a trial *de novo* is said to be a constitutional right. And see: Manufacturers R. Co. *v.* United States, 246 U. S. 457, 488–490 (1918).

[190] In two instances the courts refused to interfere with the commission's denial of reparation. Donner Steel Co. *v.* I. C. C., 8 F.(2d) 905 (1925), *certiorari denied* 270 U. S. 651; Bartlesville Zinc Co. *v.* I. C. C., 30 F.(2d) 479 (1929), *certiorari denied* 279 U. S. 856.

[191] Danzer & Co. *v.* Gulf etc. R. Co., 268 U. S. 633 (1925) (statute of limitations); News Syndicate *v.* N. Y. etc. R. Co., 275 U. S. 179 (1927) (authority

Supreme Court during the decade. In three cases where parties sought to avoid administrative action by simply criticizing the administrative process and reasoning the commission was sustained.[192] Another award of reparation was sustained on the basis of the administrative findings, the construction of the contract of sale between the consignor and consignees, and commercial practice.[193] One order of the commission arising out of the wartime

of the commission over rates from foreign countries). And see: Jeanneret *v.* Chicago etc. R. Co., 17 F.(2d) 978, *certiorari denied* 275 U. S. 531.

[192] In the first case, on suit for enforcement of the order awarding reparation the defendants offered no evidence but sought, instead, to defend on the ground that the order was unlawful on its face, alleging that no right to recovery was shown. Jurisdiction of the court and of the parties was also attacked. None of these contentions found favor with the lower federal courts. The circuit court of appeals, after referring to the *prima facie* effect to be given the order of the commission, held that "the defendants are not permitted to destroy this *prima facie* effect by internal criticisms of the commission's findings." The judgment was affirmed on appeal to the Supreme Court. Vicksburg etc. *v.* Anderson etc. Co., 256 U. S. 408 (1921).

In another case where a shipper sought to enforce the award in a district court and the carrier introduced no new evidence but relied upon criticisms of the commission's procedure, reasoning, and authority, a district court found substantial evidence in the orders of the commission, no defect in procedure or excess of authority, and enforced the commission's award of reparation. The circuit court of appeals affirmed the decision without comment, and the Supreme Court refused to review the case. St. Louis etc. Ry. *v.* Montrose Oil etc. Co., 25 F.(2d) 755 (1928), *certiorari denied* 277 U. S. 598.

In the last case on reparation orders to reach the Supreme Court during the decade the commission had determined that rates were unreasonable and awarded reparation. A district court refused to enforce part of the order of the commission on the ground that the shipments involved were intrastate and not subject to the commission's jurisdiction, but the Supreme Court sustained the commission. The proceedings in the lower courts had taken place on the record of the commission, and the Supreme Court determined that the findings of the commission, from which the existence of interstate commerce was apparent, "ought to have been accepted by the district court as conclusive, since there was ample evidence to sustain it." United States *v.* Erie R. Co., 280 U. S. 98 (1929).

[193] The commission awarded reparation for excessive freight charges. In the district court some facts were stipulated by the parties, the court appointed an auditor to examine others, witnesses testified, the proceedings and orders of the commission were introduced in evidence, jury trial was waived, and the court allowed the damages awarded by the commission except for part of the period. The circuit court of appeals granted enforcement of the order of the commission in full. The case was then taken to the Supreme Court. The contention that interest was improperly allowed for the period prior to the final award by the commission was also rejected on the basis of the practice of the

transportation tangle was reversed,[194] and another was reversed upon a complicated interpretation of the proceedings and of the statutory provisions.[195]

The necessity of revising the statutes governing reparations was

commission as sustained without question in other decisions before the Supreme Court and because of the nature of the recovery allowed in reparation cases. Two justices dissented. Louisville etc. R. Co. *v.* Sloss-Sheffield etc. Co., 269 U. S. 217 (1925).

[194] Wartime embargoes on interstate shipments of some commodities were responsible for this litigation, which culminated in 1929. The commission granted reparation for what it deemed unlawfully assessed demurrage charges. While embargoes on lumber from initial and reconsignment points were in effect in eastern markets, a shipper with knowledge of the situation consigned lumber to reconsignment points and then reconsigned to embargo points. The tariffs of the carriers contained no provision against reconsignment embargo points and, for that reason, the commission determined that the carriers were without authority to assess and collect demurrage charges for detention at points of reconsignment. The carriers urged the commission that the intent of the shipper was to evade the embargoes, but the shipper disclaimed any such intention and asserted that at the time of making the original shipments it did not know the final destinations. In the judicial proceedings for enforcement of the order, the records of the proceedings before the commission were introduced and some facts were stipulated. The lower courts (on motions for directed verdicts) determined that the shipper had intended his goods for one of the embargo points and that the demurrage charges (which had not been attacked as unreasonable) for detention at reconsignment points were properly applicable; they therefore refused to enforce the commission's award and the Supreme Court refused to review the decision. The lower courts substituted their judgment for that of the commission and the Supreme Court (the case had been before it on a point of procedure previously — 276 U. S. 389) did not interfere a second time. Krauss Bros. Lbr. Co. *v.* Milleon, 30 F.(2d) 901 (1929), *certiorari denied* 279 U. S. 872.

[195] The commission had awarded reparation and also established proper rates. The lower courts, variously interpreting the order of the commission, rendered judgment on demurrers and denied enforcement. In the Supreme Court the shipper sought to sustain the award of reparation on the basis of the long-and-short-haul and aggregate-of-intermediaries provisions. The court construed the order of the commission as finding that timely application had been made for the suspension of these provisions (which suspension was within the authority of the commission and which had the effect of protecting the rates from the operation of the provisions relied upon for damages), but that relief had been granted on the ground that the rates were (in the words of the order) "unreasonable in and to the extent that they respectively exceeded the aggregate of the intermediate rates." Since the shipper asserted his claim on the basis of the provisions of the act which were suspended by proper applications to the commission, reparation was denied. Patterson *v.* Louisville etc. R. Co., 269 U. S. 1 (1925).

pointed out by the commission as far back as 1916. The matter was extensively discussed in 1919, the recommendations were repeated in 1920 and 1922, outlined at length in 1930, and repeated in 1931.[196] The difficulties arise from the statutory development and interpretation, abuses of the reparation provisions by shippers, and the drain upon the time and energies of the commission needed for the broader aspects of regulation.

The Courts and the Commission since 1930. Since the close of the 1920–1930 decade the orders of the commission have come before the courts in a number of cases. Aside from those decisions involving the nature of carriage subject to the act,[197] federal control,[198] and non-reviewable orders,[199] further decisions do not indicate a different course of judicial control,[200] although some decisions

[196] Ann. Rep., 1916, pp. 75–78; 1919, pp. 17–21, 53; 1920, p. 78; 1921, p. 58; 1930, pp. 90-93, 98; 1931, pp. 93–94, 121.

[197] United States *v.* Munson Steamship Co., 283 U. S. 43 (1931).

[198] United States ex rel. Empire etc. Ry. Co. *v.* I. C. C., 45 F.(2d) 293 (1931), *certiorari denied* 283 U. S. 834.

[199] Standard Oil Co. *v.* U. S., 283 U. S. 235 (Apr. 13, 1931); Brady *v.* U. S., 283 U. S. 804 (May 18, 1931); Southern etc. Co. *v.* I. C. C., 283 U. S. 850, *denying certiorari* to 47 F.(2d) 411 (May 18, 1931); United States *v.* Atlanta etc. R. Co., 282 U. S. 522 (Feb. 24, 1931).

[200] Orders of the commission fixing interstate rates were sustained in one instance: Akron etc. R. Co. *v.* United States, 52 S. Ct. 26 (1931). And in another, for failure to reopen the investigation in view of changed economic circumstances (the depression), reversed: Atchison etc. Ry. *v.* United States, 52 S. Ct. 146 (1932). Orders removing discriminations due to state rates were sustained in three instances: Georgia Public Service Comm. *v.* United States, 283 U. S. 765 (1931); State of Alabama *v.* United States, 283 U. S. 776 (1931); State of Louisiana *v.* United States, 52 S. Ct. 74 (1931); and in a fourth reversed for "lack of basic or essential findings": State of Florida *v.* United States, 282 U. S. 149 (1931). An order directing carriers to discontinue the practice of moving private passenger train cars, including the so-called office cars of other carriers, free or at other than published tariff rates was sustained: Louisville etc. R. Co. *v.* United States, 282 U. S. 740 (1931); Kansas City etc. R. Co. *v.* United States, 282 U. S. 760 (1931). Orders permitting construction or abandonment were sustained: Chesapeake etc. Ry. Co. *v.* United States, 283 U. S. 35 (1931); Transit Commission of N. Y. *v.* United States, 52 S. Ct. 157 (1932). And see: Western Pacific etc. R. Co. *v.* Southern Pac. Co., 52 S. Ct. 56 (1931). An order removing discriminations in allowances to warehouse companies was sustained: Merchants Warehouse Co. *v.* United States, 283 U. S. 501 (1931). One reparation order was sustained: Lewis-Simas-Jones Co. *v.* Southern Pac. Co, 283 U. S. 654 (1931). Two reparation orders were reversed: Great Northern Ry. Co. *v.* Delmar Co., 283 U. S. 686 (1931); Arizona Grocery Co. *v.* Atchison etc. Ry. Co., 52 S. Ct. 183 (1932). A condition prescribing through routing, which the condition made one of the terms of approval of a

may be noted which indicate judicial interference rather than control.[201]

VI. Conclusion

Notwithstanding those instances in which judicial control has become judicial interference, the career of the commission in the courts since 1920 has been a continuation of the previous sympathetic (particularly as compared with the Federal Trade Commission) relationship — extending through the difficulties of interpreting and administering a new legislative policy and a revised body of statutes. Pressure upon the commission has come from other departments of government than the judiciary,[202] and the fact that attempts to bring outside influence to bear are the subject of strong public criticism speaks well for the popular estimation and independent political position of the agency to which the regulation of the national transportation system is entrusted. However, the

lease of carriers, was sustained: Atlantic Coast Line R. Co. *v.* United States, 52 S. Ct. 171 (1932).

[201] For example, in giving approval to the financial plan for reorganization of a transcontinental railway the commission attempted to retain authority over a special fund set up to compensate reorganization managers and committees; the Supreme Court's opinion played gently on the general theme of delegation of power and due process of law, insisted upon treating this special fund as one "created by contract between private persons to which the carrier was not a party," — "a transaction distinct and complete in itself without regard to its results" and "subject to the sole control of private persons," — and joined with the lower court in denying authority to the commission. Chicago etc. R. Co. *v.* United States, 282 U. S. 311 (1931). But see the different treatment of a condition in Atlantic Coast Line R. Co. *v.* United States, 52 S. Ct. 171 (1932).

In another case a portion of an order of the commission regulating charges for foreign freight cars after a nation-wide investigation was annulled — allowances of time and exemptions for certain kinds of coal cars allowed short line carriers and to which trunk lines objected were declared arbitrary; this was done (so far as appears from the opinion) on abstract grounds and without examination of the great mass of evidence from which the reasonableness of the order was apparent — in fact the court substituted its judgment for both that of the commission and the lower court. Chicago etc. Ry. Co. *v.* United States, 52 S. Ct. 87 (1931). In a third instance the commission's division of joint rates was set aside for failure to specify the future date upon which it should take effect (an intervening decision of the Supreme Court complicated the situation); with abrupt technicality the court refused to allow the obvious and statutory date to operate. United States *v.* Baltimore etc. R. R. Co., 52 S. Ct. 109 (1931).

[202] See: Sharfman, *The Interstate Commerce Commission* (1931), II, 452–476.

sparing control of the courts is undoubtedly one of the more important factors which have made the Interstate Commerce Commission the foremost example of administrative justice in the United States.

As compared with the Federal Trade Commission, the Interstate Commerce Commission is the authoritative governmental agency for the regulation of the national transportation system. Unlike the Federal Trade Commission, other duties — such as investigation and publicity [203] — are a small item. Principles of regulation have been developed by the commission.[204] There is a specialized body of practitioners.[205] The maintenance of established regulation and the process of experimentation in new matters and to meet new conditions, together with a continuation of the administrative policy of advising the Congress through recommendations for legislation [206] — these combined characterize and distinguish the Inter-

[203] There have been some investigations at the instance of Congress or on motion of the commission itself, but not comparable in extent to this feature of the work of the Federal Trade Commission: Ann. Rep. I. C. C., 1907, pp. 21–22; 1912, pp. 38–39; 1914, pp. 3–6; 1915, pp. 3–5; 1916, p. 4; 1917, p. 6; 1918, p. 22; 1920, pp. 38–42; 1921, pp. 29–30; 1923, pp. 30–34; 1924, p. 30; 1925, pp. 32–41; 1926, pp. 36–39; 1927, pp. 67–72; 1928, pp. 63–68; 1929, pp. 69–73; 1930, pp. 61–68.

[204] See for example: Ann. Rep., 1909, p. 4; 1911, p. 1.

[205] See for example: Ann. Rep., 1930, p. 74.

[206] The commission pointed out increasing needs for legislation from 1920 to the close of the decade. In 1923 and 1924 the recommendations of previous years are renewed by reference. Ann. Rep., 1923, p. 70; 1924, p. 78. Twenty pages of the report for 1930 are devoted to a comparatively extensive legislative program. The particular recommendations involve the following: *Bribery of employees:* 1920, pp. 57, 77–78; 1921, p. 58; 1922, p. 75; 1925, p. 71; 1926, p. 76; 1927, p. 79; 1928, p. 81; 1929, p. 88; 1930, p. 95. *Increase in locomotive inspection staff:* 1920, pp. 69, 78; 1921, p. 58; 1922, pp. 22–23, 75; 1923, pp. 3–4; 1924, p. 2. *Transportation of explosives:* 1920, pp. 74–77, 78. *Modification of reparation provisions:* 1920, p. 78; 1921, p. 58; 1930, pp. 90–93, 98. *Steel passenger cars:* 1920, p. 78; 1921, p. 58; 1922, p. 75; 1925, p. 71; 1926, p. 76; 1927, pp. 79–80; 1928, p. 81; 1929, p. 88; 1930, pp. 95–96. *Hours of service:* 1921, p. 58; 1922, pp. 75–76; 1925, pp. 71–72. *Electric railroad securities:* 1921, pp. 21, 58; 1922, p. 76; 1925, p. 72; 1928, pp. 79–81, 83; 1929, p. 89; 1930, p. 96. *Railroad consolidation:* 1921, pp. 18, 58–59; 1922, p. 76; 1925, pp. 13–14; 1925, p. 72; 1926, pp. 76–77; 1927, p. 80; 1928, pp. 81–82; 1929, pp. 87–88; 1930, p. 79. *Clarification of Merchant Marine Act:* 1921, pp. 13–14, 59; 1922, p. 76; 1924, pp. 3–5; 1925, pp. 2, 72–73; 1926, p. 77; 1927, p. 80; 1928, p. 82; 1929, p. 88; 1930, p. 96. *Reports from carriers by water:* 1922, p. 76; 1925, pp. 3, 72. *Installation of safety devices:* 1925, p. 72; 1926, p. 77; 1927, p. 80. *Monthly reports to Congress on equipment:* 1925, pp. 29, 73. *Deficits during federal control,*

state Commerce Commission in its relations to the other branches of the government. It is particularly the cooperation between Congress and the administrative commission which has made regulation effective. The work of the commission is of considerable popular and professional interest,[207] and while criticism of "bureaucratic" regulation still exists — now accentuated by industrial conditions [208] — the commission is an established and authoritative institution.

limitations: 1925, pp. 24–25, 73; 1926, p. 77; 1927, p. 12. *Interstate motor transportation:* 1926, pp. 41–43; 1927, pp. 75–76. *Regulation of holding companies:* 1929, pp. 79–83, 89; 1930, pp. 80, 97. *Recapture provisions:* 1926, pp. 19–20, 77; 1927, p. 80; 1928, p. 82; 1929, p. 88; 1929, p. 88; 1930, pp. 82–90, 96. *Valuation provisions:* 1926, pp. 16–17, 77; 1927, p. 80; 1928, p. 82; 1929, pp. 88, 89–90. *Penalty provisions:* 1928, pp. 16–17, 82; 1929, p. 89; 1930, p. 97. *Loan provisions:* 1929, p. 89. *Tariffs to foreign parts:* 1928, pp. 72–76, 82. *Freight forwarding companies:* 1930, pp. 81–82, 97. *Authority to delegate matters to single commissioners or employees:* 1928, pp. 82–83; 1929, pp. 88–89; 1930, pp. 94–95, 96. *Civil Service classification:* 1928, p. 83. *Long-and-short-haul provisions:* 1928, pp. 79, 89; 1929, pp. 79, 97. *Limitation on recovery of charges:* 1930, p. 97.

[207] See, for example: a series of articles by former commissioner Woodlock, *Impressions of an Ex-Commerce Commissioner*, Barron's, September 29, 1930, p. 10; October 6, 1930, p. 6; October 13, 1930, p. 22; *The Education of a Commissioner*, Barron's, October 27, 1930, p. 10; November 3, 1930, p. 5; November 10, 1930, p. 5; November 17, 1930, p. 5.

[208] For example: *Railroads and I. C. C.*, New York *Times*, June 12, Sec. 2, p. 1. And compare: Railway Age, Vol. 92, No. 13, March 26, 1932, pp. 513–520.

CHAPTER V

COMPARISON AND CONCLUSION

The experience of the two federal commissions concerned with the regulation of trade and commerce reveals differences in operation over the same span of years which are wholly explainable neither by the subject matter nor by the terms of the statutes. The Federal Trade Commission began active administration in 1919, and the Interstate Commerce Commission began the administration of a new legislative policy in 1920. Each commission is an independent establishment within the federal government — that is, each has a measure of freedom from executive or legislative interference. Appointment, supply, and authority, however, must come from the political arms of the government, and the particularized activity of each commission is subject to judicial control.

I. The Differences

Since the object of administrative justice is the establishment of a new regime — or perhaps a new body of law — in some phase of social control, the extent to which this purpose is realized should furnish the basis for critical examination of systems of commission regulation. Herein lies the most striking difference in the net result of the work of the Interstate Commerce Commission and the Federal Trade Commission.

Common-Law Precedents. Some of the legal bases for regulation are to be found in the books of common law or in the judicial decisions of American courts. Perhaps the contrast of the horse-drawn coach with the locomotive of today has been enough to start the development of a new body of law for steam and electric carriers which provide the commercial veins of a continent. The Interstate Commerce Commission has developed a new system of active and authoritative control over the national transportation system. Carriers and shippers are confined in large measure to such relief as the commission affords, while in the field of trade regulation parties are frequently referred to any action they may have at common law or under the Sherman Act. Furthermore, the common law on trade practices has been regarded as limiting the Federal Trade Commission.

Before the Federal Trade Commission was established, three judges who later sat in the Supreme Court of the United States, in denying relief, said: "We find no . . . authority in the books, and are clear in the opinion that . . . the remedy must come from the legislature, and not from the courts." [1] In one of the earlier instances of judicial review of an order of the Federal Trade Commission a circuit court of appeals quoted this judicial statement as illustrating "the reason which led Congress to enact the statute creating the Federal Trade Commission and making unfair methods of competition unlawful and empowering the commission to put an end to them." [2] The first court to review an order of the commission took the view that the commissioners were to develop regulation "quite irrespective of whether the specific practices in question have yet been denounced in common law cases." [3] But the leading decision of the Supreme Court denies change: The words "unfair method of competition," says the court, are "clearly inapplicable to practices never heretofore regarded as opposed to good morals because characterized by deception, bad faith, fraud or oppression, or as against public policy because of their dangerous tendency unduly to hinder competition or to create monopoly. The act was certainly not intended to fetter free and fair competition *as commonly understood and practiced* by honorable opponents in trade." [4] In effect, the Federal Trade Commission has been limited to pre-existing law, and many of the decisions — particu-

[1] Taft, Lurton, and Day, JJ., in American Washboard Co. *v.* Saginaw Mfg. Co., 103 Fed. 281, 286 (1900).

[2] Royal Baking Powder Co. *v.* Federal Trade Commission, 281 Fed. 744, 751–752 (1922).

[3] "The commissioners, representing the government as *parens patriae*, are to exercise their common sense, as informed by their knowledge of the general idea of unfair trade at common law, and stop all those trade practices that have a capacity or a tendency to injure competitors directly or through deception of purchasers, quite irrespective of whether the specific practices in question have yet been denounced in common law cases." Sears, Roebuck & Co. *v.* Federal Trade Commission, 258 Fed. 307, 311 (1919).

[4] Federal Trade Commission *v.* Gratz, 253 U. S. 421, 427–428 (1920). Italics inserted. And compare the opinion of a circuit court of appeals in which an order of the commission condemning entertainment of buying agents as commercial bribery was set aside on the ground that the practice had "been an incident of business from time immemorial." New Jersey Asbestos Co. *v.* Federal Trade Commission, 264 Fed. 509, 510–511 (1920).

larly those of the lower federal courts — expressly adhere to common law precedent. It has been held that the trade commission statutes did not change the law but simply set up a commission,[5] that the policy of the Sherman Act is material for interpretation of the legislation of 1914,[6] that the Clayton Act and Federal Trade Commission Act are only supplemental,[7] that the prohibitions apply only to fraudulent practices or acts,[8] that the legislation

[5] "It is not conceived that Congress, which laid down no definition whatever, intended to either limit or extend the matters which constituted unfair methods of competition prior to the passage of the Clayton Act, but that its object was the creation of a board of commissioners. . . ." Kinney-Rome Co. *v.* Federal Trade Commission, 275 Fed. 665, 667–668 (1921).

[6] "The Sherman Act is not involved . . . except in so far as it shows a declaration of public policy, to be considered in determining what are unfair methods of competition, which the Federal Trade Commission is empowered to condemn and suppress." Federal Trade Commission *v.* Beech-Nut Packing Co., 257 U. S. 441, 453 (1922). "Though differing somewhat from other laws . . . the Clayton Act, nevertheless, deals with matters within the realm of monopoly. . . . The only standard of legality with which we are acquainted is the standard established by the Sherman Act in the words 'restraint of trade or commerce' and 'monopolize, or attempt to monopolize,' and by the courts in construing the Sherman Act. . . ." Standard Oil Co. of N. J. *v.* Federal Trade Commission, 282 Fed. 81, 87 (1922). "In determining the meaning of 'unfair methods of competition' within the meaning of the Federal Trade Commission Act, a court must give due consideration to the public policy declared in the Sherman Act." L. B. Silver Co. *v.* Federal Trade Commission, 289 Fed. 985, 990 (1923). But see: "Whether any analogy [between cases under the trade commission acts and the Sherman Act] exists is a matter about which opinion may differ, but the matter is unimportant, unless the fact that a company has violated the Sherman Act . . . is evidence that it has also violated the Federal Trade Commission Act, which is not true." Eastman Kodak Co. *v.* Federal Trade Commission, 7 F.(2d) 994, 995 (1925), *affirmed* 274 U. S. 619.

[7] "The Clayton Act was intended to supplement the Sherman Act, and within its limited sphere established its own rule." Swift & Co. *v.* Federal Trade Commission, 8 F.(2d) 595, 597 (1925), reversed, 272 U. S. 554. But compare: "The Federal Trade Act . . . was intended to reach . . . unfair business methods when the Anti-Trust Law could not do so." Fox Film Corp. *v.* Federal Trade Commission, 296 Fed. 353, 356 (1924).

[8] "We are of the opinion that Congress did not intend to do more than to eliminate the almost infinite variety of fraudulent practices from business in interstate commerce." Sinclair Refining Co. *v.* Federal Trade Commission, 276 Fed. 686, 688 (1921), *affirmed* 261 U. S. 463. "Congress intended to eliminate all varieties of fraudulent practices from business in interstate commerce." National Biscuit Co. *v.* Federal Trade Commission, 299 Fed. 733, 739 (1924), *certiorari denied* 266 U. S. 613. The act "does not give the Federal Trade Commission power to regulate trade policy. It is only where the practices amount to fraud in regard to some public or private right. It is only then that

must be construed as limited to the items indicated in the legislative history,[9] and that — aside from fraud — the prohibitions include only conspiracy or concerted action.[10] Throughout the opinions there is a marked tendency not to interfere with commercial warfare.[11]

The Technical Judicial Treatment. The dissimilar state of development in the two fields is a concomitant of the technical treatment accorded the orders of the respective commissions on review in the courts. In the relations of the courts to the commissions is disclosed the procedure which converts the execution of the Federal Trade statutes into judicial process and permits a relatively administrative justice in the regulation of transportation.

The orders of the Federal Trade Commission are subject to a judicial reconsideration on the record taken before the trade commissioners, while the orders of the Interstate Commerce Commission are subject to be set aside only for excess of authority or dis-

an unfair method of competition is established." Ayer *v.* Federal Trade Commission, 15 F.(2d) 274, 277 (1926), *certiorari denied* 273 U. S. 759. But see: These defenses "have to do with the motive for the transaction. We have to do only with the 'effect' of the transaction; and with its effect only as it may 'substantially lessen competition . . . or restrain commerce, . . . or tend to create monopoly.'" Aluminum Co. of America *v.* Federal Trade Commission, 284 Fed. 401, 408 (1922), *certiorari denied* 261 U. S. 616.

[9] Mennen Co. *v.* Federal Trade Commission, 288 Fed. 774, 778–799 (1923), *certiorari denied* 262 U. S. 759.

[10] For example: Raymond Bros.-Clark Co. *v.* Federal Trade Commission, 280 Fed. 529, 531 (1922), *affirmed* 263 U. S. 565.

[11] "The great purpose of both statutes was to advance the public interest by securing fair opportunity for the play of the contending forces ordinarily engendered by an honest desire for gain. And to this end it is essential that those who adventure their time, skill, and capital should have large freedom of action in the conduct of their own affairs." Federal Trade Commission *v.* Sinclair Co., 261 U. S. 463, 476 (1923). "Effective competition requires that merchants have freedom of action in conducting their own affairs. To be successful may increase or render insuperable the difficulties that rivals must face, but it does not constitute reprehensible or fraudulent methods." National Biscuit Co. *v.* Federal Trade Commission, 299 Fed. 733, 740 (1924), *certiorari denied* 266 U. S. 613. "Competition is not an unmixed good. It is a battle for something that only one can get; one competitor must necessarily lose. The weapons in competition are various. . . . Expense attending the use of any weapon, the foolishness of it, the fact that a method is uneconomical, or that the competitor cannot meet any method or scheme of competition because it will be ruinous to him to do so, have not, or has either of them, ever been held unfair." Sinclair Refining Co. *v.* Federal Trade Commission, 276 U. S. 686, 688 (1921), *affirmed* 261 U. S. 463.

regard or insufficiency of evidence. The trade commissioners themselves have finally taken the view that the commission is an investigative body and public prosecutor in a special field.[12] The judges substitute their judgment on the evidence for whatever determination the trade commissioners may have made, but in interstate commerce the inquiry is directed to discovering whether or not there is evidence reasonably connected with the legislative policy. Of course, through the handy device of formulating a rule of law and subsuming a given state of facts a particular order of the Interstate Commerce Commission may be, and sometimes is, set aside contrary to the general trend of judicial review, the intervention of the courts on the whole is sparing, and they disclaim any inquiry into the weight of evidence or the wisdom of orders. Undoubtedly, on an abstract or doctrinaire basis the determinations of the Interstate Commerce Commission are clothed with considerable finality.

The Evidence. In examining the differences in judicial treatment of the orders of these two commissions, an extended comparison of the weight accorded evidence or the pronouncements and decisions as to what may be accepted as evidence is barren, for the courts must translate the "evidence" into evidential facts, "ultimate" facts, "inferences" or "conclusions." This gradation carries the matter into the field of "law" as distinguished from facts or evidence — converts the questions into matters of rule or policy in which the ultimate authority is judicial. Accordingly, what extensions will be made from the evidence depends upon the judicial attitude toward the legislation administered. Obviously, without some conception of the purposes and desired legal situation, a treatment of the evidence must meander into ineffectiveness.

Policy. The distinguishing difference in review of the orders of these two commissions is to be found in the acceptance of legis-

[12] "It is readily conceded by all who have given consideration to the subject that what constitutes an 'unfair method of competition' in the meaning of the statute, is a question of law to be finally decided by the court of last resort. . . . But the Commission must necessarily, in the first instance, open the trail by deciding whether or not a given practice is lawful or unlawful so as to give the court an opportunity to adjudicate the question. In doing so, the Commission, though merely an administrative and fact-finding body, acts in a quasi-judicial capacity without appearing to exalt itself into the realm of the judicial branch of the government." Memorandum, May 29, 1929, p. 1. Commissioner McCullough. Compare the study made by Henderson in 1924, *The Federal Trade Commission*, pp. 92–103, 97–98, 336–337 (on pp. 97–98 there is a comparison with the Interstate Commerce Commission).

lative and administrative policy by the courts. The policy of trade regulation is scarcely mentioned.[13] It is not surprising, therefore, that the orders of the Federal Trade Commission get nowhere in the courts. With no goal in mind it is, of course, impossible to test administrative action. The policy of transportation regulation, on the other hand, has not only been accepted by the courts but they have assisted in the development of a comprehensive program of administrative control.[14]

The restraining influence of the courts upon the Federal Trade Commission has turned the efforts of that body from authoritative regulation to investigation, conciliation, and publicity. The review of the Interstate Commerce Commission orders, on the other hand, has been such that the transportation system of the nation has been brought under authoritative regulation, and contests in the courts are comparatively rare.[15]

II. The Explanation

Superficially, dissimilarities may be explained on a number of grounds. Railroads are a public utility [16] — but the mercantile world is not. This might describe the present status of regulation; it does not, however, explain why the public interest in maintenance of competition and the statutes directed to that end have not been effective. Railroad regulation until 1906 met with no more success than the regulation of competition has at the present time. Then too, regulation of competition by the Federal Trade Com-

[13] Except for the references to common law materials such as "fraud" and "dangerous tendency toward monopoly" discussed above.

[14] *Supra*, p. 140 n. 134, p. 141 n. 135.

[15] See: Fletcher, *The Interstate Commerce Commission* in *Growth of American Administrative Law* (1923), p. 65.

[16] ". . . When Legislatures are held to be authorized to do anything considerably affecting public welfare it is covered by apologetic phrases like . . . the statement that the business concerned has been dedicated to a public use." ". . . The notion that a business is clothed with a public interest and has been devoted to the public use is little more than a fiction. . . . The truth seems to me to be that, subject to compensation when compensation is due, the Legislature may forbid or restrict any business when it has a sufficient force of public opinion behind it." Mr. Justice Holmes, dissenting, in Tyson *v.* Banton, 273 U. S. 418 (1927). And see, for example: Adler, *Business Jurisprudence*, 28 Harv. L. Rev. 135 (1914); Keezer, *Some Questions Involved in the Application of the "Public Interest" Doctrine*, 25 Mich. L. Rev. 596 (1927); Robinson, *The Public Utility Concept in American Law*, 41 Harv. L. Rev. 277–308 (1928); Hamilton, *Affectation with Public Interest*, 39 Yale L. J. 1089 (1930).

mission began after the war, — a "reactionary" period followed by commercial expansion, — but the new legislative policy of railroad regulation began at the same time.

Personnel. The more reasoned discussions of the whole problem of administrative justice in one way or another focus upon the adequacies of administrators.[17] The movement toward discretionary authority demands competent agencies for its exercise. The administrative personnel cannot be without profound effect — as was recognized in Congress when the Trade Commission Act was under consideration.[18] Accordingly, the quality of the men who sit upon the Federal Trade Commission and the Interstate Commerce Commission may furnish a clue to the very different success of these bodies as authoritative agencies for the regulation of trade and commerce.

An extended analysis of differences in personnel of the commission is impossible here. The orders and reports of the Interstate Commerce Commission from the very beginning reveal a careful and expert consideration of subject matter, and the excellence of its personnel has been the subject of much professional comment.[19] The reports of the Federal Trade Commission show a lack of vigor in administration, and then there is the failure to press necessary legislation, the noncommittal exposition of difficulties encountered, and the unprotesting turn toward other duties than authoritative regulation of competitive practices. Particular actions of each commission might be singled out for comparison, such as the ill-

[17] The training and background of the legal profession are put forth as the point of superiority of administration by courts. See, for example: Pound, *The Revival of Personal Government*, 4 Proc. N. H. Bar Ass'n 13 (1917); Pound, *Justice According to Law*, 13 Col. L. Rev. 696 (1913); Allen, *Bureaucracy Triumphant* (1931), pp. 67, 104–105. And upon the same ground the necessity of administrative justice is asserted. See: Robson, *Administrative Justice* (1928), p. 35 et seq. For a discussion of this aspect of the present state of commission regulation see: Frankfurter, *The Public and Its Government* (1930), p. 111 et seq.

[18] "It is of paramount importance that men of the first order of ability should be attracted to these positions. . . ." Report of the Senate Committee, 63d Cong., 2 Sess., No. 597, p. 11 (1914). "The proposed commission will largely justify its creation by the method and manner of the performance of its varied duties by its members." Report of the House Committee, 63d Cong., 2 Sess., No. 533, p. 2 (1914).

[19] See, for example: *Socrates among the Railroads*, Fortune, v, No. 2, p. 71 (Feb., 1932). And changes in personnel are noted; see, for example: *Interstate Commerce Commission Appointments*, Railway Age, LXXXVII, 1427; Commercial and Financial Chronicle, CXXXI, 731 (Aug. 2, 1930).

considered practice of the trade commission whereby petty matters are allowed to consume valuable time and energy. The trade commissioners, as compared with the interstate commerce commissioners, display some unfortunate want of discrimination; there has been a lack of tact and harmony, at least, in both the internal and external affairs of the trade commission.[20] However, a worthy attempt to administer the Federal Trade Commission Act and the Clayton Act has been made, and the fact that it was ineffective is not to be laid entirely to the inability of the trade commissioners *as administrators*. In a broad sense, perhaps, the differences in personnel explain the dissimilar history and judicial relations of the two commissions. It is apparently the lack of statesmanship in the Federal Trade Commission that explains some of the differences. The Interstate Commerce Commission has continually cooperated with Congress and has relied upon the national legislature for additional powers or corrective legislation as the need arose.[21]

Procedure. Somewhat related to the matter of personnel is the procedure and practice adopted by the trade commissioners. While the administrative organization of the Interstate Commerce Commission and the procedure adopted go almost without comment, there is considerable inquiry and discussion of the mode of administration of the Federal Trade Commission Act. Much of the criticism is applicable to all public administration,[22] even that of the courts, and at any event treatment of the trade commission in terms of the mechanics of its process (which is more properly open to the objection that it is too cumbersome rather than that it is unfair)[23] is to becloud more fundamental problems.

Opinions of the Commission. One item of trade commission process, however, has been singled out for particular criticism —

[20] Illustrated, for example, in a Senate discussion: Cong. Rec., LXIX, 2942 et seq., particularly at p. 2956.

[21] But of course whether more pointed appeals for federal trade legislation would have been gratified is another question. On the matter of personnel compare: "Admitting, for the purpose of the argument, that commissions are inferior in learning, disinterestedness and impartiality to the courts, the people have the constitutional right to be badly governed and it is not for the courts to remedy administrative inefficiency." Cuthbert Pound, *Constitutional Aspects of Administrative Law* in *Growth of American Administrative Law* (1923), p. 130 (printed also in 9 A. B. A. J. 409).

[22] Compare, for example, the discussion in *Public Regulation of Competitive Practices*, (National Industrial Conference Board 1925), pp. 213–214 (first paragraph).

[23] *Supra*, p. 42 n. 13.

the inadequacy of the opinions and findings of the commissioners.[24] Although the courts themselves have not remarked the absence of argumentative opinions and even where findings are made have either ignored them or have subjected them to an almost metaphysical consideration,[25] the absence of an extended administrative report on each case confirms what, in some cases, is a judicial conviction that administrative process is particularly open to the suspicion that careful consideration has not been given the evidence.[26] Where the courts point out a lack of findings, they have no hesitancy in drawing their own conclusions from the record. In comparison, the decisions or reports of the Interstate Commerce Commission are carefully drawn and treat the evidence fully, although the Supreme Court has pronounced that the courts have no concern with the soundness of the reasoning, the application of administrative precedents, or the wisdom of the action of the Interstate Commerce Commission.[27] On occasion, however, the commerce commission has been admonished to state in its reports the facts and reasons for its conclusions to facilitate judicial review.[28] Apparently, while the courts in their regular course of procedure may render decision by memorandum or deny relief "for want of equity," administrative decisions must be clothed in the garb of judicial opinion before they will be accepted by the bench as *bona fide* adjudications. Herein the federal trade commissioners have undoubtedly been remiss.

The Explanation given by the Courts. The Supreme Court has distinguished between review of Federal Trade Commission orders and those of the Interstate Commerce Commission on the basis of the language of the statutes. The language of the Federal Trade Commission Act, says the court, "is broad, and confers power of review not found in the Interstate Commerce Act." [29] But the

[24] Davies, *The Federal Trade Commission* in *Growth of American Administrative Law* (1923), pp. 85–86; Henderson, *The Federal Trade Commission* (1924), Ch. III and pp. 334–337. But compare: *Public Regulation of Competitive Practices* (1925), p. 210 n. 1.

[25] *Supra*, p. 30 et seq.

[26] See, for example, the lower court opinions in Benson *v.* Crowell, 33 F.(2d) 137, 38 F.(2d) 306, overruled on this point in the Supreme Court in 52 S. Ct. 285 (1932).

[27] *Supra*, p. 135 n. 115.

[28] Beaumont, S. L. & W. Ry. *v.* United States, 282 U. S. 74, 86 (1930).

[29] Curtis Publishing Co. *v.* Federal Trade Commission, 260 U. S. 568, 580 (1923). The court further held that decisions on review of the Interstate Com-

lower federal courts have found the difference in the nature of the powers delegated to the commission [30] or, on the basis of the language of the statutes providing for judicial review, find — the Supreme Court and the practice to the contrary notwithstanding — that the courts have less control over the trade commission than over the Interstate Commerce Commission.[31]

Doctrine. However, these attempts of the courts to explain the differences in relationship to the two commissions are not helpful.[32] The review of both commissions proceeds upon the doctrine of divisibility of law and fact. The determination of facts by the trade commission is, by statute, made conclusive. The determination of facts by the Interstate Commerce Commission was originally to be accorded only *prima facie* effect in the courts, but in 1906 — from which date authoritative regulation by the commerce commission begins — even this provision was omitted and the courts were left to work out their own principles of review.[33]

Enforcement Procedure. In one respect, however, the statutory provisions, as adapted by the courts, affect regulation. The orders of the Interstate Commerce Commission, unless set aside upon application of private parties to the courts, become effective within

merce Commission orders "while helpful as to proper practice, do not determine the present problem."

[30] ". . . The situation is wholly different from that of the Interstate Commerce Commission. There the basic question is the fixation of rates, which is a question of business discretion, and in no sense a legal, judicial, or moral one. Manifestly, Congress did not mean to confer upon the Trade Commission the power to grant injunctions in cases of business competition, where courts would not be justified in granting injunctions." Curtis Publishing Co. *v.* Federal Trade Commission, 270 Fed. 881, 909 (1921), *affirmed* 260 U. S. 568. "The powers conferred upon this commission are similar to those conferred upon the Interstate Commerce Commission, with the exception that the powers of the latter are more pronounced and potential." Chamber of Commerce *v.* Federal Trade Commission, 280 Fed. 45, 48 (1922).

[31] "If such be the holdings where the findings are made but *prima facie* true [as in the case of the Interstate Commerce Commission] how much greater their pertinancy where such findings are by statute made conclusive [as in the case of the Federal Commission]? Arkansas Wholesale Grocers' Ass'n *v.* Federal Trade Commission, 18 F.(2d) 866, 871 (1927), *certiorari denied* 275 U. S. 533.

[32] Compare: Freund, *Administrative Powers over Persons and Property* (1928), pp. 280–284.

[33] Except reparation and valuation orders. Compare a different interpretation of the statutory differences: *Public Regulation of Competitive Practices* (1925), pp. 214–216.

a specified time; [34] but the Federal Trade Commission must apply to the courts for enforcement of each order. In the regulation of competition, therefore, the administrative agency must appear at the bar of a circuit court of appeals and justify its decision, while in the case of regulation of transportation the burden is shifted to those who contest the administrative determination.[35] The procedure provided for the Federal Trade Commission delays enforcement.[36] Also, in this aspect, courts are influenced by the general conception of special procedure and extraordinary remedies, such as the procedure under the common law discretionary writs of injunction and mandamus, wherein the party seeking judicial action must undertake to show clearly a situation which will move the court to act. As one court said in reviewing an order of the Trade Commission, "injunction [against commercial practices] is so drastic and prohibitive a remedy, its issuance by a court of equity so carefully safeguarded, that to have substantial question of the wisdom of such issue often suffices to withhold. To doubt is to decide, and this well-founded principle of equity in itself would lead a court of original jurisdiction to deny the strong arm of injunctive relief." [37] The injunctive analogy is also felt in the troublesome question of enforcement of orders of the trade commission irrespective of their validity.[38]

In each of these particulars — the division of authority between the commissions and the courts and the provisions for enforcement of orders — the courts have themselves developed principles of review hardly foreseeable from the language of the statutes. It may be significant, however, that when the Interstate Commerce Commission (to 1906) was under the same burden in enforcing its or-

[34] Except reparation orders.

[35] Compare the remarks of Thayer: "In general he who seeks to move a court in his favour . . . must satisfy the court of the truth and adequacy of his claim, both in point of fact and law. But he, in every case, who is the true *reus* or defendant, holds, of course, a very different place in the procedure. He simply awaits the action of his adversary, and it is enough if he repel him. He has no duty of satisfying the court; it may be doubtful, indeed extremely doubtful, whether he is not legally in the wrong and his adversary legally in the right; indeed he may probably be in the wrong, and yet he may gain and his adversary lose, simply because the inertia of the court has not been overcome. . . ." *Cases on Evidence* (2 ed., 1900), p. 69.

[36] Henderson, *The Federal Trade Commission* (1924), p. 87 et seq.

[37] Curtis Publishing Co. *v.* Federal Trade Commission, 270 Fed. 881, 914 (1921), *affirmed* 260 U. S. 568.

[38] See *supra*, p. 74 et seq.

ders, the authority of the commission was very seriously curtailed by the courts.

Form of the Legislation. Perhaps a more accurate judicial statement of the reasons for different treatment of the orders of the commissions is that the powers of the Interstate Commerce Commission "are more pronounced and potential." [39] The form of the legislative charter of authority for each commission is much the same. The delegation of authority is in terms of legal standard such as "reasonable rates" or "tending to create monopoly." Sometimes the standard, thus clothed with authority of law, is given a moral color — "unfair competition," "undue prejudice," "unjust discrimination." But these standards, as between the two commissions, differ in scope or particularity of subject matter. The standards which the Interstate Commerce Commission must apply are more specifically related to particular situations — rates, services, facilities, and so on. But the standard entrusted to the Federal Trade Commission — the maintenance of competition or prevention of monopoly — embraces the whole commercial field; [40] the authority to prevent monopoly is particularized in only three instances — price discrimination, full line forcing, and the acquisition of capital or share stock of competitors — while the authority to prevent "unfair methods of competition" is unlimited and the commission is left to work out the particular practices which are to be prohibited. However, the differences in scope of subject matter to which the standards are directed does not explain the differences in treatment by the courts, for even those particularized portions of the statutes which the Federal Trade Commission administers have not been excepted from the general course of review of trade regulation orders. The differences in the scope or particularity of the statutory authority are explainable by legislative history. In fact, it is in the legislation of nearly half a century that the significant difference in the character and work of the commissions is disclosed.

Legislative History: The Federal Trade Commission. The first statutes under which the two commissions were established and operated were much the same in origin. Since the commissions were set up, however, their legislative history has diverged sharply. The authority of the Federal Trade Commission was originally contained in four sections of the Clayton Act and one sentence of the Trade Commission Act. There was no agreement on the mean-

[39] *Supra*, n. 30. [40] *Supra*, pp. 10–11 n. 19.

ing of the statutes when passed, and nothing has been added to the legislation of 1914 except the extension of the scope of the field of regulation to include foreign trade. On the other hand, successive statutes have either expressly or by implication vested the regulation of certain industries or phases of commercial practice in other agencies of the federal government. The commission's annual reports to Congress do not advocate legislation. Most of the recommendations of the trade commission have resulted from investigations instituted at the direction of Congress; thus the commission has not — as compared with the Interstate Commerce Commission — been the active force in legislation but has contented itself with the role of special investigator under the direction of Congress.[41]

[41] In contrast with the cooperation of Congress and the commerce commission the legislative recommendations of the Federal Trade Commission are negligible. At first the trade commission (although engaged in assimilating the investigative functions of the Bureau of Corporations, Ann. Rep., 1915, p. 5) followed the procedure of the Interstate Commerce Commission in the matter of making recommendations to Congress. The personnel of the commission changed rapidly. Commissioner Davies, who was responsible for the studies in the law of unfair competition, resigned in 1918, and after the war, which interrupted the regular development of the recently established commission, legislative recommendations are almost negligible and those made are not strongly pressed except a recommendation for amplification of investigative powers.

Recommendations for legislation, 1915–1931: Export trade: 1916, pp. 34–36, 60–61; 1917, p. 32. (Investigation was specifically provided in the Federal Trade Commission Act. Compare also the remarks of President Wilson, Address at Indianapolis, January 8, 1915, *Messages and Papers of the Presidents*, XVII, 8024 at 8030. Report of Senate Committee, 63d Cong., 2 Sess., No. 597, p. 13 [1914].)

Appropriations: 1916, p. 36. *Quarters:* 1916, pp. 36–37; 1919, p. 5. *Salary limitation:* 1916, p. 37; 1917, p. 32. *Authority to require reports and make investigations:* 1917, pp. 29–31; 1918, pp. 84–86; 1929, pp. 9, 28–29; 1930, p. 14; 1931, p. 6. *Costs in litigation:* 1927, pp. 5–6. *Resale price maintenance:* 1929, pp. 69–71; 1930, p. 36; 1931, pp. 28–31 (legislation disfavored).

Other general legislative recommendations have been made, but not for furthering or strengthening the regulative function of the commission. Some of these are made in connection with investigations conducted at the request of Congress. See, for example: *Commercial bribery:* 1920, pp. 52–54. *Meat packing industry:* 1918, pp. 5, 22–25. *Price fixing of necessities during wartime:* 1917, pp. 30–31. *Petroleum industry:* 1917, pp. 31–32; 1925, pp. 85–86. *Canned foods:* 1918, pp. 26–27. *Alien enemy patents:* 1918, pp. 7–8. *Trading with the enemy act:* 1918, pp. 50–51. *Marketing of perishable foods:* 1920, pp. 39–40. *Tobacco industry:* 1921, p. 37. *Grain marketing:* 1922, pp. 41, 51; 1923, pp. 62–65; 1926, pp. 59–60. *Coal industry:* 1922, pp. 43–44; 1925, pp. 83–85. *Cotton trade:* 1924, pp. 80–82; 1925, pp. 89–90. *Open price associations:* 1929, pp. 68–69. *Newsprint-paper industry:* 1930, pp. 47–48.

For the most part, lack of authority and reverses at the hands of the courts are reported noncommittally. The attempt at authoritative regulation which first came before the courts in 1919 was so restricted judicially that by 1926 the efforts of the commission were turned in other directions and the character of the commission completely changed by the end of the decade. Unable to regulate competition, the commission turned to investigation, conciliation, and publicity.

The Interstate Commerce Commission. Space does not permit treatment of the legislative history of the Interstate Commerce Commission to bring out the full contrast. From the year of its establishment, 1887, until 1906 the history of the commission parallels that of the trade commission. The year 1896 marked the judicial veto of administrative exercise of authority (comparable to the year 1926 in the work of the Federal Trade Commission), and until 1906 the commerce commission could do little more than protest.[42] Unlike the more recent Federal Trade Commission, however, the Interstate Commerce Commission kept up an insistent demand for legislation. Ten years after the courts had so seriously cut down the authority of the commission Congress responded with legislation. In 1906 the statutes, which the courts had found lacking, were amplified and the system of enforcing the orders of the commission through the courts abandoned. In 1910 the statutory authority of the commission was further defined to remedy the situation under judicial decisions and effectuate the legislative policy of the first Act to Regulate Commerce. From 1910 legislation is frequent. In 1920 the entire scheme of railway regulation was revised, the previous authority of the commission amplified in many particulars, and important additional duties imposed. The commission, with the cooperation of the courts, has moulded this new body of legislation into a comprehensive policy. In fact, difficulties may be expected from the great load and the diversity of duties [43] — and particularly from the broad grants of authority such as emergency powers and financial regulation.

[42] To 1903 "out of 43 applications to the courts, there are only two in which the commission has been finally sustained." Newcomb, *Work of the Interstate Commerce Commission* (1905), p. 15.

[43] "Such shortcomings . . . as may emerge in an appraisal of the Commission's work will find their source, for the most part, in positive rather than in negative defects. In other words, the difficulties surrounding the Commission's activities are largely due to the wide extent and diverse character of the powers and duties imposed upon it . . . rather than to any conspicuous Con-

Delegation of Authority and Successful Administration. The regulation of carriers has not been achieved by the simple device of delegating authority to a competent administrative agency. Rather, the standards laid down in legislation have been a permission for administrative experimentation under the supervision of the courts. When this process has not been satisfactory, the commission has secured further legislation. It is the cooperation between the commission and Congress and the cumulated and vigorous legislative policy that distinguishes the regulation of carriers from regulation of competition in general trade. The history of trade regulation was similar up to the establishment of the commission, but the only effect of the statutes was to prolong and shift the controversy for a while. The original purpose of Congress to establish a trade commission which would cooperate in the development of a body of legislation [44] has not been achieved. Whereas the history of the Federal Trade Commission since 1914 has been an interplay between the courts and the commission with final authority in the former, the relations of the Interstate Commerce Commission since 1906 have been three-cornered — the

gressional failure to endow it with sufficient authority. . . ." Sharfman, *The Interstate Commerce Commission* (1931), I, 12.

[44] It is clear from the reports of the committees that experimentation and further legislation were contemplated. "Had we submitted the administration of the antitrust act to an impartial quasi-judicial tribunal similar to the Interstate Commerce Commission . . . we would by this time have made gratifying progress in the regulation and control of trusts, through the quasi-judicial investigations of a competent commission and through legislation based upon its recommendations." The proposed Trade Commission's "subsequent recommendations to Congress will be fortified with actual knowledge of practical conditions. . . . If conditions . . . warrant, there will be a natural growth in the power of this body." Report of the Senate Committee, 63d Cong., 2 Sess., No. 597, pp. 6, 10 (1914).

"The history of the Interstate Commerce Commission is conclusive evidence that the best legislation regarding many of the problems to come before the interstate-trade commission will be produced from time to time as the result of the reports of the commission after exhaustive inquiries and investigations. No one can foretell the extent to which the complex interstate business of a great country like the United States may require, alike for the benefit of the business man and for the protection of the public, new legislation in the form of Federal regulations, but such legislation should come by a sound process of evolution. . . . It is largely the experience of the independent commission itself that will afford Congress the accurate information necessary to give to the country from time to time the additional legislation which may be needed." Report of the House Committee, 63d Cong., 2 Sess., No. 533, p. 8 (1914).

commission, the courts, and Congress have each taken an active part. Although the restriction of the authority of the Federal Trade Commission seems for the most part unwarranted under the terms of the statutes, the position of the courts in the matter is strengthened by the failure of Congress to come to the aid of the commission.

III. Conclusion

The field of trade and commerce regulation is no exception to the rule of experience that there are no sharp turns in government, and it must be admitted — as compared with the time span of changes in other fields — that the experience in commission regulation is brief. But the yield of nearly two decades of contemporaneous administration by the Federal Trade Commission and the Interstate Commerce Commission reveals differences which are not entirely explained by the necessities of trial and error.

The very different operation of these two commissions under statutes delegating general authority brings into sharp relief the differences in the effect of legislation upon related subject matter. Political and economic history and tradition have so affected the application of the legislation entrusted to the commissions that a comparison of the texts explains little. Behind the legislative history of the Interstate Commerce Act lies a public interest of long standing, although fear of monopoly and the public interest in the maintenance of competition (entrusted to the Federal Trade Commission) is much in the mind of the citizen.[45] The nature of the transportation system, however, is peculiarly monopolistic, and

[45] Compare: "How did it happen that, outside the Commission, no serious protest was ever raised against . . . spirited repulses of the Commission by the courts, and . . . judicial assimilation of the anti-trust legislation of 1914 into the Sherman Act? The reason is that public opinion, since 1914, has reversed itself, and turned its back on the ideas that produced the atmosphere and anti-trust legislation of 1914." Montague, *Anti-Trust Laws and the Federal Trade Commission: 1914–1926*, 13 A. B. A. J. 328, 331 (1927). "Anti-trust legislation . . . has lost a good deal of the emotional appeal adhering to it in the days when Mr. Roosevelt was trust busting." "There is today less tumult and shouting concerning the trust problems, partly because few of our contemporary corporations can be summed up in terms of one extremely unpopular individual and partly because most of the larger corporations whose consolidating activities might be open to question have at their disposal legal advisers to tell them what is or is not permissible." Fortune, II, No. 3, pp. 94, 96.

the legislation has not been entirely a victory over the contrary ideas of the carriers, for at times it has been the carriers themselves that have urged legislation and regulation. Fears of monopoly on the one hand and the inevitable unification and elimination of competition in transportation on the other have been compromised, if not solved, by regulation. But in the broader field of trade and commerce the same conditions are coming to be recognized.

Much-discussed changes are taking place in commerce and industry — particularly the modification of the competitive system.[46] Public regulation is a large factor in these trends.[47] As the

[46] ". . . The sacredness of free competition is sorely strained, and it may well be true that it has ceased to be a freedom and has become a license." Cabot, *The Vices of Free Competition*, Yale Review, September, 1928, pp. 38, 46. "In general, one might say that the present depression was forced upon industry by mass thinking, particularly as it involved lack of understanding among manufacturers and misunderstanding as to the meaning of the word 'competition.' In agriculture, production, distribution, and finance, in the relationship between government and business, and in our social life, many important changes have recently taken place which have not been understood or assimilated. We are using modern tools with minds accustomed to old ones." Doriot, *Our Sick Industries*, Yale Review, April 6, 1931, pp. 443–444. And see the dissenting opinion of Mr. Justice Brandeis in New State Ice Co. *v.* Liebmann, 52 S. Ct. 371, 385–387 (1932).

"Few aspects of the changes in our economic organization have been more striking or have aroused wider public attention and discussion than the trend towards the merger or consolidation of industrial enterprises into large-scale industrial units, which has characterized the last fifty years of American business history and has been specially emphasized in recent years." *Mergers in Industry* (National Industrial Conference Board, 1929), pp. v–vi. And see, for example: Curtis, *The Trusts and Economic Control* (1931); Fetter, *The Masquerade of Monopoly* (1931); Homan, *Industrial Combination as Surveyed in Recent Literature*, Quarterly Journal of Economics, Vol. 44, p. 345 (Feb., 1930); Laidler, *Concentration of Control in American Industry* (1931); Marquand, *Dynamics of Industrial Combination* (1931); Seager and Gulick, *Trust and Corporation Problems* (1929); Handler, *The Federal Anti-Trust Laws* (A symposium) (1932).

[47] ". . . With one minor exception, every effective exemption granted in the fifteen years since the amendment of the Sherman Act has become more or less of a legislative habit has been made upon the condition that the interests exempted shall be subject . . . to the supervision and regulation of some governmental administrative agency." *Mergers and the Law* (National Industrial Conference Board, 1929), p. 131. The policies of other countries show "a liberality toward monopolistic combinations, subject, when the public interest required, to governmental regulation. . . ." Seager and Gulick, *op. cit.*, p. 663. "Great monopolies with uncontrolled discretion are certainly dangerous and no democratic society is likely to allow them. Nevertheless the dangers of un-

relation between a new or inevitably changing economic order and government develops, administration will become a consideration of first importance, and judicial action — "the limitations set by courts upon experimentation in the fields of social and economic science"[48] — will be a force to be carefully reckoned. In the regulation of transportation, a course of legislation since 1906 has provided a more modern economic basis for public control along with a modified administrative-judicial relationship. In the maintenance and regulation of general business practice, however, the national legislature has failed to continue the experiment begun in 1914 or, at least, has failed to insist upon experimentation by the administrative commission — instead, Congress has been a party

bridled fair competition are just as great and unfortunately lack the popular appeal inherent in anti-monopolistic attacks. The necessity for some method of making legal agreements which can stop senseless competition with its threat to the stability of established industrial groups and its shocking economic wastes is becoming more and more apparent. In the course of working out any such reappraisal, legislation will be essential." Donham, *Business Adrift* (1931), pp. 141–142. There is a discussion of the methods of government regulation in Seager and Gulick, *op. cit.*; and from a political and legal point of view Freund, *Administrative Powers over Persons and Property* (1928), is a comparatively exhaustive inquiry (see particularly pp. 578–585).

"In my message of a year ago I commented on the necessity of congressional inquiry into the economic action of the antitrust laws. There is wide conviction that some change should be made especially in the procedure under these laws." President Hoover, Annual Message to Congress, 75 Cong. Rec. 25 (Dec. 8, 1931). Copeland, *Revising the Anti-Trust Laws*, Harvard Business Review, x, 292 (Apr., 1932); Donovan, *Should the Anti-Trust Laws be Modified?* Harvard Business Review, x, 129 (Jan., 1932); Donovan, *We Need a New Business Tribunal*, Nations Business, xviii, 158 (Mar., 1930); Jones, *Significance of Current Attempts to Amend the Anti-Trust Laws*, The Annalist, xxxviii, 101 (July 17, 1931); Keezer and May, *Public Control of Business* (1930); Spreckels, *Changing Conditions Require Changed Laws*, Printers Ink, cliii, 33 (Oct. 2, 1930); Strawn, *Are Our Anti-Trust Laws Out of Date?*, Nations Business, xix, 132 (May, 1931); Swope, *The Swope Plan* (1931); Thorp, *The Persistence of the Merger Movement*, American Economic Review, xxi, 77 (Mar., 1931); Verity, *Should Anti-Trust Laws Be Modified?*, Commerce and Finance, Vol. xxi, No. 6 (Feb. 10, 1932); *Business Is Dragging Its Brakes*, Business Week, p. 47 (Dec. 11, 1929); *A Federal Trade Court*, Business Week, p. 5 (Mar. 12, 1930). But compare: ". . . The present Sherman and Clayton Acts in some ways go too far in the industrial field. . . . As a result they may bring greater evils than those they cure, though by judicial decisions these acts are gradually being adapted to social needs." Donham, *Business Looks at the Unforeseen* (1932), p. 52.

[48] Mr. Justice Brandeis, dissenting, in New State Ice Co. *v.* Liebmann, 52 S. Ct. 371, 386 (1932).

to turning the efforts of the Federal Trade Commission in other directions.

As the veto power of the courts is less and less to be explained on the basis of a *laissez faire* philosophy, judicial interference with administrative regulation will become increasingly objectionable. However, the judiciary — as shown by the experience of the Interstate Commerce Commission — does respond to a determined legislative policy. For effective regulation of transportation, Congressional cooperation with the administrative tribunal must continue. To vitalize the regulation of trade and industry, Congress and the executive have yet to provide a capable body of administrators, and now the statutes must be revised. In the substantive portions of such legislation a policy must be stated and maintained as administration progresses. On the procedural side, if the regulation is to be administrative and not judicial, the determinations of the administrative agency must be made effective without resort to the courts. This was the legislative program which revived the regulation of interstate transportation in 1906 and 1910.

In the absence of clear and continuous manifestation of legislative policy, the courts fall back upon the common law and deny administrative authority. Legislation in the field of transportation over a period of forty-five years — a vigorous legislative policy since 1906 — has provided a charter for authoritative regulation by the Interstate Commerce Commission. The legislation of 1914 for the regulation of trade practices has not been amplified, and the relatively inferior personnel of the Federal Trade Commission is further evidence of executive and Congressional indifference; thus the trade commission has been diverted to investigation, conciliation, and publicity — precisely the status existing before the legislation was put on the statute books.

Friction is inevitable where administration is entrusted to the joint action of judicial and administrative agencies — differently constituted and traditionally opposed institutions. Effective regulation under such a system is secured by the active cooperation of the legislature with the administrative arm of government.

REFERENCES AND AUTHORITIES

REFERENCES AND AUTHORITIES

Books and Treatises

Allen: Bureaucracy Triumphant (1931) 16, 17, 33, 37, 176

Bernhardt: The Interstate Commerce Commission (1923) 101, 110
Blaisdell: The Federal Trade Commission (1932) 39, 99
Briggs: Federal Regulation of Interstate Commerce, 1862–1913 (1913) 101
Butler: The Supreme Issue of 1912 (1912) 23
Butler and Lynde: The Federal Trade Commission (1915) 39

Cardozo: The Growth of the Law (1924) 5
Cardozo: The Nature of the Judicial Process (1921) 16, 18
Clark on Interstate Commerce (1919) 127
Clark: The Federal Trust Policy (1931) 23, 39
Curtis: The Trusts and Economic Control (1931) 39, 186

Dicey: Law and Public Opinion (Reprinted, 1920) 113
Dicey: Law of the Constitution (8 ed., 1927) 13
Dickinson: Administrative Justice and the Supremacy of Law (1927) 3, 6, 10, 12, 13, 16, 17, 20, 23, 24, 25, 29, 35
Donham: Business Adrift (1931) 187
Donham: Business Looks at the Unforeseen (1932) 187
Durand: The Trust Problem (1915) 39

Fetter: The Masquerade of Monopoly (1931) 186
Fifoot: English Law and Its Background (1932) 26
Frankfurter: The Public and Its Government (1930) 176
Frankfurter and Landis: The Business of the Supreme Court (1927) 37, 119
Freund: Administrative Powers over Persons and Property (1928) 3, 4, 20, 24, 179, 187

Gaskill: Price Control in the Public Interest (2 ed., 1931) 97
Ghose: Comparative Administrative Law (1919) 12
Goodnow: Politics and Administration (1900) 5
Gray: The Nature and Sources of the Law (1909) 18

Haines: Revival of Natural Law Concepts (1930) 15
Handler: The Federal Anti-Trust Laws (A Symposium, 1932) 186
Haney: A Congressional History of Railways in the United States, v. I (1909), v. II (1910) 101
Harland and McCandless: The Federal Trade Commission (1916) . 39

Henderson: The Federal Trade Commission (1924)
23, 39, 40, 49, 60, 64, 91, 92, 97, 174, 178, 180
Henderson: The Position of Foreign Corporations in American Constitutional Law (1918) 71
Hewart: The New Despotism (1929) 13, 14, 16
Holt: The Federal Trade Commission (1922) 39

Jones: The Trust Problem in the United States (1921) 39

Keezer and May: The Public Control of Business (1930) 41, 187

Laidler: Concentration of Control in American Industry (1931) ... 186
Laski: Introduction to Politics (1931) 16

MacIver: The Modern State (1926) 5
Marquand: Dynamics of Industrial Combination (1931) 186
Marriott: The Crisis of English Liberty (1930) 16
Mergers in Industry (Nat. Ind. Conf. Bd., 1929) 186
Miller: Legislative Evolution of the Interstate Commerce Act (1930) 101

Newcomb: Work of the Interstate Commerce Commission (1905) 110, 183

Parker: The Three Powers of Government (1869) 5
Plucknett: Statutes and their Interpretation in the Fourteenth Century (1922) 18
Port: Administrative Law (1929) 33
Pound: Introduction to the Philosophy of Law (1922) 19, 38
Public Regulation of Competitive Practices (Nat. Ind. Conf. Bd., 1925) 39, 79, 80, 98, 177, 178, 179

Robson: Administrative Justice (1928) 176

Seager and Gulick: Trust and Corporation Problems (1929)
19, 39, 40, 41, 100, 186
Seligman and Love: Price Cutting and Price Maintenance (1932) . 97
Sharfman: The Interstate Commerce Commission (1931)
6, 22, 100, 108, 110, 119, 127, 130, 132, 133, 143, 151, 167
Swope: The Swope Plan (1931) 187

Thayer: Preliminary Treatise on Evidence (1898) 25, 26, 27

Vander Eycken: Methode positive de l'Interpretation juridique .. 16
Vinogradoff: Introduction to Historical Jurisprudence (1920) 25

Wigmore: Evidence (2 ed., 1923) 30
Wigmore: Principles of Judicial Proof (2 ed., 1931) 32
Wilson: Constitutional Government in the United States (1911) .. 14

Casebooks

Frankfurter and Davison: Cases on Administrative Law (1932) ... 12
Frankfurter and Katz: Cases on Federal Jurisdiction (1931) 23
McLaughlin: Cases on the Federal Anti-Trust Laws (1930) 97
Thayer: Cases on Evidence (2 ed., 1900) 180

Articles and Essays

A Federal Trade Court, Business Week, Mar. 12, 1930, p. 5 187
Adler: Business Jurisprudence, 28 Harv. L. Rev. 135 (1914) 175
Albertsworth: Judicial Review of Administrative Action by the Supreme Court, 35 Harv. L. Rev. 129 (1921) 24

Berle: Expansion of American Administrative Law, 39 Harv. L. Rev. 430 (1917) 12
Bondy: Separation of Governmental Powers, Columbia University Studies, V, 139 (1896) 5
Brown: The Right to Refuse to Sell, 25 Yale L. J. 194 (1916) 15
Burgess: Recent Efforts to Immunize Commission Orders against Judicial Review, 55 A. B. A. Rep. (1930) 16
Business Is Dragging Its Brakes, Business Week, Dec. 11, 1929, p. 47 187

Cabot: The Vices of Free Competition, Yale Review, Sept., 1928, p. 38 186
Carrington: Unfair Competition, 7 Va. L. Rev. 361 (1921) 42
Clayton Act, Section 3, and Patent Protection, Comment 40 Yale L. J. 954 (1931) 93
Copeland: Revising the Anti-Trust Laws, Harv. Bus. Rev., X, 292 (1932) 187

Daish: The Federal Trade Commission, 24 Yale L. J. 43 (1914) .. 39
Davies: The Federal Trade Commission (in Growth of American Administrative Law, 1923; reprinted in 18 Fla. S. B. A. 93, 1925) 39, 64, 178
Dicey: Development of Administrative Law in England, 31 Law Q. Rev. 148 (1915) 13
Dickinson: Judicial Control of Administrative Discretion, 22 Am. Pol. Sci. Rev. 275 (1928) 21
Donovan: Should the Anti-Trust Laws Be Modified? Harv. Bus. Rev., X, 129 (1932) 187
Donovan: We Need a New Business Tribunal, Nations Business, XVIII, 158 (1930) 187
Doriot: Our Sick Industries, Yale Review, April 6, 1931, p. 443 .. 186
Duff and Whiteside: Delegata Potestas non Potest Delegari: A Maxim of American Constitutional Law, 14 Corn. L. Q. 168 (1929) 7

Eastman: The Place of the Independent Commission, 12 Const. Rev. 95 (1928) 11

Esch: The Breadth of the Commerce Clause, Nat. Assn. of Railroad and Utilities Commissioners, Nov. 10, 1926 127

Fayne: The Federal Trade Commission: The Development of the Law Which Led to Its Establishment, 9 Am. Pol. Sci. Rev. 57 (1915) 39

Federal Trade Commission as Special Master in Anti-Trust, 30 Harv. L. Rev. 168 98

Fletcher: The Interstate Commerce Commission (in Growth of American Administrative Law, 1923) 175

Frank: Are Judges Human? 80 U. Pa. L. Rev. 17 (1931) 23

Frankfurter and Landis: A Study in Separation of Powers, 37 Harv. L. Rev. 1010 (1924) 6

Freund: Historical Survey of American Administrative Law (in Growth of American Administrative Law, 1923) 14, 20, 26, 30

Freund: Shifting Theories of Control, 7 A. B. A. J. 656 (1921)..... 34

Gallagher: The Federal Trade Commission, 10 Ill. L. Rev. 31 (1915) 42

Grimm: Administrative Determinations, 3 St. Louis L. Rev. 140 (1919) 24

Haines: Efforts to Define Unfair Competition, 29 Yale L. J. 1 (1919) 42

Hamilton: Affectation with Public Interest, 39 Yale L. J. 1089 (1930) 175

Handler: Constitutionality of Investigations by the Federal Trade Commission, 28 Col. L. Rev. 708 (1928) 41

Handler: Jurisdiction of the Federal Trade Commission over False Advertising, 31 Col. L. Rev. 527 (1931) 94

Hankin: Conclusiveness of the Federal Trade Commission Findings as to Facts, 23 Mich. L. Rev. 233 (1925) 24, 39

Hankin: Constitutionality of the Federal Trade Commission Act, 19 Ill. L. Rev. 17 (1924) 8

Hankin: Functions of the Federal Trade Commission, 6 Ill. L. Q. 183 (1914) 39

Hankin: Jurisdiction of the Federal Trade Commission's Orders, 6 Ill. L. Q. 264 (1924) 39

Haycroft: Attempts of Congress to Promote Free Competition, 8 Nat. U. L. Rev. 39 (1928) 39

Hening: The Interstate Commerce Commission before the Federal Courts, 31 Am. L. Reg. (n.s.) 156 (1892) 110

Homan: Industrial Combination as Surveyed in Recent Literature, Quarterly Journal of Economics, v. 44, p. 345 (1930) 186

Hughes: Some Observations, New York Times, June 22, 1920, p. 11 20

Interstate Commerce Commission Appointments, Railway Age, LXXXVII, 1427; Commercial and Financial Chronicle, CXXXI, 731, Aug. 2, 1930 176

Interstate Commerce Commission, Railway Age, v. 92, No. 13, March 26, 1932, p. 513 169

Irvine: Uncertainties of Section 7 of the Clayton Act, 14 Cornell L. Q. 28 (1928) ... 93

Isaacs: Judicial Review of Administrative Findings, 30 Yale L. J. 781 (1921) ... 4, 24

Jacobs: The Interstate Commerce Commission and Interstate Railroad Reorganization, 45 Harv. L. R. 855 (1932) ... 128, 158

Jones: Historical Development of the Law of Business Competition, 35 Yale L. J. 905, 36 Id. 42, 207 (1926), 36 Id. 351 (1927) ... 39, 109, 114, 187

Jones: Significance of Current Attempts to Amend the Anti-Trust Laws, The Annalist, XXXVIII, 101 (1931) ... 187

Judicial Interpretation of Section 7 of the Clayton Act, Comment 39 Yale L. J. 1042 (1930) ... 93

Judicial Power to Set Aside Orders of the Interstate Commerce Commission, Note 41 Harv. L. Rev. 381 (1928) ... 135

Katz: Federal Legislative Courts, 43 Harv. L. Rev. 894 (1930) ... 37

Keezer: Some Questions Involved in the Application of the "Public Interest" Doctrine, 25 Mich. L. Rev. 596 (1927) ... 175

Kerr: The Trade Commission and the Courts, 9 Ill. L. Rev. 338 (1914) ... 42

Landis: Note on "Statutory Interpretation," 43 Harv. L. Rev. 886 (1930) ... 18

Law and Fact, 2 Edinburgh Law Journal 144 (1837) ... 26, 27

Levy: A Decade of the Federal Trade Commission, 11 Va. L. Rev. 21, 111 (1924), 169, 372 (1925) ... 39

Montague: Anti-Trust Laws and the Federal Trade Commission: 1914–1926, 27 Col. L. Rev. 650, 13 A. B. A. J. 328 (1927) 10, 39, 185

Montague: Unfair Methods of Competition, 25 Yale L. J. 20 (1915) 93

Needham: Judicial Determinations by Administrative Commissions, 10 Pol. Sci. Rev. 235 (1916) ... 11

Needham: The Federal Trade Commission, 16 Col. L. Rev. 175 (1916) ... 42

Newcomb: Force and Effect of the Orders of the Interstate Commerce Commission, 23 Harv. L. Rev. 12 (1909) ... 120

Paul: Unfair Competition and Its Late Developments, 6 St. Louis L. Rev. 73 (1921) ... 42

Pillsbury: Administrative Tribunals, 36 Harv. L. Rev. 405 (1923) 12

Pound, Cuthbert: Constitutional Aspects of Administrative Law (in Growth of American Administrative Law, 1923; reprinted in 9 A. B. A. J. 409) ... 10, 12, 24, 35, 37, 177

Pound, Roscoe: Administrative Application of Legal Standards, 44 A. B. A. Rep. 445 (1919) ... 18, 19, 23, 25

Pound: Justice According to Law, 13 Col. L. Rev. 696 (1913), 14 Id. 1, 103 (1914) 13, 19, 20, 21, 101, 176
Pound: Scope and Purpose of Sociological Jurisprudence, 25 Harv. L. Rev. 489 (1912) 22, 36
Pound: The Ideal Element in American Judicial Decisions, 45 Harv. L. Rev. 136 (1931) 16
Pound: The New Feudalism, 16 A. B. A. J. 553 (1930) 12
Pound: The Revival of Personal Government, 4 Proc. N. H. Bar Ass'n 13 (1917) 176
Powell: Conclusiveness of Administrative Determinations in the Federal Government, 1 Am. Pol. Sci. Rev. 583 (1907) 24
Powell: Separation of Powers: Administrative Exercise of Legislative and Judicial Power, 27 Pol. Sci. Q. 215 (1912), 28 Id. 34 (1913) 4, 12

Radin: Statutory Interpretation, 43 Harv. L. Rev. 863 (1930) ... 18
Railroads and I. C. C., New York Times, June 12, 1932, Sec. 2, p. 1.. 169
Randolph: Inquisitorial Power Conferred by the Trade Commission Bill, 23 Yale L. J. 672 (1914) 41
Robinson: The Hoch-Smith Resolution and the Future of the Interstate Commerce Commission, 42 Harv. L. Rev. 610 (1929) 130
Robinson: The Public Utility Concept in American Law, 41 Harv. L. Rev. 277 (1928) 175
Rogers: Unfair Competition, 17 Mich. L. Rev. 490 (1919) 42
Rosenberry: Administrative Law and the Constitution, 23 Am. Pol. Sci. Rev. 32 (1929) 11, 12, 28, 35, 36
Ross: Applicability of Rules of Evidence in Proceedings before Workmen's Compensation Commissions, 36 Harv. L. Rev. 263 (1923) 30
Rublee: The Original Plan and Early History of the Federal Trade Commission, Proc. Acad. Pol. Sci., XI, 666 (1924–1926) 39

Sankey: Foreword (to Port's Administrative Law, 1929).......... 37
Scope of the Jurisdiction of the Federal Trade Commission over False and Misleading Advertising, Comment 40 Yale L. J. 617 (1931) 94
Seligson: Extent of Jurisdiction of the Federal Trade Commission over Unfair Competition, 9 A. B. A. J. 689, 23 Col. L. Rev. 758 (1923) 93
Simpson: The Interstate Commerce Commission and Railroad Consolidation, 43 Harv. L. Rev. 192 (1931) 158
Socrates Among the Railroads, Fortune, V, No. 2, p. 71 (1932) ... 176
Spreckels: Changing Conditions Require Changed Laws, Printers Ink, CLIII, 33 (1930) 187
Stevens: Resale Price Maintenance and Unfair Competition, 19 Col. L. Rev. 265 (1919) 95
Stevens: Unfair Competition, 29 Pol. Sci. Q. 282 (1916) 42
Stevens: What Has the Federal Trade Commission Accomplished? 15 Am. Econ. Rev. 625 (1925) 62
Strawn: Are Our Anti-Trust Laws Out of Date? Nations Business, XIX, 132 (1931) 187

Tennant: Administrative Finality, 6 Can. Bar. Rev. 497 (1928) ... 24
The Clayton Act, Fortune II, No. 2, p. 94 185
Thorp: The Persistence of the Merger Movement, Am. Econ. Rev., XXI, 77 (1931) 187
Tollefson: Administrative Finality, 29 Mich. L. Rev. 839 (1931) 24, 34
Tollefson: Judicial Review of the Decisions of the Federal Trade Commission, 4 Wis. L. Rev. 257 (1927) 8, 33, 39
Tollefson: Judicial Review of Decisions of the Interstate Commerce Commission, 11 Minn. L. Rev. 389 (1927) 120, 133

Vanderblue: The Long and Short Haul Clause since 1910, 36 Harv. L. Rev. 426 (1923) 36, 128
Verity: Should Anti-Trust Laws Be Modified? Commerce and Finance, v. XXI, No. 6 (1932) 187
von Hippel: Die Verschiebung der Machtverhältnisse im Alten und Neuen Deutschland, Dargestellt an der Lehre Montesquieu's, und die Praktische Bedeutung dieses Prinzips fur die Juristische Konstruktion, 43 Rechtsgeleerd Magazijn 59, 85–89 (1924) ... 13

Watkins: An Appraisal of the Work of the Federal Trade Commission, 32 Col. L. Rev. 272 (1932) 99
Wigmore: Administrative Board Rules, 17 Ill. L. Rev. 263 (1922) 30
Wilson: Law and the Facts, 5 Am. Pol. Sci. Rev. 1 (1911) 26
Woodlock: Impressions of an Ex-Commissioner, Barron's, Sept. 29, 1930, p. 10; Oct. 6, 1930, p. 6; Oct. 13, 1930, p. 22; The Education of a Commissioner, Barron's, Oct. 27, 1930, p. 10; Nov. 3, 1930, p. 5; Nov. 10, 1930, p. 5; Nov. 17, 1930, p. 5 169

MISCELLANEOUS PUBLICATIONS AND PUBLIC DOCUMENTS

Congressional Record, LXIX, 2942 177
Davies: Trust Laws and Unfair Competition, Dept. of Commerce, Bureau of Corporations (1915) 39
Executive Order of the President, June 15, 1917, Messages and Papers of the Presidents, XVIII, 8366 at 8370 43
Hearings on Extension of Tenure of Government, 65th Cong., 3 Sess., v. 2, 3 126
Hoover: Annual Message to Congress, 75 Cong. Rec. 25, Dec. 8, 1931 187
Interstate Commerce Act Annotated (1929) 125, 127
Proceedings on the Death of Chief Justice White, 257 U. S. v, xxv–xxvi (1922) 7
Report on Car Supply Investigation, 42 I. C. C. 657 (1917) 124
Report of the House Committee, 63d Cong., 2 Sess., No. 533 (1914) 40, 176, 184
Report of the Senate Committee on Interstate Commerce, 63d Cong., 2 Sess., No. 597 (1914) 9, 10, 40, 42, 176, 182, 184

FEDERAL TRADE COMMISSION, ANNUAL REPORTS TO CONGRESS

INTERSTATE COMMERCE COMMISSION, ANNUAL REPORTS

STATUTES

Court Orders, Decisions and Opinions

INDEX

INDEX

Bei Fragen zur Produktsicherheit wenden Sie sich bitte an:
If you have any questions regarding product safety,
please contact:

Walter de Gruyter GmbH
Genthiner Straße 13
10785 Berlin
productsafety@degruyterbrill.com